Editor's Note

Most of the text here used is from the Edinburgh Edition of Stevenson's works. Of that edition it is Volume III, issued in 1895. A prefatory statement dated January of that year deplores the author's death a month earlier and states that "the successive volumes will be prepared for press by Mr. Sidney Colvin, with the author's corrections so far as they have been sent home." The assumption, therefore, is that Stevenson had given approval to the text of Volume III issued so soon after his death, and that this first collected edition incorporates his last corrections. The present edition differs from the Edinburgh Edition in that single quotation marks are changed to double, in keeping with Stevenson's manuscript. Occasionally it has been necessary to delete a word or a short phrase added by Colvin in order to return to the original manuscript text. One typographical error, which resulted in the misspelling of Stevenson's "Glenlivet," has been altered.

The Edinburgh Edition is divided into three major sections: *The Amateur Emigrant, The Old and New Pacific Capitals,* and *The Silverado Squatters.* The larger part of the first section, dealing with Stevenson's crossing of the Atlantic, had not been published before and was bowdlerized at the insistence of family and friends. In the present edition the finished but previously unpublished text is made available thanks to the courtesy of the Beinecke Rare Book and Manuscript Library at Yale University. It is inserted, within diamond brackets, in its proper place. The second part of *The Amateur Emigrant* had been printed separately in 1892 under its subtitle, *Across the Plains,* and some of its text that had been deleted from the first edition was also kept out of the Edinburgh Edition. The missing text is here for the first time reinstated from the same source and in the same way. In the restored manuscript material for both parts of *The Amateur Emigrant,* minor and meaningless misspellings have been silently corrected, but ones that have significance have been retained and annotated. For the sake of consistency a period has also been inserted after the abbreviations "No" and "Mr" in the restored material. Included here, too, in the footnotes to the chapter "Despised Races" is some text printed in *Longman's Magazine* in serialization (July and August 1883) but never in book form.

The two essays on the Pacific Coast capitals were first gathered together under their common title in the Edinburgh Edition, although they had appeared respectively in *Fraser's Magazine* of November 1880 and *The Magazine of Art* of May 1883. Of Stevenson's two other essays about Monterey that are included in the present volume, "San Carlos Day" has not appeared before in a book, and "Simoneau's at Monterey" is here printed for the first time.

"San Carlos Day" was first published in the Monterey *Californian* of November 11, 1879. "The Monterey Barbarian," the author's pseudonym, was first identified by George R. Stewart on several convincing counts: (1) Stevenson's letter of November 15 to Edmund Gosse mentioning the enclosure of "a Monterey paper where the works of R.L.S. appear"; (2) the style and the allusions, which suit Stevenson; and (3) the quotation of the couplet from Richard Barnfield's "The Address to the Nightingale," which appears again in *The Wrecker,* once more slightly misquoted, as is not uncommon in a work committed to memory. Although Stewart did not mention it, the couplet had previously been quoted by Stevenson in "The Best Thing in Edinburgh," an address delivered in 1873 but first published in 1923. The article, with Stewart's introduction, appeared in *Scribner's Magazine,* LXVIII, No. 2 (August 1920), 209–211; and of it Lloyd Osbourne wrote in the same issue, "The article is undoubtedly genuine, and to the ardent Stevensonian is of real charm and value." This is the only article in the Monterey *Californian* that can be clearly attributed to Stevenson, although there has long been a belief that he wrote others.

"Simoneau's at Monterey," to which has been given a title quoted from the text, is here published for the first time from manuscripts 6589 and 6846 in the Beinecke Rare Book and Manuscript Library of Yale University. The first two paragraphs and a little less than half of the third belong to manuscript 6846. In his *Life of Robert Louis Stevenson* (New York, 1901), Vol. I, p. 200, Graham Balfour rather accurately quotes the second paragraph and part of the third but declares that "the fragment breaks off." Actually the conclusion of the single page of manuscript 6846 leads directly to the first words of manuscript 6589. The four pages of that incomplete manuscript are numbered 2–3, 13–14, the latter pair in some part repeating in slightly variant form some of the material of the earlier pages. Deletion of the repetition leaves a clear sequential text. It is here presented as Stevenson wrote and corrected it except for the excision of the repetitive section, the transfer of one short sentence from that section to the appropriate place in the first and seemingly better version, the deletion of one incomplete sentence on Bronson and three terminal but incomplete paragraphs on the subject of California wines, and the correction of two misspellings and one miswritten word.

The final text, *The Silverado Squatters*, has added to its footnotes a few brief passages that appeared in its serialization in *Century Magazine* (November and December 1883) but that were not carried over into the first book edition of 1883 or into the Edinburgh Edition, although they add to the significance of the work.

The title of this volume was created for this edition. It is considered to be both more accurate and more comprehensive than "Travels and Excursions," which Sidney Colvin devised for the third volume of the Edinburgh Edition.

The Beinecke Rare Book and Manuscript Library of the Yale University Library and the Graduate Department of Yale University have generously granted permission to publish those parts of the manuscript of *The Amateur Emigrant* that have not been previously printed as well as the manuscripts that are here printed for the first time as "Simoneau's at Monterey." Mr. Alan Osbourne, executor of Stevenson's estate, has also kindly given permission for the printing of these manuscripts. The Society of Authors has granted permission to print two stanzas of a poem first published in Stevenson's *New Poems* in 1918. The Henry E. Huntington Library and Art Gallery generously furnished the text of the rare, perhaps unique broadside "Padre Dos Reales," which Stevenson wrote in Monterey in 1879 and which has never since been reprinted.

Mr. George L. McKay, the bibliographer of the Beinecke collection, was helpful in answering questions at the outset of this project, and further appreciated assistance along the way came from Miss Marjorie G. Wynne of the Beinecke Library and Mr. Robert W. Hill, Keeper of Manuscripts of the New York Public Library. Others who assisted in my quests for information are Professors Maynard A. Amerine, Bradford A. Booth, B. H. Bronson, Gilbert Highet, and John E. Jordan. Many years ago my good friend George R. Stewart wrote his master's dissertation on Stevenson in California, and to that work and to the always rewarding talk with him I am much indebted. Finally, it is a pleasure to thank Gordon O. Taylor, a graduate student in the Department of English at Berkeley, who zealously and ingeniously helped to run down many of the matters needed for the book's annotation.

J.D.H.

Berkeley, California
March 1966

Contents

Illustrations

INTRODUCTION

The story of Stevenson's voyage from Scotland to California begins with his earlier, easier travels. The impetus to cross the Atlantic and the American continent in 1879 came from a relationship created during holiday excursions to France in 1875 and 1876.

In July 1875 the twenty-four-year-old Stevenson grudgingly fulfilled his father's desire that he enter a stable profession by being admitted to the bar in Edinburgh, but instead of settling down to practice, he was soon off for a visit to France. He was accompanied by his favorite cousin Bob, formally known as Robert Alan Mowbray Stevenson, a slightly older and slightly more bohemian companion, who was now dabbling at painting and who introduced him to the artists' colonies of the Barbizon region. The young man who wanted to be an author rather than a barrister was so attracted by the area that a year later he was back again, this time on a canoe trip that ended at "a place called Grez, a pretty and very melancholy village on the plain," where he admired "a low bridge of many arches choked with sedge; great fields of white and yellow water-lilies; poplars and willows innumerable." [1] The bridge, endlessly painted in all its quaintness by amateurs and professionals alike, crossed the Loing River, beyond the forest of Fontainebleau, in the area that Stevenson so nicely called "the great *al fresco* school of art of modern France." [2] Although the famous

1. Sidney Colvin (ed.), *The Letters of Robert Louis Stevenson to Family and Friends* (London, 1899), I, 104.
2. "Fontainebleau," *The Works of Robert Louis Stevenson* (New York, 1906), IX, 94.

Millet had died the year of Stevenson's first visit to the region, so that the green shutters of his modest house were closed and his daughters were in mourning, there were plenty of other artists around — many of them, as Stevenson observed, seated under their white umbrellas, planted where the inn's garden met the river, doggedly painting that picturesque old bridge.

On the 1876 visit the young Stevenson men soon heard rumors that an alien element had been introduced into the artists' colonies. Just two years before Henry James drew that classic portrait of an American lady, Daisy Miller — "an inscrutable combination of audacity and innocence" disturbing the sophisticated society of Europe — Stevenson learned that women from the United States were invading the old French settlements for painters. Of course, a few women had been there before, as models and as mistresses, but this was a new type, hard to know how to handle. As Stevenson said, "when that essentially modern creature, the . . . American girl-student, began to walk calmly into his favourite inn as if into a drawing-room at home, the French painter owned himself defenceless; he submitted or he fled." [3] Submission was particularly likely to be inspired by the peculiar invasion of Grez, for to it came not one but two American girl students; worse yet, one was a mother and the other her daughter.

The mother was known as Fanny Osbourne. She had been christened Frances Matilda Vandegrift, but after childhood she was always known by her nickname — an interesting informality since even after marriage she always used her family name, aristocratically enhanced by a spelling change to Van de Grift. The married name she bore, presumably without much enthusiasm, was Mrs. Samuel Osbourne. She had had the name for nineteen years since her marriage in her native Indianapolis to a blond, handsome Kentuckian, charming in a Southern style. It had been an unsettled marriage, in which the easygoing Osbourne had not only shifted jobs frequently but had been gone two years or more soldiering in the Civil War. Then,

3. *Ibid.*, p. 96.

First Stevenson made a quick trip to London, probably to seek an assignment as a special foreign correspondent from a newspaper and to say good-bye to his friends, all of whom urged him to stay home and to develop his literary career. But as he told Edmund Gosse less than ten days before leaving, "I envy you your wife, your home, your child — I was going to say your cat. There would be cats in my home too if I could but get it. I may seem to you 'the impersonation of life,' but my life is the impersonation of waiting." [17] And so, against all advice and without a farewell to his family, he set forth. As he said in *Virginibus Puerisque*, "Falling in love is the one illogical adventure . . . the effect is out of all proportion with the cause."

Stevenson had little money and slight prospect of getting much more because only his friend Charles Baxter, who acted as an intermediary with his parents, was given an American address, with strict instructions that it be told "to *no one*, not even the Queen." Under the slight disguise of Robert Stephenson he embarked on August 7, 1879, aboard the *Devonia*, a steamer of 4,270 tons. The ship had three classes of accommodation, and Stevenson selected the middle at a cost of eight guineas rather than taking the even meaner steerage, for which one paid six guineas and provided one's own bedding and mess utensils. The second cabin was bad enough, as his account of the rough crossing makes clear. He wrote his friend Henley that by the end of the voyage he had lost fourteen pounds "and got the itch. I could not eat, and I could not sh—— hush! — the whole way." But he worked and worked, and "in a slantindicular cabin with the table playing bob-cherry with the ink bottle" [18] he wrote the thirty-one pages of "The Story of a Lie" and many more pages that were eventually transmuted into the first part of *The Amateur Emigrant*.

On the evening of the tenth day Stevenson finally debarked

---

17. Colvin, *Letters to Family and Friends*, I, 137–138.
18. DeLancey Ferguson and Marshall Waingrow (eds.), *R. L. S., Stevenson's Letters to Charles Baxter* (New Haven, 1956), pp. 66, 68.

at New York in a downpour that lasted throughout his stay. As he wrote Colvin: "The only American institution which has yet won my respect is the rain. One sees it is a new country, they are so free with their water." [19] On that dreary Sunday night, his first ashore, at the cheap Reunion House, he wrote Henley he "did not close an eye, but sat on the floor in my trousers and scratched myself from ten P.M. to seven, when I arose much the better for the exercise." [20] During his single day in the city he tried to find publishers who would be interested in his writings but had no success, although he wrote Colvin: "Bought a copy of my own work, and the man said 'by Stevenson.' — 'Indeed,' says I. — 'Yes, sir,' says he. — Scene closes." [21] He loaned the work, *Travels with a Donkey*, about his recent and more pleasant excursion through the Cévennes, to a serving girl in his rooming house, "a little Irish girl just bursting into figure, but dirty." She read it aloud to her sister, and Stevenson observed, "They chuckle and I feel flattered. Now they yawn and I am indifferent: such a wisely conceived thing is vanity!" [22]

Since the news from California sent to him at General Delivery in New York was bad — "F. has inflammation of the brain" — he started immediately to make the land trip of three thousand miles across the continent in the fastest but cheapest way possible, by emigrant train. Leaving behind some of his water-soaked clothes but adding the six fat volumes of George Bancroft's *History of the United States* to his slender baggage of a small valise, a knapsack, and a railway rug, Stevenson began the eleven-day trek on the hideously uncomfortable cars that he described so graphically in "Across the Plains." The experience was an unpleasantly practical one, counteracting his romantic conception of the New World. "America was to me a sort of promised land," he wrote in his narrative; and

19. Colvin, *Letters to Family and Friends*, I, 144.
20. *Letters to Charles Baxter*, pp. 66–67.
21. Colvin, *Letters to Family and Friends*, I, 144.
22. *Letters to Charles Baxter*, p. 67.

if there was a somewhat humorous note in the message he had
sent on the eve of departure to Charles Baxter — "I read
Aimard's novels to teach me independence and philosophy and
learn something of the ways of New York" [23] — Stevenson's
views were not wholly alien to this Dumas of the Indians, who
had regaled boys with such books as *Loyal Heart; or, The
Trappers of Arkansas, The Pirates of the Prairies,* and *The
Gold Seekers.* Indeed, he admitted in *The Amateur Emigrant*
that Ohio "had early been a favourite home of my imagination," for when he was still unbreeched he had listened to his
nurse Cummy read a wonderful adventure story set there.
Even as he was traveling through the land, he was stirred by
its rich poetical nomenclature, redolent of the romance and af-
firmation that he associated with Whitman's *Leaves of Grass*
and other great works of American literature.

Realism soon shouldered out romance, however, on this
transcontinental crossing. If Bancroft's fact-studded volumes
gave him a less sentimental view, so did his days and nights in
the crowded, fetid cars. Once again he could feel, as he did
on the *Devonia,* that "There is nothing more agreeable to picture and nothing more pathetic to behold. The abstract idea, as
conceived at home, is hopeful and adventurous . . . [but]
the more I saw of my fellow-passengers, the less I was tempted
to the lyric note." It was no wonder that he should suffer
some dark moods, for as he told Henley, "What it is to be
ill in an emigrant train let those declare who know." And he
wrote Gosse, "I had no feeling one way or the other, from
New York to California, until, at Dutch Flat, a mining camp
in the Sierra, I heard a cock crowing with a home voice; and
then I fell to hope and regret both in the same moment." [24]
So he arrived with some happiness in San Francisco as the sunrise slid over Mount Tamalpais and down across the city and
the bay, shimmering in summer daylight. He had come at last
almost to the end of a hard but sentimental journey.

23. *Ibid.,* pp. 65–66.
24. Colvin, *Letters to Family and Friends,* I, 147, 151.

At the very end of August, three weeks after leaving home and the Clyde, Stevenson finally ended his travels at Monterey, a secluded, seaside town some hundred and thirty miles south of San Francisco, where Fanny had gone to recuperate. The population of Monterey, Stevenson wrote to Colvin, "is about that of a dissenting chapel on a wet Sunday in a strong church neighbourhood. They are mostly Mexican and Indian — mixed." [25] Although the land and the economy were in the hands of the Americans, the town was essentially Mexican, an indolent place of a few streets and a few more lanes, generally unpaved, except by the ever-drifting sand of the seashore. Here Stevenson found Fanny, staying with her children and her sister Nellie in the quaint home of a Spanish senorita who had been loved by General Sherman when he was a young officer stationed at this Pacific outpost at the end of the Mexican War.

It was a moving yet ambiguous reunion for the lovers. They themselves have left no record, although she fancifully and primly wrote from Monterey, "My literary friend from Scotland has accepted an engagement to come to America and lecture." [26] The children, like everyone else, saw through this easily enough. Isobel grumbled, "Maybe my mother saw in this contrast to my father the security from infidelity that had wrecked their marriage. At any rate she was happy when he was near, and I, standing in awe of her inflexible decisions, had no hopeful moments that she would not marry this penniless foreigner. At seventeen [sic] I would sit in judgment to be regretted in shame for the rest of my life!" [27] Her brother Sam remembered, "He looked ill even to my childish gaze; the brilliancy of his eyes emphasized the thinness and pallor of his face. His clothes, no longer picturesque but merely shabby, hung loosely on his shrunken body." [28]

25. *Ibid.*, I, 150.
26. McKay, *A Stevenson Library*, VI, 2504.
27. Elsie N. Caldwell, *Last Witness for Robert Louis Stevenson* (Norman, Oklahoma, 1960), p. 10.
28. Osbourne, *An Intimate Portrait*, p. 16.

It was a sad irony that Fanny had recovered while her beloved had become seriously sick, in large part because of the rigors of his incessant traveling to reach her bedside. He had suffered from too little food, much of it unnourishing, and too little sleep, all of it irregular. He had experienced the constant pressure of intense work and bad weather. As a result, his nerves were now stretched as thin as his body — a body wracked with pleurisy and covered with eczema. Worst of all, he was deeply dispirited because Fanny was still uncertain about a divorce, talking endlessly with her husband about it, either at Monterey, to which he occasionally made weekend trips, or at their Oakland home, to which she still returned. Remembering that he had felt better after making easy outdoor excursions in France, Stevenson only ten days after his arrival decided to leave Monterey and its endless sea fogs. To his friend Baxter he wrote a pathetic letter: "My news is nil. I know nothing, I go out camping, that is all I know. Today I leave, and shall likely be three weeks in camp. I shall send you a letter from there with more guts than this, and now say good bye to you, having had the itch and a broken heart." [29]

In low spirits Stevenson turned his back on the ocean and rode up into the Santa Lucia Mountains in the hope of finding health. Instead, he got sicker, until finally he could not move at all, and for two nights he "lay out under a tree in a sort of stupor," [30] listening to an unearthly distant tinkling of bells. They turned out to be around the necks of angora goats belonging to some frontiersmen, who rescued him and brought him to their ranch eighteen miles from Monterey. They helped him into their simple house, where he lay "in an upper-chamber nearly naked, with flies crawling all over me and a clinking of goat bells in my ears." [31] Finally he recovered under their good care and went back to Monterey to pick up the threads of existence.

29. *Letters to Charles Baxter*, p. 68.
30. Balfour, *Life*, I, 198.
31. *Letters to Charles Baxter*, p. 70.

He became sick there again and was treated by Dr. J. P. E. Heintz, the "little French doctor" with whom he lodged and from whom he often cadged a meal. Another Frenchman who took even better care of him was Jules Simoneau, a jolly, "fifty-eight-year-old wreck of a good-hearted, dissipated, and once wealthy Nantais tradesman," [32] whose fine little French restaurant advertised "meals at all hours. Good cheer and a good reception." [33] There Stevenson ate one fine dinner a day for the sum of just twenty-five cents, and with the proprietor he played chess between times, or over a friendly glass of wine or brandy discussed the universe. It was Simoneau who, worried by Stevenson's absence from his usual table for two days, went to the room where the exhausted traveler lay stricken by a bad fever, unable to get up or to take care of himself, and thus perhaps saved his life.

Although he wrote Baxter that he was "sick both at heart and in body," Stevenson also said that he had "done towers of work since I have been here." [34] In October and November he wrote so much that he wondered if he "might have affected the price of paper on the Pacific coast." Yet he worried endlessly about his work and about the payments it might bring, and all the letters to his friends are filled with concern that he "must make money a great deal quicker than I used." [35] He was terribly conscious that he had to make every moment and every experience count. Over the years he had in one way or another offended the upper-middle-class sensibilities of his dour, respectable father, hurting him much by failing to follow the profession of his family of engineers, Scotland's most eminent lighthouse builders, and then, on top of that, refusing to practice the law in which his father had finally persuaded him to be trained. To have become a bohemian writer of sto-

32. Colvin, *Letters to Family and Friends*, I, 148.
33. The Monterey *Californian*, November 4, 1879, p. 4.
34. *Letters to Charles Baxter*, p. 72.
35. Colvin, *Letters to Family and Friends*, I, 153, 161.

ries and personal tales was bad enough; worse by far was to have left home and homeland without so much as a good-bye in order to travel to the uttermost bounds of the English-speaking world in pursuit of a married woman whom he could only vaguely hope would get a divorce so as to marry him. The two Stevensons, father and son, could not communicate with one another save through intermediaries, and it was through them the son learned that the father was sick and deeply desirous of having his sole child return home to Edinburgh. In this extremity he wrote to his old friend Baxter to ask plaintively, "how for God's sake about my father? Tell me, please, Charles. Since I have gone away I have found out for the first time how much I love that man; he is dearer to me than all except F." [36] Yet his family was not corresponding with him, nor was any allowance coming his way. Although his mother and father were deeply devoted to him, the rupture was such that he could declare to Colvin from Monterey, "With my parents, all looks dead black." [37] He therefore had to write not only as well but as much as he could.

He worked first on the opening section of *The Amateur Emigrant,* about which he enthusiastically told Colvin, "I believe it will be more popular than any of my others; the canvas is so much more popular and larger too." Next he devoted time to *The Pavilion on the Links,* which he sent off to Henley for placement as a "grand carpentry story in nine chapters, and I should hesitate to say how many tableaux. Where is it to go? God knows. It is the dibbs that are wanted . . . Dibbs and speed are my mottoes." By way of change he laid aside the sixty-eight pages of *The Amateur Emigrant* to try his hand at a new novel, to be called either *A Chapter in the Experience of Arizona Breckonridge* or *A Vendetta in the West,* or a combination of the two. By the middle of November it was more than half done, and he told Colvin that "the scene from Chap-

36. *Letters to Charles Baxter*, p. 70.
37. McKay, *A Stevenson Library*, III, 946.

ter IV. to the end lies in Monterey and the adjacent country;
of course, with my usual luck, the plot of the story is somewhat scandalous, containing an illegitimate father for piece of
resistance." However, although he kept mentioning the tale
in letter after letter, even as late as June 1880, and presumably
took the manuscript back to Scotland, it was always shoved
off while other writing took first place. Work planned or in
progress included essays for *The Cornhill* and "a short story of
50 pp., which shall be finished to-morrow, or I'll know the
reason why." [38] Finally, he wrote Colvin to ask whether he
could place an article about a camp in the redwoods, illustrated
by Joe Strong, the young, bohemian San Francisco artist who
married Isobel while Stevenson was waiting in Monterey to
marry her mother; but the projected collaboration was never
published.

Despite sickness and long hours of work, Stevenson found
Monterey "a lovely place, which I am growing to love." [39]
For setting there was the bay and the ocean, with long beaches
enticing to a walker. He liked looking upon the slow rolling
green waves, the sea gulls hovering over them, the sandpipers
darting along the shore, and farther back toward the mountains, the hardy live oaks, the pine trees heavy with Spanish
moss, the glades, thickets, and groves, above which hung a soft
fog at evening, followed by starry nights, full of inland perfume. There was good company, too. Isobel recalls "riding
parties to Point Lobos, picnics on the beach, swimming off the
wharf, and the gay weekly fandangos where we soon learned
the old Spanish dances." [40] Of course, this was a young girl's
view, as she made clear only a few words later when she wrote,
"on a commode beside the bed, we always kept a candle and
matches, for the charming Spanish custom of the serenade still
prevailed, and the only response expected was to show a light."
For a man, slightly older, there were other pleasures of com-

38. Colvin, *Letters to Family and Friends,* I, 149, 151–152, 157.
39. *Ibid.,* I, 153.
40. Field, *This Life I've Loved,* p. 118.

panionship. They centered on Fanny when she was present. During her absences he found friends in the saloon of the handsome young Adulpho Sanchez, soon to marry Nellie Van de Grift, or at the dinner table in Simoneau's little whitewashed back room. At either place he usually met Crevole Bronson, the new editor of the town's weekly newspaper, the Monterey *Californian*, who put Stevenson on the payroll at $2 a week, surreptitiously supplied by Simoneau and other friends to help him in his impoverished condition.

Stevenson found fellowship and sport in one piece of writing printed in Monterey for which he expected neither pay nor public recognition. With Bronson, Simoneau, and an Italian fisherman, Stevenson entered into a conspiracy against the local padre, Father Casanova. Ironically, the father should have delighted Stevenson, for he worked hard to get funds to roof the Carmel Mission, as Stevenson had urged in an article for the *Californian*; but his niggardliness in personal charity caused him to be the subject of a poster written by Stevenson and printed by Bronson, and apparently not printed again since that November night of 1879.[41] It read:

PADRE DOS REALES.

On the night of Sunday, 16th November, BIAGGINI, an Italian Swiss, from the same village as the Padre of Monterey and born in a house opposite to that of the Padre's family, came to the latter's door for charity. BIAGGINI had only to reach San Luis Obispo, where welcome and work were ready for him. He was now penniless, but naturally thought that all would be well since he had found his countryman. The Padre gave him —TWO BITS; and sent him for further help to —THE ITALIAN FISHERMEN. It will not be forgotten that the Apostles were fishermen.

41. Reprinted from the rare, perhaps unique, original in the Henry E. Huntington Library and Art Gallery.

> How long, O Lord, how long? People of Mon-
> terey, have you not a Bishop? Let us be done
> with PADRE DOS REALES.

Two hundred copies were posted in the dark of night, and
they had almost all been destroyed by eight in the morning
when the local citizenry were about. "But," Stevenson wrote
to Colvin, "I think the nickname will stick. Dos Reales; deux
réaux; two bits; twenty-five cents; about a shilling; but in
practice it is worth from ninepence to threepence: thus two
glasses of beer would cost two bits." [42]

Although he had become part of the life of Monterey, there
was not much reason to remain after Fanny had returned to
Oakland for good to settle affairs with her husband. In late
December he moved to San Francisco to be nearer her. He
found the city large and lonely after the intimacy of Monterey.
Christmas came and went, and he had no one with whom to exchange even a greeting except his warm-hearted Irish landlady
Mrs. Carson, her husband, and her children, or the waiters at
restaurants where he dined over a cheap but good table d'hôte,
with a book as company. "This is not a gay way to pass Christmas, is it?" he wrote Colvin, "and I must own the guts are a
little knocked out of me." [43]

At this time, of all times, his friends at home began to turn
against him, or rather tried to turn him from his own ways to
what they thought were better ones. With their parochial outlook they thought his writing would inevitably deteriorate if
he persisted in remaining long in America and, more deplorable,
in allying himself to an American woman who was older than
he, still married, and the mother of a grown daughter and
young son. Colvin frankly admitted to Baxter, "My own object is to get L. back, if without Mrs. S., so much the better; if
with her, then as the best of a bad job." [44] Accordingly, he
wrote Stevenson that he found the first part of *The Amateur*

42. Colvin, *Letters to Family and Friends*, I, 158.
43. *Ibid.*, I, 161.
44. McKay, *A Stevenson Library*, IV, 1270.

Emigrant "a spiritless record of squalid experiences," little likely to advance a "still only half-established reputation." [45] Henley and Gosse added their own dark words. With remarkable good humor Stevenson observed to his still loyal friend Charles Baxter that he had recently received a good deal of "correspondence that would have taken the starch out of Mark Tapley. People rolled letters on to me like boulders, and then ran away and pelted me with notes like road metal. I feared to open an envelope: there was sure to be some damned torpedo or, at the least, some Waterloo Cracker that would singe my whiskers." [46]

With this mood upon his English friends, Stevenson was unable to get "a roving commission from a paper" [47] in London for which he had asked Henley's help. He seems to have tried to get work from some of the local newspapers. There have long been stories that the San Francisco *Bulletin* and perhaps one or two other papers bought special feature pieces, but the texts have never been definitely identified. Even if there were such articles, they were certainly slight and did not bring him the kind of money he desperately needed.

Although he was in frightful health and had to drop from a fifty-cent to a two-bit dinner taken in the middle of the day, the poor man's hour, he relished the charm of the city, appreciating the local color of which he later wrote so warmly in "A Modern Cosmopolis" and the chapter called "Faces on the City Front" in *The Wrecker*. And though he had plenty of bleak days throughout his stay, he found some good friends too. One was Virgil Williams, director of the California School of Design, where Fanny had first studied art. Williams got him a visitor's card at the Bohemian Club, and there he met a local author, Charles Warren Stoddard, in whose aerie atop Telegraph Hill, decorated with paddles and baskets and plumes

---

45. Colvin, *Letters to Family and Friends,* I, 149, 165.
46. *Letters to Charles Baxter,* p. 76.
47. Anne Roller Issler, *Happier for His Presence* (Stanford, California, 1949), p. 90.

From Scotland to Silverado

from the South Seas, Stevenson heard idylls of tropical life and got a further sense of romance through the copies of *Typee* and *Omoo* to which Stoddard introduced him. Best of all, Fanny came to the city about twice a week, when they would dine together at a French or Italian restaurant, in his room at Mrs. Carson's house, or with the Williamses.

As the wet spring of San Francisco continued, Mrs. Carson's younger son, Robbie, became seriously ill with pneumonia. This four-year-old, "bright-haired innocent" was a favorite of the man he called "de author," and Stevenson suffered great, tiring pangs of pity as he sat up for hours nursing the child. When Robbie recovered, his older namesake collapsed. With his background of malaria and malnutrition, Stevenson fell into what he called a galloping consumption, which was marked by a high fever, cold sweats, frustrating attacks of coughing, and sinking fits in which he wholly lost the power of speech. As he wrote Colvin, "I was near the other side of Jordan." [48] Even after he began to recover under the dedicated nursing of Fanny and Mrs. Carson, Stoddard said that his "itinerary was very limited; he usually travelled from his couch to his lounge, possibly touching at the arm-chair on the way."

Yet at the very time that Stoddard thought him "but a disembodied intellect . . . submerged in billows of bedclothes," [49] he was writing. He was pushing ahead on the unfinished works he had brought up from Monterey, as well as recording his impressions of that indolent old Pacific capital. He found materials wherever he could, such as the observations from his walks about San Francisco, which were turned into an essay on the new Pacific capital, or the passage from a letter written by his landlady's brother, Martin Mahoney, which was quoted in "Across the Plains." He even contemplated a work, perhaps as long as *Prince Otto*, to be called *Adventures of John Carson in Several Quarters of the World*, presumably the recollections of the brother-in-law of that same landlady. He wrote some of

48. Colvin, *Letters to Family and Friends*, I, 163, 171.
49. J. A. Hammerton (ed.), *Stevensoniana* (London, 1903), p. 48.

a cramp. The next morning Fanny mashed her thumb while making repairs. Later she came down with a nervous chill. By the sixth day mother and son were both sick with diphtheria and had to be taken to Calistoga by open cart. There they stayed for about a week. After they had returned to their tumbled-down cabin, but without the China boy that Stevenson had hoped to get as help, they were plagued by the laziness of their hired man, Irvine Lovelands, an ignorant, indolent backwoodsman typical of the Pike County genus characterized by Bayard Taylor as "the Anglo-Saxon relapsed into semi-barbarism." [58]

Despite the unpleasantnesses, Stevenson cast an Arcadian air over his life when he described it in *The Silverado Squatters.* Perhaps, indeed, it was the fulfillment of that for which he had longed in France when he wrote, "to live out of doors with the woman a man loves is of all lives the most complete and free." [59] Certainly Fanny, combining mother, mistress, manager, and nurse, knew how to make his life happy. Writing to her yet unmet mother-in-law about "my dear boy," she declared, "taking care of Louis is, as you must know, very like angling for shy trout; one must understand when to pay out the line, and exercise the greatest caution in drawing him in." [60] Fanny had him fast hooked, and Isobel noticed that "the change in Louis was amazing; he was like a different man," [61] as she watched him working on a first draft of *The Silverado Squatters,* finishing off *The Amateur Emigrant,* and polishing other pieces begun at Monterey and San Francisco. Life turned pleasant, and the crudities of the place were obscured during the last month of their stay. The mine platform became a verandah on which Louis could sit and write or sun himself under the clear blue skies, enjoying a mid-morning rum punch frothy with cream and topped with a sprinkle of cinnamon,

58. Bayard Taylor, *At Home and Abroad, Second Series* (New York, 1862), p. 51.
59. "A Night Among the Pines," *Travels with a Donkey.*
60. Sanchez, *Life of Mrs. Stevenson,* p. 79.
61. Field, *This Life I've Loved,* pp. 128–129.

talking with their visitors, including the Joe Strongs, Fanny's sister Nellie, and the Virgil Williamses, or dining out-of-doors on venison, a pigeon, or a wild duck bought from a neighbor and stored in the mouth of the old mine along with cans of fresh milk. It was, at last, a delightful conclusion to Stevenson's rough voyage to America and across the continent, as well as to his long, often unhappy, and sickly life in California.

By the end of July, Stevenson seemed well enough to risk the discomforts of travel and of a less benign climate, so the newly wed couple decided to set off for his native Scotland. After a brief stop in San Francisco he, Fanny, and Sam boarded a Pullman — emigrant trains were for him a thing of the past — and journeyed safely to New York, whence they embarked first-class on the *City of Chester* on August 7, 1880 — coincidentally, just one year to the day after he had set forth on his travels aboard the *Devonia*.

That year apparently marked the change from youth to maturity. During those twelve months Stevenson was without homeland, family, and friends. He began by living in squalid conditions as an experiment, and he almost ended by dying in mean circumstances because he could afford no better. For the first time he had to write in order to support himself, and later a family, while his old friends were telling him that his works were no longer the free and fanciful pieces they had formerly enjoyed. More than once he was so sick that both the doctors and he despaired of his recovery, and he admitted, "I felt unable to go on farther with that rough horseplay of human life." [62] But he had lived, and he had found a wife, and a ready-made family too, as he moved from his twenties to his thirtieth year and left behind the days of his youth.

The two most important works that Stevenson wrote before going to California — *An Inland Voyage* and *Travels with a Donkey* — were records of pleasure trips, undertaken in part simply to provide material for books. Earlier he had tuned the instrument of his prose to playing pretty melodies, imitating

62. Colvin, *Letters to Family and Friends*, I, 170.

one great writer after another in order to learn their mannerisms and achieve facility; but even when he found himself ready to write in his own style, he had to create a subject by going out in search of it on holiday excursions rather than by obtaining it from basically meaningful personal experiences. It was in a style too artfully playful that he wrote in *An Inland Voyage:* "we lunched on a meadow inside a parallelogram of poplars. The leaves danced and prattled in the wind all round about us. The river hurried on meanwhile, and seemed to chide at our delay. Little we cared. The river knew where it was going; not so we; the less our hurry, where we found good quarters, and a pleasant theatre for a pipe." [63]

The tougher travels of his year in America made these mannerisms mostly a thing of the past, and in the place of an attractive but often rather precious youthfulness there came into his travel writings a new mood of maturity, and a sense of substance. Yet paradoxically, some of the rougher, more realistic aspects of the writings born of this maturity have been concealed from Stevenson's readers. During his lifetime and afterward some of his manuscripts and letters were edited to present a different image of the man, more in keeping with what was wanted by family and friends — particularly by his father; Fanny; Graham Balfour, his second cousin and official biographer; and Sidney Colvin, his old friend and the compiler of his correspondence. As Malcolm Elwin said, it was their view "that nothing should be admitted to disturb the popular conception of a *beau chevalier* of letters." [64] Even while he was in California, his mother wrote to her "dearest Lou" about some example of bad taste that she had detected in *Travels with a Donkey,* "I am shocked to find that you really put in that horrid bit in your book that I objected so much to — scarcely modified." [65] In part, as Henley so bitterly declared in his furious review of Balfour's biography, his protectors recog-

---

63. "Down the Oise."
64. Elwin, *The Strange Case of Robert Louis Stevenson,* p. vii.
65. McKay, *A Stevenson Library,* IV, 1609.

nized that "his personality was a marketable thing"; in part, they themselves were dedicated to certain proprieties and wanted to make him "smooth, and smiling, and ladylike." They therefore concocted what Henley called "this Seraph in Chocolate, this barley-sugar effigy of a real man." [66]

As a small part of creating and preserving this view, family and friends insisted that *The Amateur Emigrant* be pruned, either by the author or by others, even though that which was excised not only was every bit as finished as the parts deemed publishable but also was integral to an understanding of the situation as Stevenson saw it and to the work as a whole.

Begun aboard ship, at least in the form of notes, written and tinkered with in Monterey and San Francisco, the first part of *The Amateur Emigrant* was at last sent off to Colvin in December 1879. It went to him not only for placement with a magazine or book publisher but also with marginal inquiries asking for the verification of a quotation or whether a particular technical word had been properly employed. Colvin saw himself, rightly enough, as free to comment upon and to do some editing of the text, but he went beyond that into general disparagement. He appointed himself a leader of what Richard Aldington called "the little Sanhedrin which determined what Stevenson should and should not publish." [67] Stevenson found Colvin so "eminently descriptive, and even eloquent in dispraise" of the work that he had to complain "you rolled such a lot of polysyllables over me that a better man than I might have been disheartened." [68] Since he was not disheartened, he moved ahead on the next section of the manuscript. Late in the spring of 1880 Colvin received that second part, "Across the Plains" (some of it had actually been written on the back of Colvin's letter objecting to the first

66. William Ernest Henley, "R. L. S.," *The Pall Mall Magazine*, XXV, 104 (December 1901), pp. 505–514.
67. Richard Aldington, *Portrait of a Rebel* (London, 1957), p. 108.
68. Colvin, *Letters to Family and Friends*, I, 165.

part), and it satisfied him moderately well. "From the Clyde to Sandy Hook" was so strongly disapproved that the idea of publication was dropped by Stevenson, and it did not appear in print until his works were gathered in the posthumous Edinburgh Edition, from which the rougher passages were deleted, presumably by Colvin, the editor. "Across the Plains," however, was allowed to appear in a magazine in 1883, although its offending passages were also withheld at the request of Colvin and Stevenson's other protectors.

The tone of the whole work, as Stevenson wrote it, was different from his earlier travel accounts, as it should have been, for in it he told of hard and often sordid experiences. Although the idea of setting off on a sea voyage across three thousand miles of ocean on a journey to reach his sweetheart seemed romantic enough, rough fellow passengers and rougher surroundings had produced a different subject matter and attitude from that to which he and his associates had become accustomed and which they had taught the public to expect. Nevertheless, at the suggestion of his friends, *The Athenaeum* of Feb. 7, 1880, indicated to readers that they could expect the same mixture as before, for it announced that Stevenson was preparing "a third set of his charming *impressions de voyage*." But he knew that a different situation demanded a different response. As he said early in the work, "a writer of the school of M. Zola would here find an inspiration for many pages," and deciding that to be the proper line, he followed it, even though ordinarily he would not have traded one chapter of Dumas "for the whole boiling of the Zolas." [69] Although Colvin found the work "squalid" because it contained more than he liked of the Zolaesque view, he also had other reasons to consider some of the manuscript unsuitable. It would not have required a lawyer like his friend Charles Baxter to point out that the Anchor Line might find actionable material in the text, that some of the officers or crew of its *Devonia* could possibly

69. Colvin, *Letters to Family and Friends*, I, 234.

discover libelous statements, and that the instructions on how best to stow away and which line to select would hardly be welcomed by steamship companies.

The passages and even whole pages of carefully wrought prose that were cut from the manuscript have not reappeared in their proper places until the publication of this present edition. On the occasion of the dedication of The Beinecke Rare Book and Manuscript Library at Yale University, where this manuscript is housed, the deletions on pages 92–95 were printed in a limited keepsake edition, but the rest are here published for the first time, thanks to the kind permission of that library. The previously deleted portions of the work deepen and extend the sense of Stevenson's second-class passage. However, if they add to the tone of the work, they do not change its subject. Although upon occasion the wind sings in the rigging and we sense the buffeting of the waves, our view of the voyage is essentially limited to that which occurs on board ship. What we are given is a description of humanity huddled together in a microcosm that might almost as well be in some isolated enclosure ashore as at sea. It is this sense of enclosure that is more fully and vividly bodied forth in the uncut text, for the filth of men, women, and children living together in close quarters is pungently forced upon us, and we get a real feeling why Stevenson should call them "human animals" and refer to their habitation as "stalls" and "pens."

The individuals who are singled out as subjects for separate vignettes are also more forcefully evoked in the extended text. "The Sick Man," who receives a chapter to himself, is made a good deal sicker and a good deal more unpleasantly so in the original manuscript. He is also made a good deal more of a person because we are allowed to observe the "courtliness of a good heart" that led him to offer a handkerchief so that Stevenson might clean off the vomit in which he had kneeled. Similarly the stowaway Alick is made not only more perfidious but also more blackguardly as we see a little further into his nasty way with women. In both parts of *The Amateur Emi-*

grant we get franker views of common people, of the mean-
nesses of surly employees of steamship company and railroad
line alike, and even of why Stevenson himself should often
have been in such poor temper. A bit of fever and some general discomfort Colvin could tolerate in print, but he could
not allow a description of the vermin-infested body of Stevenson that had made him a mass of sores and reduced him to endless scratching.

The deletions cut about thirty per cent of "From the Clyde
to Sandy Hook" — passages quite as good as the more seemly
ones that were allowed to remain. All had been written in terrible pain. "God only knows how much courage and suffering
is buried in that MS.," he told Colvin, and there was a single
passage, "about having got to shore, and sich, which must
have cost me altogether six hours of work as miserable as ever
I went through." [70] The deletions from "Across the Plains"
were fewer (only about five pages out of fifty-seven), for in it
there was no vomit from seasickness; but still there were
smells of unwashed human bodies too long confined in too
small a space, and still there were unpleasant references to
sharp railroad practices and to the American character, and
these had to go. Yet the work was not so bad that it could not
be allowed in print long before its predecessor, even though
Stevenson had thought that it would be only the second section, titled "The Emigrant Train," to follow "The Emigrant
Ship," as part of one work, *The Amateur Emigrant.* Alone it is
not only short but seems a bit odd, for it begins flatly, like a
snatch of diary, and without an antecedent for the reference
to "our own" emigrant ship.

Although the whole manuscript was presumably acceptable
to Kegan Paul and Company, which had published his two
previous books, the galley proofs were considerably marked
up for deletion. When his family cabled to San Francisco that
he might expect a good allowance thereafter, his first act was
to write Colvin to "recover the sheets of the *Emigrant,* and

70. *Ibid.,* I, 172

post them registered to me," [71] and he took the sheets with him
to Silverado, there to work painfully over excision and rewrit-
ing of the first part. Even that did not satisfy the family, and
more than a year after his return home his father told him, "I
think it not only the worst thing you have done, but altogether
unworthy of you." [72] Therefore Stevenson allowed his father
to pay the publishers a hundred pounds to withdraw the work
that showed the scion of a good professional Edinburgh family
traveling with dirt and disease and associating with poor people. Not until after the author's death was the opening and
longest section of his book issued, and then in a bowdlerized
form that partly concealed what Richard Aldington rightly
calls "the most mature piece of work Stevenson had yet produced." [73]

The sketches that came out of his California residence were
far more satisfactory to Stevenson's official literary guardians.
The one on Monterey opens with a softly descriptive, charm-
ingly picturesque view of the lovely natural setting. The
second part evokes the mood of an idyllic pastoral life based on
the Spanish and Mexican past. It concludes with the coming of
a luxury resort and the plaint: "Alas for the little town! it is
not strong enough to resist the influence of the flaunting
caravanserai, and the poor, quaint, penniless native gentlemen
of Monterey must perish, like a lower race, before the millionaire vulgarians of the Big Bonanza." There one has the precur-
sor of the Steinbeck manner and mood, a half-century before
Tortilla Flat, and it was as appealing to sentimentalists then as
later.

Having written about the old Pacific capital, Stevenson
gathered impressions for a later essay on the new Pacific capital; but he presumably considered it a lesser affair since, although it was written in 1882 and printed in a magazine the

71. *Ibid.,* I, 172.
72. George L. McKay, *Some Notes on Robert Louis Stevenson: His
Finances and His Agents and His Publishers* (New Haven, 1958), p. 16.
73. Aldington, *Portrait of a Rebel,* p. 109.

next year, he never included it in any of his several collections of essays, leaving book publication to wait until the first edition of his collected works. If not in his most mature style, the essay is nevertheless smoothly pleasing with its colorful, personal tone. Three words — romance, quaint, and foreign — run through the work like a refrain. Other imagery and diction are also consciously repeated, such as the "forest of masts" toward the opening, echoed in the "forest of spars" near the end. Alliteration and assonance are so contrived that Mexicans must appear as "countrymen of Cortes." Yet despite all the "literaryisms," as Stevenson later called them, the work is an attractively evocative essay.

The Silverado Squatters is a far more substantial work, not only in length but in achievement. It belongs with his two preceding travel books — *An Inland Voyage* and *Travels with a Donkey* — as well as with one based on his recent trip to California. Whereas the subject has the charm inherent in the earlier works, the treatment has the character developed in the more recent one. It grew directly out of the experiences he recorded in his *Journal* at Silverado; in fact, what he wrote in the *Journal*, as the admirable edition by Professor John E. Jordan points out, is "not the raw material of a book; it is the rough draft." Stevenson feared that he was presenting the new subject matter in his same youthful manner, simply pouring new wine into old bottles — "large vats, small bottles," he called it.[74] Although the work does have a good deal of what Henry James called Stevenson's "literary surface," the obviously cadenced phrase and decoration for its own sake are far less common than they were in his earliest books. He struggled against the speciously fine figure of speech, and he looked askance at the expression "flower-dotted" when he observed it in the Boston edition, declaring, "I never wrote that, O American printer, but what did I write. — maybe I did though." [75]

Of course, as he realized, the work is not without its manner-

74. Jordan, *Silverado Journal*, pp. xxxv, xxxix.
75. McKay, *A Stevenson Library*, VI, 2253–2254.

isms. They begin with its title, *The Silverado Squatters*, which is made playfully romantic by careful alliteration, an exotic place name, and the adventuresome overtones imparted by the use of the word "squatters" rather than "campers." He still toyed with antiquarian diction, such as "marish," a poetic and obsolete word for marshy, or "malvoisies," an archaism for malmsey grapes. Even spelling had its effect, for the "e" added to "ranch" seems to take it out of the dirt of Far West farming and into the domain of a Spanish hacienda. Someone else — perhaps Colvin or the printer — endowed another word with a color even beyond Stevenson's, for in his *Journal* kept at Silverado he always alluded to a "canyon," whereas in the printed work it was transmuted into the more Spanish "cañon."

Despite the exotic diction and spelling, and regardless of the literary atmosphere engendered by a spate of quotations from authors as disparate as the Elizabethan Sir Henry Wotton, the contemporary American John T. Trowbridge, Victor Hugo, Dryden, and Thomas Dekker, *The Silverado Squatters* never becomes bookish. Since it grew out of life in the open air, the surroundings are tremendously significant. Always there is a sense of setting. Even before the incidents comes the site. Just as his essay on Monterey is introduced by a vivid image of topography, and his piece on San Francisco begins with a description of the city's location as seen on a map, this work opens with the observation that the summit of Mount Saint Helena affords a place for "an excellent lesson of geography." The very first sentence sets the matter of interest before the reader: "The scene of this little book is on a high mountain." Having established his mountain, Stevenson moves into the community of men, where "life in its shadow goes rustically forward." Yet often the natural scene substitutes for human association, so that he writes, "there was scarce any trace of man but the road we followed . . . but we had the society of these bright streams," or "around the foot of the mountain the silence of nature reigns in a great measure unbroken," or yet again, "that part of the mountainside, which is very open and free, was tenanted by no living creatures but ourselves and the insects; and nothing stirred but the cloud manufactory upon the mountain summit." Sometimes the setting is the entire subject, as in that tour de force "The Sea Fogs," a chapter whose soft outlines and quiet coloring have the effect of a Japanese print or an impressionist painting.

This attractive ambiance is often made to seem as fanciful as the forest of Arden. As Stevenson says of the old mine, "it was a promising scene for the imagination," and his imagination invests it and its people with a charming legendry. Having humorously chosen for his title page a quotation from Cicero comparing men who live in the country to kings, he playfully extends this figure elsewhere in the book. He writes of himself and his wife as "the King and Queen of Silverado"; young Sam is "the Crown Prince, on horseback, who led the way like an outrider"; and even Chuchu, their mongrel setter crossed with spaniel, is known as "the Grand Duke." When mother and son are stricken with diphtheria, the reader learns only that there was "an interregnum." Although at many points the description of people and places is plain enough, the arch and amused manner makes even the most forthright remarks appear agreeable. Life tends to become a great game in this sequestered realm of his creation. In the sylvan wonderland the scenes melt one into another with a dreamy beauty remotely reminiscent of *The Faerie Queene,* or perhaps even more of an eighteenth-century Spenserian poem like James Thomson's *Castle of Indolence* — a work, indeed, whose title Stevenson bestows upon the local inn. The light-hearted tone, less full-bodied than is appropriate to the Spenserian tradition, indulges in the sort of mock-heroic analogies that Washington Irving enjoyed, as when Stevenson conjures up spires for the pines and gargoyles for the abandoned mine. Thus, the atmosphere of the honeymoon scene is made at once quaint and whimsical, romantic and appealing.

Into this "great solitude of four-and-twenty mountain hours" are introduced fine set pieces, vivid vignettes of the moment,

like the coming of the stagecoach to the Toll House, recalling
perhaps one of Washington Irving's sketches and enlivened by
such characters as "the ogling well-shod lady with her troop
of girls" or the "burly, thickset, powerful Chinese desperado,
six long bristles upon either lip," who flash momentarily across
the bucolic scene and then are gone, leaving Stevenson's quiet
world alone and far behind. That world produced its own people too, in abundance, and they receive fuller development
than the strangers who but whisk through it. Unlike *An Inland
Voyage* or *Travels with a Donkey*, which have no fully developed characters, Stevenson's books about travel to and
through the United States are replete with vivid personalities.
They are quickly sketched or lightly treated in the two earlier
works, but in *The Silverado Squatters* their development is almost as great as would be expected in a piece of fiction. Perhaps only three or four of the chapters are fully devoted to
characterization, like "The Scot Abroad," "To Introduce Mr.
Kelmar," and "The Hunter's Family," yet they are not the
only ones to establish firmly realized persons. Alongside the
great clan of Kelmar and the rustic Hansons with their brutish
brother-in-law Irvine are such fine though lighter-sketched
figures as Petrified Charley Evans, "a far more delightful curiosity" to Stevenson than all his natural phenomena, suited only
to make the heart of a geologist beat quicker. Some people are
exaggerated for literary purposes, so that they occasionally
seem as quaint as Dickensian caricatures, but they are not for
that reason to be conceived as the subject of contempt or prejudice. The reference to the Jewish storekeepers in "Monterey" or
the treatment of the Kelmar family are matters for amusement,
not antipathy. Therefore, it is understandable that Stevenson
was truly amazed when a Scottish lady suggested that he might
be anti-Semitic. To him it was certainly "a strange idea," since
"Isaiah and David and Heine are good enough for me; and I
leave more unsaid." [76] So close did Stevenson feel to his charac-

76. Adelaide A. Boodle, *R. L. S. and His Sine Qua Non* (London,
1926), p. 140.

ters that he even violated a Victorian tradition by treating his own family in a personal way. Notwithstanding the gentility of Richard Watson Gilder, the editor of *The Century* where *The Silverado Squatters* first appeared, Stevenson alludes to his wife as "Fanny" toward the end of the work, although previously he has properly mentioned her only as "my wife," and his stepson appears generally as "Sam," as he was then commonly called, or occasionally under his middle name of Lloyd.

Stevenson's year in the United States had been a significant one, and the country where he gained a wife and family remained thereafter one of the nations to which he felt close. In his *Silverado Journal* he wrote, "I am a Scotchman, touch me and you will find the thistle; I am a Briton, and live and move and have my being in the greatness of our national achievements; but am I to forget the long hospitality of that beautiful and kind country, France? or has not America done me favours to confound my gratitude? Nay, they are all my relatives; I love them all dearly." [77] Much as he liked the new world, he saw it not only as it was but in terms of the other countries that he knew and loved well. So it was that his writings, no matter in which country they were created, borrowed the language or allusions of one or another of his favorite lands. When he came to write of his life in the United States, he drew sometimes upon experiences of Europe, such as his comparison of the Toll House to a Davos resort or his treatment of California wines in terms of Valtellines met in Switzerland. His native Scottish diction was always strongly with him too. In the opening of *The Silverado Squatters* he describes the Napa Valley as "a long green strath," while in his essay on San Francisco he calls the mouth of the Columbia River "a firth." Even more purposefully provincial and striking Scotticisms occur, such as those toward the end of *The Silverado Squatters*, where he uses the word "scaurs" for the more usual "rocks" and compares the size of a California kangaroo rat to the badge on a MacGregor bonnet.

77. Jordan, *Silverado Journal*, pp. 18–19.

During his remaining fourteen years he always remembered America as "a great place for kindness." [78] He saw the United States only once more — in 1887–88 on the way to his final home in Samoa — but again and again his mind reverted to his days in California. Three years after he left America, he published *Treasure Island*, his most popular book. Although it is a romantic tale of adventures occurring on an imaginary island, Stevenson admitted to Colvin, "The scenery is Californian in part, and in part *chic*." [79] Years ago, George R. Stewart carefully analyzed what was Californian and what was *chic*, and showed that there was a good deal more of the former. One needs but glance at the opening pages of "Monterey" to see how much the breakers that roared upon the beach there are like the ocean around Treasure Island where, although "the sun might blaze overhead, the air be without a breath, the surface smooth and blue, but still these great rollers would be running along all the external coast, thundering and thundering by day and night; and I scarce believe there is one spot in the island where a man would be out of earshot of their noise." And how similar to the peninsula of Monterey is the land through which Jim Hawkins adventures, "undulating, sandy country, about a mile long, dotted with a few pines, and a great number of contorted trees, not unlike the oak in growth, . . . the boughs curiously twisted, the foliage compact, like thatch." As Jim climbs upward out of the marshes and sands, he leaves behind the land of Monterey and, like Stevenson, strikes up into terrain akin to that of Silverado. When he innocently walks by some snakes, "one raised his head from a ledge of rock and hissed at me with a noise not unlike the spinning of a top," [80] just as Stevenson had noted often encountering a snake in the Silverado woodpile who "thrust up his small head between two logs, and hissed at the intrusion," its rattles whizzing

78. Janet Adam Smith, *Henry James and Robert Louis Stevenson* (London, 1948), p. 123.
79. Colvin, *Letters to Family and Friends*, I, 321.
80. *Treasure Island,* chaps. XIV, XXII.

"like spinning-wheels." On the hillside Jim delights in vegetation like that which Stevenson saw from the platform of the abandoned mine: "a heavy-scented broom and many flowering shrubs had almost taken the place of grass. Thickets of green nutmeg trees were dotted here and there with the red columns and the broad shadow of the pines; and the first mingled their spice with the aroma of the others. The air, besides, was fresh and stirring, and this, under the sheer sunbeams, was a wonderful refreshment to our senses." Over all looms the profile peculiar to Mount Saint Helena, flat-topped as seen from the south, in the novel called Spyglass Hill, running up sheer from almost every side, and then suddenly cut off at the top "like a pedestal to put a statue on." [81]

It is apparent that more than a summer residence had emerged from what Stevenson calls in the essay "our first prospect of Juan Silverado." As the name makes plain, Long John Silver came from it, too. If there was play-acting at Calistoga about being "here in a land of stage-drivers and highwaymen: a land, in that sense, like England a hundred years ago," and lighthearted romancing about the realm of Silverado, so there is boyish adventure in the novel's romantic and imaginary scenes that the region suggested. Both *The Silverado Squatters* and *Treasure Island* are first person narratives, each in its way a picaresque adventure story in which scene and situation depend one upon another. Even part of the situation for the novel came out of local matters, for the Monterey *Californian* reported during Stevenson's stay that an old rumor of a buried treasure had been verified when a resident of the area, out hunting quail, came across a newly dug hole and near it found one old coin, like the solitary piece discovered by the mutineer Morgan.

Not only in *Treasure Island*, written at the time that *The Silverado Squatters* was revised into a book, did Stevenson remember California. In the poem "To My Name-child," writ-

81. *Treasure Island*, chaps. XIII, XXXI.

ten for little Louis Sanchez, the son of Fanny's sister, he imagines the youngster

> Seeking shells and seaweed on the sands of Monterey,
> Watching all the mighty whalebones lying buried by the
> breeze,
> Tiny sand-pipers and the huge Pacific seas

and tenderly tells him

> And that while you thought of no one, nearly half the
> world away
> Some one thought of Louis on the beach of Monterey!

There were other works too that came out of his California experience. In *The Ebb Tide*, written the very year of his death, the story never reaches San Francisco, but as Stewart says, "the presence and power of the city hangs upon the edge of the story as Captain Flint hovers just outside the action of *Treasure Island*." [82] In *The Wrecker* one gets an even fuller sense of what the region meant to him. The tale is told by a sea captain in the Marquesas Islands in the style of Conrad, and although his adventures take him over half the world, including Paris, Edinburgh, and the South Pacific, it is on San Francisco that they center. From there come the characters named the Speedys, modeled on the Carsons, Stevenson's landlord and landlady of years before; and the unnamed "youngish, good-looking fellow" [83] who writes his own adventures and loans his friend a copy of Melville's *Omoo* is a portrait of Charles Warren Stoddard. In San Francisco, too, Stevenson had heard the bawling and swearing of Kearney, the demagogic labor leader, and his sandlot followers, wandered through the Italian town of North Beach, climbed the "endless crazy wooden stairs" of little Mexico, so much like the description in his essay on the modern cosmopolis, and poked into the mysteries of Chinatown, "undermined with opium cellars," all

82. George R. Stewart, Jr., "Stevenson in California. A Critical Study," Master's thesis, University of California, Berkeley, 1921, p. 83.
83. *The Wrecker*, chap. IX.

recalled among other sights and sounds of "the city front" in *The Wrecker.*

Clearly, Stevenson had found San Francisco fascinating, even though he was once so sick there that he began "to grow weary and timid in this big jostling city," [84] fearing he might die in it. Instead, it lived forever in his mind, as did all the surrounding region. Out of one year's experience coming to and living in California, Stevenson created three books and as many sketches, and even after he had formally completed his personal narratives based on his own experiences, the region kept entering and shaping other works. His twelve months of suffering and joy in the United States continued to reverberate through Robert Louis Stevenson's writings down to the very last year of his life.

JAMES D. HART

84. Colvin, *Letters to Family and Friends*, I, 160.

The Amateur Emigrant

Robert Alan Mowbray Stevenson

Our friendship was not only founded before we were born by a community of blood, but is in itself near as old as my life. It began with our early ages, and, like a history, has been continued to the present time. Although we may not be old in the world, we are old to each other, having so long been intimates. We are now widely separated, a great sea and continent intervening; but memory, like care, mounts into iron ships and rides post behind the horseman. Neither time nor space nor enmity can conquer old affection; and as I dedicate these sketches, it is not to you only, but to all in the old country, that I send the greeting of my heart.

R. L. S.

1879.

PART I

From the Clyde to Sandy Hook

THE SECOND CABIN

I first encountered my fellow-passengers on the Broomie-law[1] in Glasgow. Thence we descended the Clyde in no familiar spirit, but looking askance on each other as on possible enemies. A few Scandinavians, who had already grown acquainted on the North Sea, were friendly and voluble over their long pipes; but among English speakers distance and suspicion reigned supreme. The sun was soon overclouded, the wind freshened and grew sharp as we continued to descend the widening estuary; and with the falling temperature the gloom among the passengers increased. Two of the women wept. Any one who had come aboard might have supposed we were all absconding from the law. There was scarce a word interchanged, and no common sentiment but that of cold united us, until at length, having touched at Greenock, a pointing arm and a rush to the starboard bow announced that our ocean steamer was in sight. There she lay in mid-river, at the tail of the Bank,[2] her sea-signal flying: a wall of bulwark, a street of white deck-houses, an aspiring forest of spars, larger than a church, and soon to be as populous as many an incorporated town in the land to which she was to bear us.

1. A section of the Glasgow dock area from which river boats took passengers twenty-two miles to the port at Greenock, where the Clyde River widened enough to allow the entry of ocean-going vessels.
2. A large sandbank off Greenock, affording a fine anchorage in the Clyde.

I was not, in truth, a steerage passenger. Although anxious to see the worst of emigrant life, I had some work to finish on the voyage, and was advised to go by the second cabin, where at least I should have a table at command. The advice was excellent; but to understand the choice, and what I gained, some outline of the internal disposition of the ship will first be necessary. In her very nose is Steerage No. 1, down two pair of stairs. A little abaft, another companion, labelled Steerage No. 2 and 3, gives admission to three galleries, two running forward towards Steerage No. 1, and the third aft towards the engines. The starboard forward gallery is the second cabin. Away abaft the engines and below the officers' cabins, to complete our survey of the vessel, there is yet a third nest of steerages, labelled 4 and 5. The second cabin, to return, is thus a modified oasis in the very heart of the steerages. Through the thin partition you can hear the steerage passengers being sick, the rattle of tin dishes as they sit at meals, the varied accents in which they converse, the crying of their children terrified by this new experience, or the clean flat smack of the parental hand in chastisement.

There are, however, many advantages for the inhabitant of this strip. He does not require to bring his own bedding or dishes, but finds berths and a table completely if somewhat roughly furnished. He enjoys a distinct superiority in diet; but this, strange to say, differs not only on different ships, but on the same ship according as her head is to the east or west. In my own experience, the principal difference between our table and that of the true steerage passenger was the table itself, and the crockery plates from which we ate. But lest I should show myself ungrateful, let me recapitulate every advantage. At breakfast, we had a choice between tea and coffee for beverage; a choice not easy to make, the two were so surprisingly alike. I found that I could sleep after the coffee and lay awake after the tea, which is proof conclusive of some chemical disparity; and even by the palate I could distinguish a smack of snuff in the former from a flavour of boiling and dish-cloths in the

second. As a matter of fact I have seen passengers, after many
sips, still doubting which had been supplied them. In the way
of eatables at the same meal we were gloriously favoured; for
in addition to porridge, which was common to all, we had
Irish stew, sometimes a bit of fish, and sometimes rissoles. The
dinner of soup, roast fresh beef, boiled salt junk, and potatoes,
was, I believe, exactly common to the steerage and the second
cabin; only I have heard it rumoured that our potatoes were of
a superior brand; and twice a week, on pudding days, instead
of duff, we had a saddle-bag filled with currants under the
name of a plum-pudding. At tea we were served with some
broken meat from the saloon; sometimes in the comparatively
elegant form of spare patties or rissoles; but as a general thing,
mere chicken-bones and flakes of fish neither hot nor cold. If
these were not the scrapings of plates their looks belied them
sorely; yet we were all too hungry to be proud, and fell to
these leavings greedily. These, the bread, which was excellent,
and the soup and porridge which were both good, formed my
whole diet throughout the voyage; so that except for the
broken meat and the convenience of a table I might as well
have been in the steerage outright. Had they given me porridge
again in the evening, I should have been perfectly contented
with the fare. As it was, with a few biscuits and some whisky
and water before turning in, I kept my body going and my
spirits up to the mark.

The last particular in which the second cabin passenger remarkably stands ahead of his brother of the steerage is one altogether of sentiment. In the steerage there are males and females; in the second cabin ladies and gentlemen. For some time
after I came aboard I thought I was only a male; but in the
course of a voyage of discovery between decks, I came on a
brass plate, and learned that I was still a gentleman. Nobody
knew it, of course. I was lost in the crowd of males and females,
and rigorously confined to the same quarter of the deck. Who
could tell whether I housed on the port or starboard side of
steerage No. 2 and 3? And it was only there that my superior-

ity became practical; everywhere else I was incognito, moving among my inferiors with simplicity, not so much as a swagger to indicate that I was a gentleman after all, and had broken meat to tea. Still, I was like one with a patent of nobility in a drawer at home; and when I felt out of spirits I could go down and refresh myself with a look of that brass plate.

For all these advantages I paid but two guineas. Six guineas is the steerage fare; eight that by the second cabin; and when you remember that the steerage passenger must supply bedding and dishes, and, in five cases out of ten, either brings some dainties with him, or privately pays the steward for extra rations, the difference in price becomes almost nominal. Air comparatively fit to breathe, food comparatively varied, and the satisfaction of being still privately a gentleman, may thus be had almost for the asking. Two of my fellow-passengers in the second cabin had already made the passage by the cheaper fare, and declared it was an experiment not to be repeated. As I go on to tell about my steerage friends, the reader will perceive that they were not alone in their opinion. Out of ten with whom I was more or less intimate, I am sure not fewer than five vowed, if they returned, to travel second cabin; and all who had left their wives behind them assured me they would go without the comfort of their presence until they could afford to bring them by saloon.

Our party in the second cabin was not perhaps the most interesting on board. Perhaps even in the saloon there was as much good-will and character. Yet it had some elements of curiosity. There was a mixed group of Swedes, Danes, and Norsemen, one of whom, generally known by the name of "Johnny," in spite of his own protests, greatly diverted us by his clever, cross-country efforts to speak English, and became on the strength of that an universal favourite — it takes so little in this world of shipboard to create a popularity. There was, besides, a Scots mason, known from his favourite dish as "Irish Stew," three or four nondescript Scots, a fine young Irishman, O'Reilly, and a pair of young men who deserve a special word of condemnation. One of them was Scots: the other claimed to be American; admitted, after some fencing, that he was born in England; and ultimately proved to be an Irishman born and nurtured, but ashamed to own his country. He had a sister on board, whom he faithfully neglected throughout the voyage, though she was not only sick but much his senior, and had nursed and cared for him in childhood. In appearance he was like an imbecile Henry the Third of France. The Scotsman, though perhaps as big an ass, was not so dead of heart; and I have only bracketed them together because they were fast friends, and disgraced themselves equally by their conduct at the table.

Next, to turn to topics more agreeable, we had a newly married couple, devoted to each other, with a pleasant story of how they had first seen each other years ago at a preparatory school, and that very afternoon he had carried her books home for her. I do not know if this story will be plain to Southern readers; but to me it recalls many a school idyll, with wrathful swains of eight and nine confronting each other stride-legs, flushed with jealousy; for to carry home a young lady's books was both a delicate attention and a privilege.

Then there was an old lady, or indeed I am not sure that she was as much old as antiquated and strangely out of place, who had left her husband, and was travelling all the way to Kansas by herself. We had to take her own word that she was married; for it was sorely contradicted by the testimony of her appearance. Nature seemed to have sanctified her for the single state; even the colour of her hair was incompatible with matrimony, and her husband, I thought, should be a man of saintly spirit and phantasmal bodily presence. She was ill, poor thing; her soul turned from the viands; the dirty table-cloth shocked her like an impropriety; and the whole strength of her endeavour was bent upon keeping her watch true to Glasgow time till she should reach New York. They had heard reports, her husband and she, of some unwarrantable disparity of hours between these two cities; and with a spirit commendably scientific, had seized on this occasion to put them to the proof. It was a good thing for the old lady; for she passed much leisure time in studying the watch. Once, when prostrated by sickness, she let it run down. It was inscribed on her harmless mind in letters of adamant that the hands of a watch must never be turned backwards; and so it behoved her to lie in wait for the exact moment ere she started it again. When she imagined this was about due, she sought out one of the young second-cabin Scotsmen, who was embarked on the same experiment as herself and had hitherto been less neglectful. She was in quest of two o'clock; and when she learned it was already seven on the shores of Clyde, she lifted up her voice and cried "Gravy!" I had not heard this innocent expletive since I was a young child; and I suppose it must have been the same with the other Scotsmen present, for we all laughed our fill.

Last but not least, I come to my excellent friend Mr. Jones. It would be difficult to say whether I was his right-hand man, or he mine, during the voyage. Thus at table I carved, while he only scooped gravy; but at our concerts, of which more anon, he was the president who called up performers to sing, and I but his messenger who ran his errands and pleaded privately with the over-modest. I knew I liked Mr. Jones from the moment I saw him. I thought him by his face to be Scottish; nor could his accent undeceive me. For as there is a *lingua franca* of many tongues on the moles and in the feluccas of the Mediterranean, so there is a free or common accent among English-speaking men who follow the sea. They catch a twang in a New England Port; from a cockney skipper even a Scotsman sometimes learns to drop an *h*; a word of a dialect is picked up from another hand in the forecastle; until often the result is undecipherable, and you have to ask for the man's place of birth. So it was with Mr. Jones. I thought him a Scotsman who had been long to sea; and yet he was from Wales, and had been most of his life a blacksmith at an inland forge; a few years in America and half a score of ocean voyages having sufficed to modify his speech into the common pattern. By his own account he was both strong and skilful in his trade. A few years back, he had been married and after a fashion a rich man; now the wife was dead and the money gone. But his was the nature that looks forward, and goes on from one year to another and through all the extremities of fortune undismayed; and if the sky were to fall to-morrow, I should look to see Jones, the day following, perched on a step-ladder and getting things to rights. He was always hovering round inventions like a bee over a flower, and lived in a dream of patents. He had with him a patent medicine, for instance, the composition of which he had bought years ago for five dollars from an American pedlar, and sold the other day for a hundred pounds (I think it was) to an English apothecary. It was called Golden Oil; cured all maladies without exception; and I am bound to say that I partook of it myself with good results. It is a character of the man that he was not only perpetually dosing himself with Golden Oil, but wherever there was a head aching or a finger cut, there would be Jones with his bottle.

If he had one taste more strongly than another, it was to study character. Many an hour have we two walked upon the deck dissecting our neighbours in a spirit that was too purely scientific to be called unkind; whenever a quaint or human trait slipped out in conversation, you might have seen Jones and me exchanging glances; and we could hardly go to bed in comfort till we had exchanged notes and discussed the day's experience. We were then like a couple of anglers comparing a day's kill. But the fish we angled for were of a metaphysical species, and we angled as often as not in one another's baskets. Once, in the midst of a serious talk, each found there was a scrutinising eye upon himself; I own I paused in embarrassment at this double detection; but Jones, with a better civility, broke into a peal of unaffected laughter, and declared, what was the truth, that there was a pair of us indeed.

EARLY IMPRESSIONS

We steamed out of the Clyde on Thursday night, and early on the Friday forenoon we took in our last batch of emigrants at Lough Foyle, in Ireland, and said farewell to Europe. The company was now complete, and began to draw together, by inscrutable magnetisms, upon the deck. There were Scots and Irish in plenty, a few English, a few Americans, a good handful of Scandinavians, a German or two, and one Russian; all now belonging for ten days to one small iron country on the deep.

As I walked the deck and looked round upon my fellow-passengers, thus curiously assorted from all northern Europe, I began for the first time to understand the nature of emigration. Day by day throughout the passage, and thenceforward across all the States, and on to the shores of the Pacific, this knowledge grew more clear and melancholy. Emigration, from a word of the most cheerful import, came to sound most dismally in my ear. There is nothing more agreeable to picture and nothing more pathetic to behold. The abstract idea, as conceived at home, is hopeful and adventurous. A young man, you fancy, scorning restraints and helpers, issues forth into life, that great battle, to fight for his own hand. The most pleasant stories of ambition, of difficulties overcome, and of ultimate success, are but as episodes to this great epic of self-help. The epic is composed of individual heroisms; it stands to them as the victorious war which subdued an empire stands to the personal act of bravery which spiked a single cannon and was adequately rewarded with a medal. For in emigration the young men enter direct and by the shipload on their heritage of work; empty continents swarm, as at the bo'sun's whistle, with industrious hands, and whole new empires are domesticated to the service of man.

This is the closet picture, and is found, on trial, to consist mostly of embellishments. The more I saw of my fellow-passengers, the less I was tempted to the lyric note. Comparatively few of the men were below thirty; many were married and encumbered with families; not a few were already up in years; and this itself was out of tune with my imaginations, for the ideal emigrant should certainly be young. Again, I thought he should offer to the eye some bold type of humanity, with bluff or hawk-like features, and the stamp of an eager and pushing disposition. Now those around me were for the most part quiet, orderly, obedient citizens, family men broken by adversity, elderly youths who had failed to place themselves in life, and people who had seen better days. Mildness was the prevailing character; mild mirth and mild endurance. In a word I was not taking part in an impetuous and conquering sally, such as swept over Mexico or Siberia, but found myself, like Marmion, "in the lost battle, borne down by the flying."

Labouring mankind had in the last years, and throughout Great Britain, sustained a prolonged and crushing series of defeats. I had heard vaguely of these reverses; of whole streets of houses standing deserted by the Tyne, the cellar-doors broken and removed for firewood; of homeless men loitering at the street-corners of Glasgow with their chests beside them; of closed factories, useless strikes, and starving girls. But I had never taken them home to me or represented these distresses livingly to my imagination. A turn of the market may be a calamity as disastrous as the French retreat from Moscow; but it hardly lends itself to lively treatment, and makes a trifling figure in the morning papers. We may struggle as we please, we are not born economists. The individual is more affecting than the mass. It is by the scenic accidents, and the appeal to the carnal eye, that for the most part we grasp the significance of tragedies. Thus it was only now, when I found myself involved in the rout, that I began to appreciate how sharp had been the battle. We were a company of the rejected; the drunken, the incompetent, the weak, the prodigal, all who had been unable to prevail against circumstances in the one land, were now fleeing pitifully to another; and though one or two might still succeed, all had already failed. We were a shipful of failures, the broken men of England. Yet it must not be supposed that these people exhibited depression. The scene, on the contrary, was cheerful. Not a tear was shed on board the vessel. All were full of hope for the future, and showed an inclination to innocent gaiety. Some were heard to sing, and all began to scrape acquaintance with small jests and ready laughter.

The children found each other out like dogs, and ran about the decks scraping acquaintance after their fashion also. "What do you call your mither?" I heard one ask. "Mawmaw," was the reply, indicating, I fancy, a shade of difference in the social scale. When people pass each other on the high seas of life at so early an age, the contact is but slight, and the relation more like what we may imagine to be the friendship of flies than that of men; it is so quickly joined, so easily dissolved, so open in its communications and so devoid of deeper human qualities. The children, I observed, were all in a band, and as thick as thieves at a fair, while their elders were still ceremoniously manœuvring on the outskirts of acquaintance. The sea, the ship, and the seamen were soon as familiar as home to these half-conscious little ones. It was odd to hear them, throughout the voyage, employ shore words to designate portions of the vessel. "Co' 'way doon to yon dyke," I heard one say, probably meaning the bulwark. I often had my heart in my mouth, watching them climb into the shrouds or on the rails while the ship went swinging through the waves; and I admired and envied the courage of their mothers, who sat by in the sun and looked on with composure at these perilous feats. "He'll maybe be a sailor," I heard one remark; "now's the time to learn." I had been on the point of running forward to interfere, but stood back at that, reproved. Very few in the more delicate classes have the nerve to look upon the peril of one dear to them; but the life of poorer folk, where necessity is so much more immediate and imperious, braces even a mother to this extreme of endurance. And perhaps, after all, it is better that the lad should break his neck than that you should break his spirit.

And since I am here on the chapter of the children, I must mention one little fellow, whose family belonged to Steerage No. 4 and 5, and who, wherever he went, was like a strain of music round the ship. He was an ugly, merry, unbreeched child of three, his lint-white hair in a tangle, his face smeared with suet and treacle; but he ran to and fro with so natural a step, and fell and picked himself up again with such grace and good-humour, that he might fairly be called beautiful when he was in motion. To meet him, crowing with laughter and beating an accompaniment to his own mirth with a tin spoon upon a tin cup, was to meet a little triumph of the human species. Even when his mother and the rest of his family lay sick and prostrate around him, he sat upright in their midst and sang aloud in the pleasant heartlessness of infancy.

Throughout the Friday, intimacy among us men made but few advances. We discussed the probable duration of the voyage, we exchanged pieces of information, naming our trades, what we hoped to find in the new world, or what we were fleeing from in the old; and, above all, we condoled together over the food and the vileness of the steerage. One or two had been so near famine that you may say they had run into the ship with the devil at their heels; and to these all seemed for the best in the best of possible steamers. But the majority were hugely discontented. Coming as they did from a country in so low a state as Great Britain, many of them from Glasgow, which commercially speaking was as good as dead, and many having long been out of work, I was surprised to find them so dainty in their notions. I myself lived almost exclusively on bread, porridge, and soup, precisely as it was supplied to them, and found it, if not luxurious, at least sufficient. But these working men were loud in their outcries. It was not "food for human beings," it was "only fit for pigs," it was "a disgrace." Many of them lived almost entirely upon biscuit, others on their own private supplies, and some paid extra for better rations from the ship. This marvellously changed my notion of the degree of luxury habitual to the artisan. I was prepared to hear him grumble, for grumbling is the traveller's pastime; but I was not prepared to find him turn away from a diet which was palatable to myself. Words I should have disregarded, or taken with a liberal allowance; but when a man prefers dry biscuit there can be no question of the sincerity of his disgust.

With one of their complaints I could most heartily sympathise. A single night of the steerage had filled them with horror. I had myself suffered, even in my decent second-cabin berth, from the lack of air; and as the night promised to be fine and quiet, I determined to sleep on deck, and advised all who complained of their quarters to follow my example. I daresay a dozen of others agreed to do so, and I thought we should have been quite a party. Yet when I brought up my rug about seven bells, there was no one to be seen but the watch. That chimerical terror of good night-air, which makes men close their windows, list their doors, and seal themselves up with their own poisonous exhalations, had sent all these healthy workmen down below. One would think we had been brought up in a fever country; yet in England the most malarious districts are in the bedchambers.

I felt saddened at this defection, and yet half-pleased to have the night so quietly to myself. The wind had hauled a little ahead on the starboard bow, and was dry but chilly. I found a shelter near the fire-hole, and made myself snug for the night. The ship moved over the uneven sea with a gentle and cradling movement. The ponderous, organic labours of the engine in her bowels occupied the mind, and prepared it for slumber. From time to time a heavier lurch would disturb me as I lay, and recall me to the obscure borders of consciousness; or I heard, as it were through a veil, the clear note of the clapper on the brass and the beautiful sea-cry, "All's well!" I know nothing, whether for poetry or music, that can surpass the effect of these two syllables in the darkness of a night at sea.

The day dawned fairly enough, and during the early part we had some pleasant hours to improve acquaintance in the open air; but towards nightfall the wind freshened, the rain began to fall, and the sea rose so high that it was difficult to keep one's footing on the deck. I have spoken of our concerts. We were indeed a musical ship's company, and cheered our way into exile with the fiddle, the accordion, and the songs of all nations. ⟨Night after night we gathered at the aftermost limit of our domain, where it bordered on that of the saloon. Performers were called up with acclamation, some shame-faced and hanging the head, others willing and as bold as brass.⟩ Good, bad, or indifferent — Scottish, English, Irish, Russian, German or Norse, — the songs were received with generous applause. Once or twice, a recitation, very spiritedly rendered in a powerful Scottish accent, varied the proceedings; and once we sought in vain to dance a quadrille, eight men of us together, to the music of the violin. The performers were all humorous, frisky fellows, who loved to cut capers in private life; but as soon as they were arranged for the dance, they conducted themselves like so many mutes at a funeral. I have never seen decorum pushed so far; and as this was not expected, the quadrille was soon whistled down, and the dancers departed under a cloud. Eight Frenchmen, even eight Englishmen from another rank of society, would have dared to make some fun for themselves and the spectators; but the working man, when sober, takes an extreme and even melancholy view of personal deportment. A fifth-form schoolboy is not more careful of dignity. He dares not be comical; his fun must escape from him unprepared, and above all, it must be unaccompanied by any physical demonstration. I like his society under most circumstances, but let me never again join with him in public gambols.

But the impulse to sing was strong, and triumphed over modesty and even the inclemencies of sea and sky. On this rough Saturday night, we got together by the main deck-house, in a place sheltered from the wind and rain. Some clinging to a ladder which led to the hurricane deck, and the rest knitting arms or taking hands, we made a ring to support the women in the violent lurching of the ship; and when we were thus disposed, sang to our hearts' content. Some of the songs were appropriate to the scene; others strikingly the reverse. Bastard doggerel of the music-hall, such as, "Around her splendid form, I weaved the magic circle," sounded bald, bleak, and pitifully silly. "We don't want to fight, but, by Jingo, if we do," was in some measure saved by the vigour and unanimity with which the chorus was thrown forth into the night. I observed a Platt-Deutsch mason, entirely innocent of English, adding heartily to the general effect. And perhaps the German mason is but a fair example of the sincerity with which the song was rendered; for nearly all with whom I conversed upon the subject were bitterly opposed to war, and attributed their own misfortunes, and frequently their own taste for whisky, to the campaigns in Zululand and Afghanistan.

Every now and again, however, some song that touched the pathos of our situation was given forth; and you could hear by the voices that took up the burden how the sentiment came home to each. "The Anchor's Weighed" was true for us. We were indeed "Rocked on the bosom of the stormy deep." How many of us could say with the singer, "I'm lonely to-night, love, without you," or "Go, some one, and tell them from me, to write me a letter from home!" And when was there a more appropriate moment for "Auld Lang Syne" than now, when the land, the friends, and the affections of that mingled but beloved time were fading and fleeing behind us in the vessel's wake? It pointed forward to the hour when these labours should be overpast, to the return voyage, and to many a meeting in the sanded inn,[1] when those who had parted in the spring of youth should again drink a cup of kindness in their age. Had

1. Country inns often had their floors strewn with sand for cleanliness and ornament.

not Burns contemplated emigration, I scarce believe he would have found that note.

⟨This was the first fusion of our little nationality together. The wind sang shrill in the rigging; the rain fell small and thick; the whole group, linked together as it was, was shaken and swung to and fro as the swift steamer shore into the waves. It was a general embrace, both friendly and helpful, like what one imagines of old Christian Agapes. I turned many times to look behind me on the moving desert of seas, now cloud-canopied and lit with but a low nocturnal glimmer along the line of the horizon. It hemmed us in and cut us off on our swift-travelling oasis. And yet this waste was part a playground for the stormy petrel; and on the least tooth of reef, outcropping in a thousand miles of unfathomable ocean, the gull makes its home and dwells in a busy polity. And small as was our iron world, it made yet a large and habitable place in the Atlantic, compared with our globe upon the seas of space.⟩

All Sunday the weather remained wild and cloudy; many were prostrated by sickness; only five sat down to tea in the second cabin, and two of these departed abruptly ere the meal was at an end. The Sabbath was observed strictly by the majority of the emigrants. I heard an old woman express her surprise that "the ship didna gae doon," as she saw some one pass her with a chess-board on the holy day. Some sang Scottish psalms. Many went to service, and in true Scottish fashion came back ill pleased with their divine. "I didna think he was an experienced preacher," said one girl to me.

It was a bleak, uncomfortable day; but at night, by six bells, although the wind had not yet moderated, the clouds were all wrecked and blown away behind the rim of the horizon, and the stars came out thickly overhead. I saw Venus burning as steadily and sweetly across this hurly-burly of the winds and waters as ever at home upon the summer woods. The engine pounded, the screw tossed out of the water with a roar, and shook the ship from end to end; the bows battled with loud reports against the billows; and as I stood in the lee-scuppers and looked up to where the funnel leaned out over my head, vomiting smoke, and the black and monstrous topsails blotted, at each lurch, a different crop of stars, it seemed as if all this trouble were a thing of small account, and that just above the mast reigned peace unbroken and eternal.

STEERAGE SCENES

Our companion (Steerage No. 2 and 3) was a favourite resort. Down one flight of stairs there was a comparatively large open space, the centre occupied by a hatchway, which made a convenient seat for about twenty persons, while barrels, coils of rope, and the carpenter's bench afforded perches for perhaps as many more. The canteen, or steerage bar, was on one side of the stair; on the other, a no less attractive spot, the cabin of the indefatigable interpreter. I have seen people packed into this space like herrings in a barrel, and many merry evenings prolonged there until five bells, when the lights were ruthlessly extinguished and all must go to roost.

It had been rumoured since Friday that there was a fiddler aboard, who lay sick and unmelodious in Steerage No. 1; and on the Monday forenoon, as I came down the companion, I was saluted by something in Strathspey time.[1] A white-faced Orpheus was cheerily playing to an audience of white-faced women. It was as much as he could do to play, and some of his hearers were scarce able to sit; yet they had crawled from their bunks at the first experimental flourish, and found better than medicine in the music. Some of the heaviest heads began to nod in time, and a degree of animation looked from some of the palest eyes. Humanly speaking, it is a more important matter to play the fiddle, even badly, than to write huge works upon recondite subjects. What could Mr. Darwin have done for these sick women? But this fellow scraped away; and the world was positively a better place for all who heard him. We have yet to understand the economical value of these mere

---

1. Music for a dance that originated in northeast Scotland, somewhat like but slightly slower than a reel.

accomplishments. I told the fiddler he was a happy man, carrying happiness about with him in his fiddle-case, and he seemed alive to the fact.

"It is a privilege," I said. He thought a while upon the word, turning it over in his Scots head, and then answered with conviction, "Yes, a privilege."

That night I was summoned by "Merrily danced the Quaker's wife" into the companion of Steerage No. 4 and 5. This was properly speaking, but a strip across a deck-house, lit by a sickly lantern which swung to and fro with the motion of the ship. Through the open slide-door we had a glimpse of a grey night sea, with patches of phosphorescent foam flying, swift as birds, into the wake, and the horizon rising and falling as the vessel rolled to the wind. In the centre the companion ladder plumped down sheerly like an open pit. Below, on the first landing, and lighted by another lamp, lads and lasses danced, not more than three at a time for lack of space, in jigs and reels and hornpipes. Above, on either side, there was a recess railed with iron, perhaps two feet wide and four long, which stood for orchestra and seats of honour. In the one balcony, five slatternly Irish lasses sat woven in a comely group. In the other was posted Orpheus, his body, which was convulsively in motion, forming an odd contrast to his somnolent, imperturbable Scots face. His brother, a dark man with a vehement, interested countenance, who made a god of the fiddler, sat by with open mouth, drinking in the general admiration and throwing out remarks to kindle it.

"That's a bonny hornpipe now," he would say; "it's a great favourite with performers; they dance the sand dance to it." [2] And he expounded the sand dance. Then suddenly, it would be a long "Hush!" with uplifted finger and glowing, supplicating eyes; "he's going to play 'Auld Robin Gray' on one string!" And throughout this excruciating movement, — "On one string, that's on one string!" he kept crying. I would have

2. A step dance, of which a hornpipe is one type, performed on a sanded floor.

given something myself that it had been on none; but the hearers were much awed. I called for a tune or two, and thus introduced myself to the notice of the brother, who directed his talk to me for some little while, keeping, I need hardly mention, true to his topic, like the seamen to the star. "He's grand of it," he said confidentially. "His master was a music-hall man." Indeed the music-hall man had left his mark, for our fiddler was ignorant of many of our best old airs; "Logie o' Buchan," for instance, he only knew as a quick, jigging figure in a set of quadrilles, and had never heard it called by name. Perhaps, after all, the brother was the more interesting performer of the two. I have spoken with him afterwards repeatedly, and found him always the same quick, fiery bit of a man, not without brains; but he never showed to such advantage as when he was thus squiring the fiddler into public note. There is nothing more becoming than a genuine admiration; and it shares this with love, that it does not become contemptible although misplaced.

The dancing was but feebly carried on. The space was almost impracticably small; and the Irish wenches combined the extreme of bashfulness about this innocent display with a surprising impudence and roughness of address. Most often, either the fiddle lifted up its voice unheeded, or only a couple of lads would be footing it and snapping fingers on the landing. And such was the eagerness of the brother to display all the acquirements of his idol, and such the sleepy indifference of the performer, that the tune would as often as not be changed, and the hornpipe expire into a ballad before the dancers had cut half a dozen shuffles.

In the meantime, however, the audience had been growing more and more numerous every moment; there was hardly standing-room round the top of the companion; and the strange instinct of the race moved some of the new-comers to close both the doors, so that the atmosphere grew insupportable. It was a good place, as the saying is, to leave.

The wind hauled ahead with a head sea. By ten at night

heavy sprays were flying and drumming over the forecastle;
the companion of Steerage No. 1 had to be closed, and the
door of communication through the second cabin thrown open.
Either from the convenience of the opportunity, or because
we had already a number of acquaintances in that part of
the ship, Mr. Jones and I paid it a late visit. Steerage No. 1
is shaped like an isosceles triangle, the sides opposite the equal
angles bulging outward with the contour of the ship. It is lined
with eight pens of sixteen bunks apiece, four bunks below and
four above on either side. ⟨The companion lands about the
middle of the greater length, and thus cuts the open space
between the pens into two unequal apartments, as a drawing
room and boudoir. Each of these is furnished with a table and
fixed benches; that in the forward space being shaped to a
point, a triangle within a triangle, to fit the inclination of the
ship's timbers.⟩ At night the place is lit with two lanterns, one
to each table. As the steamer beat on her way among the rough
billows, the light passed through violent phases of change, and
was thrown to and fro and up and down with startling swiftness. You were tempted to wonder, as you looked, how so
thin a glimmer could control and disperse such solid blackness.
⟨Even by day much of the steerage enjoyed but a groping
twilight. I presume (for I never saw it) that some cleansing
process was carried on each morning; but there was never light
enough to be particular; and in a place so full of corners and
so much broken up by fixtures and partitions, dirt might lie for
years without disturbance. The pens, stalls, pews — I know
not what to call them — were besides, by their very design,
beyond the reach of bucket and swab. Each broad shelf with
its four deep divisions, formed a fourfold asylum for all manner
of uncleanness. When the pen was fully occupied, with sixteen
live human animals, more or less unwashed, lying immersed
together in the same close air all night, and their litter of meat,
dirty dishes and rank bedding tumbled all day together in foul
disorder, the merest possibilities of health or cleanliness were
absent.

If it was impossible to clean the steerage, it was no less impossible to clean the steerage passenger. All ablution below was rigorously forbidden. A man might give his hands a scour at the pump beside the galley, but that was exactly all. One fellow used to strip to his waist every morning and freshen his chest and shoulders; but I need not tell you he was no true steerage passenger. To wash outside in the sharp sea air of the morning is a step entirely foreign to the frowsy, herding, over-warm traditions of the working class; and a human body must apparently have been nurtured in some luxury, before it courts these rude shocks and surprises of temperature in which many men find health and vigour. Thus, even if the majority of passengers came clean aboard at Greenock, long ere the ten days were out or the shores of America in sight, all were reduced to a common level, all, who here stewed together in their own exhalations, were uncompromisingly unclean. A writer of the school of M. Zola would here find an inspiration for many pages; but without entering farther into detail, let me mention the name of sea sickness, and leave its added horrors to the imagination of the reader.

I have said that, on our voyage, the ship was a good deal below her full complement of passengers. Perhaps not half of the pens numbered their complete sixteen; and every here and there an empty bunk afforded elbow-room and something like a wardrobe to the neighbours. Steerage No. 1 was especially intended for single men; yet more than one family was here installed among the others. It was strange to note how the different nationalities had drawn apart; for all English speakers were in the foremost bunks, and Germans and Scandinavians had clustered aft into a couple of pens upon the starboard side. This separation was marked and openly recognised. I remember coming down one morning to look for the Russian, and being told that I should find him "back there wi' the Germans".) When Jones and I entered we found a little company of our acquaintances seated together at the triangular foremost table. A more forlorn party, in more dismal circumstances, it would be hard to imagine. The motion here in the ship's nose was very violent; the uproar of the sea often overpoweringly loud. The yellow flicker of the lantern spun round and round and tossed the shadows in masses. The air was hot, but it struck a chill from its fœtor. From all round in the dark bunks, the scarcely human noises of the sick joined into a kind of farm-yard chorus. In the midst, these five friends of mine were keeping up what heart they could in company. ⟨They looked white and heavy-eyed; nor was it wonderful if they were indisposed; for aside from the suggestive noises which assailed the ear, there was forced upon the mind, in this quarter of the ship, a strong and almost disquieting sense of the swiftness of her advance and the rudeness of her conflict with the sea.⟩ Singing was their refuge from discomfortable thoughts and sensations. One piped, in feeble tones, "O why left I my hame?" which seemed a pertinent question in the circumstances. Another, from the invisible horrors of a pen where he lay dog-sick upon the upper shelf, found courage, in a blink of his sufferings, to give us several verses of the 'Death of Nelson'; and it was odd and eerie to hear the chorus breathe feebly from all sorts of dark corners, and "this day has done his dooty" rise and fall and be taken up again in this dim *inferno*, to an accompaniment of plunging, hollow-sounding bows and the rattling spray-showers overhead. ⟨It seemed to me the singer, at least, that day had done his duty. For to sing in such a place and in such a state of health is cheerfully heroic. Like a modern Theseus, he thus combatted bad air, disease and darkness, and threw abroad among his fellows some pleasant and courageous thoughts.⟩

All seemed unfit for conversation; a certain dizziness had interrupted the activity of their minds; and except to sing they were tongue-tied. There was present, however, one tall, power-ful fellow of doubtful nationality, being neither quite Scotsman nor altogether Irish, but of surprising clearness of conviction on the highest problems. He had gone nearly beside himself on the Sunday, because of a general backwardness to indorse his definition of mind as "a living, thinking, substance which cannot be felt, heard, or seen" — nor, I presume, although he failed to mention it, smelt. Now he came forward in a pause with another contribution to our culture.

"Just by way of change," said he, "I'll ask you a Scripture riddle. There's profit in them too," he added ungrammatically.

This was the riddle—

> "C and P
> Did agree
> To cut down C;
> But C and P
> Could not agree
> Without the leave of G.
> All the people cried to see
> The crueltie
> Of C and P."

Harsh are the words of Mercury after the songs of Apollo! We were a long while over the problem, shaking our heads and gloomily wondering how a man could be such a fool; but at length he put us out of suspense and divulged the fact that C and P stood for Caiaphas and Pontius Pilate. (The more I study his enigma, which is given here with critical exactitude, the more deeply am I astonished by its feebleness and historical inaccuracy. It touches moreover, in an insidious, unsettling way, on a serious problem of faith; and is probably, take it for all in all, the work of an infidel propaganda in collaboration. Or perhaps it is a *memoria technica* for some exceedingly complicated date? I advise the reader to get it off by heart, for someday, who knows? it might be useful to him. For my own part, I shall never forget either the riddle or the time and place in which I heard it; and as for its propounder, though I cannot think either philosophy or history to be his forte, he seemed a brave and a warm-hearted man, and he was good to hear when he spoke about his wife and children.)

I think it must have been the riddle that settled us; but the motion and the close air likewise hurried our departure. We had not been gone long, we heard next morning, ere two or even three out of the five fell sick. We thought it little wonder on the whole, for the sea kept contrary all night. I now made my bed upon the second cabin floor, where, although I ran the risk of being stepped upon, I had a free current of air, more or less vitiated indeed, and running only from steerage to steerage, but at least not stagnant; and from this couch, as well as the usual sounds of a rough night at sea, the hateful coughing and retching of the sick and the sobs of children, I heard a man run wild with terror beseeching his friend for encouragement. "The ship's going down!" he cried with a thrill of agony. "The ship's going down!" he repeated, now in a blank whisper, now with his voice rising towards a sob; and his friend might re-assure him, reason with him, joke at him — all was in vain, and the old cry came back, "The ship's going down!" There was something panic and catching in the emotion of his tones; and I saw in a clear flash what an involved and hideous tragedy was a disaster to an emigrant ship. If this whole parishful of people came no more to land, into how many houses would the news-paper carry woe, and what a great part of the web of our cor-porate human life would be rent across for ever!

The next morning when I came on deck I found a new world indeed. The wind was fair; the sun mounted into a cloudless heaven; through great dark blue seas the ship cut a swathe of curded foam. The horizon was dotted all day with companionable sails, and the sun shone pleasantly on the long, heaving deck.

We had many fine-weather diversions to beguile the time. There was a single chess-board and a single pack of cards. Sometimes as many as twenty of us would be playing dominoes for love. Feats of dexterity, puzzles for the intelligence, some arithmetical, some of the same order as the old problem of the fox and goose and cabbage, were always welcome; and the latter, I observed, more popular as well as more conspicuously well done than the former. ⟨A party of gentlemen (I speak in the sense of caste alone) would have excelled my workman friends at hop-step-and-jump or push-the-stick, but they would scarce have displayed the same patience in these lesser exercises of the mind.⟩ We had a regular daily competition to guess the vessel's progress; and twelve o'clock, when the result was published in the wheel-house, came to be a moment of considerable interest. But the interest was unmixed. Not a bet was laid upon our guesses. From the Clyde to Sandy Hook I never heard a wager offered or taken. We had, besides, romps in plenty. Puss in the Corner, which we had rebaptized, in more manly style, Devil and Four Corners, was my own favourite game; but there were many who preferred another, ⟨nameless as far as I know, which was diverting enough to the onlookers, but must have developed a tendency to headache in those who played. The humour of the thing⟩ was to box a person's ears until he found out who had cuffed him. ⟨The harder the smacks, the better we were all pleased. I have watched it for half an hour at a time; nor do I think it was a sense of personal dignity alone, which moved me to refrain from joining.⟩

This Tuesday morning we were all delighted with the change of weather, and in the highest possible spirits. We got in a cluster like bees, sitting between each other's feet under lee of the deck-houses. Stories and laughter went around. The children climbed about the shrouds. White faces appeared for the first time, and began to take on colour from the wind. I was kept hard at work making cigarettes for one amateur after another, and my less than moderate skill was heartily admired. Lastly, down sat the fiddler in our midst and began to discourse his reels, and jigs, and ballads, with now and then a voice or two to take up the air and throw in the interest of human speech.

Through this merry and good-hearted scene there came three cabin passengers, a gentleman and two young ladies, picking their way with little gracious titters of indulgence, and a Lady-Bountiful air about nothing, which galled me to the quick. I have little of the radical in social questions, and have always nourished an idea that one person was as good as another. But I began to be troubled by this episode. It was astonishing what insults these people managed to convey by their presence. They seemed to throw their clothes in our faces. Their eyes searched us all over for tatters and incongruities. A laugh was ready at their lips; but they were too well-mannered to indulge it in our hearing. Wait a bit, till they were all back in the saloon, and then hear how wittily they would depict the manners of the steerage. We were in truth very innocently, cheerfully, and sensibly engaged, and there was no shadow of excuse for the swaying elegant superiority with which these damsels passed among us, or for the stiff and waggish glances of their squire. Not a word was said; only when they were gone Mackay sullenly damned their impudence under his breath; but we were all conscious of an icy influence and a dead break in the course of our enjoyment. ⟨We had been made to feel ourselves a sort of comical lower animal. Such a fine thing it is to have manners!

One compliment I must make to the Saloon passengers: this was the only invasion of our territory that I witnessed from beginning to end of the voyage. It was a piece of very natural and needful delicacy. We were not allowed upon their part of the ship; and so they were, and ought, to be chary of intruding upon ours. Reciprocity can alone justify such a privilege. I do not say but that a cabin passenger may once in a while slink forward under cover of night, just as some careful householders, when the servants are once in bed, descend to the kitchen for a cigar. We also, when night had fallen, installed ourselves along the hot water pipes with our backs to the saloon deckhouse. But except in some exceptional, anonymous or apologetic fashion, I give it as my experience, the visit of a cabin passenger, will be regarded as an intrusion in the steerage.⟩

STEERAGE TYPES

⟨The type of man in our steerage was by no means one to
be despised. Some were handy, some intellectual, and almost all
were pleasantly and kindly disposed. I had many long and
serious talks, and many a good bout of mirth with my fellow
passengers and I thought they formed, upon the whole, an
agreeable and well informed society.⟩

We had a fellow on board, an Irish-American, for all the
world like a beggar in a print by Callot; one-eyed, with great,
splay crow's-feet round the sockets; a knotty squab nose coming down over his moustache; a miraculous hat; a shirt that had
been white, ay, ages long ago; an alpaca coat in its last sleeves;
and, without hyperbole, no buttons to his trousers. Even in
these rags and tatters, the man twinkled all over with impudence like a piece of sham jewellery; and I have heard him
offer a situation to one of his fellow-passengers with the air of
a lord. Nothing could overlie such a fellow; a kind of base success was written on his brow. He was then in his ill days; but
I can imagine him in Congress with his mouth full of bombast
and sawder.[1] As we moved in the same circle, I was brought
necessarily into his society. I do not think I ever heard him say
anything that was true, kind, or interesting; but there was
entertainment in the man's demeanour. You might call him a
half-educated Irish Tigg.[2]

Our Russian made a remarkable contrast to this impossible
fellow. Rumours and legends were current in the steerages

1. A slang word for flattery, like "blarney."
2. Tigg, of Dickens's *Martin Chuzzlewit*, is the swindler who directs
the Anglo-Bengalese Disinterested Loan and Life Insurance Company,
whose worthless stock he sells by means of artful persuasion and
blackmail.

about his antecedents. Some said he was a Nihilist escaping; others set him down for a harmless spendthrift, who had squandered fifty thousand roubles, and whose father had now despatched him to America by way of penance. Either tale might flourish in security; there was no contradiction to be feared, for the hero spoke not one word of English. I got on with him lumberingly enough in broken German, and learnt from his own lips that he had been an apothecary. He carried the photograph of his betrothed in a pocketbook, and remarked that it did not do her justice. The cut of his head stood out from among the passengers with an air of startling strangeness. The first natural instinct was to take him for a desperado; but although the features, to our Western eyes, had a barbaric and unhomely cast, the eye both reassured and touched. It was large and very dark and soft, with an expression of dumb endurance, as if it had often looked on desperate circumstances and never looked on them without resolution.

He cried out when I used the word. "No, no," he said, "not resolution."

"The resolution to endure," I explained.

And then he shrugged his shoulders, and said, "*Ach, ja,*" with gusto, like a man who has been flattered in his favourite pretensions. Indeed, he was always hinting at some secret sorrow; and his life, he said, had been one of unusual trouble and anxiety; so the legends of the steerage may have represented at least some shadow of the truth. Once, and once only, he sang a song at our concerts, standing forth without embarrassment, his great stature somewhat humped, his long arms frequently extended, his Kalmuck head thrown backward. It was a suitable piece of music, as deep as a cow's bellow and wild like the White Sea. He was struck and charmed by the freedom and sociality of our manners. At home, he said, no one on a journey would speak to him, but those with whom he would not care to speak; thus unconsciously involving himself in the condemnation of his countrymen. But Russia was soon to be changed; the ice of the Neva was softening under the sun of civilisation; the new ideas, *"wie ein feines Violin,"* were audible among the big, empty drum-notes of Imperial diplomacy; and he looked to see a great revival, though with a somewhat indistinct and childish hope.

We had a father and son who made a pair of Jacks-of-all-Trades. It was the son who sang the "Death of Nelson" under such contrarious circumstances (and who contributed on many other occasions to make the voyage a happy period for all). He was by trade a shearer of ship plates; but he could touch the organ, had led two choirs, and played the flute and piccolo in a professional string band. His repertory of songs was, besides, inexhaustible, and ranged impartially from the very best to the very worst within his reach. Nor did he seem to make the least distinction between these extremes, but would cheerfully follow up "Tom Bowling" with "Around her splendid form."

The father, an old, cheery, small piece of manhood, could do everything connected with tinwork from one end of the process to the other, use almost every carpenter's tool, and make picture-frames to boot. "I sat down with silver plate every Sunday," said he, "and pictures on the wall. I have made enough money to be rolling in my carriage. But, sir," looking at me unsteadily with his bright rheumy eyes, "I was troubled with a drunken wife." He took a hostile view of matrimony in consequence. "It's an old saying," he remarked: "God made 'em, and the devil he mixed 'em."

I think he was justified by his experience. It was a dreary story. He would bring home three pounds on Saturday, and on Monday all the clothes would be in pawn. Sick of the useless struggle, he gave up a paying contract, and contented himself with small and ill-paid jobs. "A bad job was as good as a good job for me," he said; "it all went the same way." Once the wife showed signs of amendment; she kept steady for weeks on end; it was again worth while to labour and to do one's best. The husband found a good situation some distance from home, and, to make a little upon every hand, started the wife in a cook-shop; the children were here and there, busy as mice; savings began to grow together in the bank, and the golden age of hope had returned again to that unhappy family. But one week my old acquaintance, getting earlier through with his work, came home on the Friday instead of the Saturday, and there was his wife to receive him, reeling drunk. He "took and gave her a pair o' black eyes," for which I pardon him, nailed up the cook-shop door, gave up his situation, and resigned himself to a life of poverty, with the workhouse at the end. As the children came to their full age they fled the house, and established themselves in other countries; some did well, some not so well; but the father remained at home alone with his drunken wife, all his sound-hearted pluck and varied accomplishments depressed and negatived.

Was she dead now? or, after all these years, had he broken the chain, and run from home like a schoolboy? I could not discover which; but here at least he was, out on the adventure, and still one of the bravest and most youthful men on board.

"Now, I suppose, I must put my old bones to work again," said he; "but I can do a turn yet."

And the son to whom he was going, I asked, was he not able to support him?

"Oh yes," he replied. "But I'm never happy without a job on hand. And I'm stout; I can eat a'most anything. You see no craze about me."

⟨I should say, to finish this sketch, that he was usually more given to listen than to speak; he was indeed an indefatigable hearer, always on the edge of the group, pipe in hand, with his best ear upraised; and though unlettered and, I think, ignorant, loved to hear serious things discussed. It is strange that I should have permitted myself to use the word ignorant, about a man who understood and could successfully practise so great a variety of trades; and yet the word must remain, for there is no other to convey my meaning. Thus I have known people to declare both painters and musicians stupid, because their thoughts, lying out of the literary path, are not suited for display in company. Colours or sounds, chisels or vices, about whatever the mind may be occupied, it is still enlarged and invigorated; and yet it remains a question, whether these thoughts which cannot be clothed and rendered commonplace in words, may not be after all the most bracing and veracious. At least it would be ignorance itself to think my old acquaintance ignorant. Although one profession may be dully acquired betwixt sleep and waking, to change from one to another implies both activity and courage of the mind. For no inducement that I can fancy, would I set myself to learn another business; because the mind has grown slothful and dreads to grapple with a mass of fresh details.)

This tale of a drunken wife was paralleled on board by another of a drunken father. He was a capable man, with a good chance in life; but he had drunk up two thriving businesses like a bottle of sherry, and involved his sons along with him in ruin. Now they were on board with us, fleeing his disastrous neighbourhood.

Total abstinence, like all ascetical conclusions, is unfriendly to the most generous, cheerful, and human parts of man; but it could have adduced many instances and arguments from among our ship's company. I was one day conversing with a kind and happy Scotsman, running to fat and perspiration in the physical, but with a taste for poetry and a genial sense of fun. I had asked him his hopes in emigrating. They were like those of so many others, vague and unfounded: times were bad at home; they were said to have a turn for the better in the States; and a man could get on anywhere, he thought. That was precisely the weak point of his position; for if he could get on in America, why could he not do the same in Scotland? But I never had the courage to use that argument, though it was often on the tip of my tongue, and instead I agreed with him heartily, adding, with reckless originality, "If the man stuck to his work, and kept away from drink."

"Ah!" said he slowly, "the drink! You see, that's just my trouble."

He spoke with a simplicity that was touching, looking at me at the same time with something strange and timid in his eye, half-ashamed, half-sorry, like a good child who knows he should be beaten. You would have said he recognised a destiny to which he was born, and accepted the consequences mildly. Like the merchant Abudah,[3] he was at the same time fleeing from his destiny and carrying it along with him, the whole at an expense of six guineas.

As far as I saw, drink, idleness, and incompetency were the three great causes of emigration, and for all of them, and drink first and foremost, this trick of getting transported overseas appears to me the silliest means of cure. ⟨It is like turning in bed when you are down with a fever; you will find the new position as uneasy as the last.⟩ You cannot run away from a weakness; you must some time fight it out or perish; and if that be so, why not now, and where you stand? *Cœlum non animam.*[4] Change Glenlivet[5] for Bourbon, and it is still whisky, only not so good. A sea-voyage will not give a man the nerve to put aside cheap pleasure; emigration has to be done before we climb the vessel; an aim in life is the only fortune worth the finding; and it is not to be found in foreign lands, but in the heart itself.

Speaking generally, there is no vice of this kind more contemptible than another; for each is but a result and outward sign of a soul tragically ship-wrecked. In the majority of cases, cheap pleasure is resorted to by way of anodyne. The pleasure-seeker sets forth upon life with high and difficult ambitions; he meant to be nobly good and nobly happy, though at as

3. James Ridley's *The Tales of the Genii* (1764), written under the pseudonym Sir Charles Morell and supposedly translated from the Persian, describes a legendary Bagdad merchant, Abudah, who can be freed of the hag who nightly haunts him only by discovering the talisman of Oromanes. The hag represents conscience and the talisman enjoins one to fear God and to keep His commandments.

4. The Latin tag comes from the line in Horace's *Epistles* (I, xi, 27), "Cœlum non animum mutant qui trans mare currunt" (They change their sky, not their soul, who run across the sea).

5. A fine Scotch whiskey.

little pains as possible to himself; and it is because all has failed in his celestial enterprise that you now behold him rolling in the garbage. Hence the comparative success of the tee-total pledge; because to a man who had nothing it sets at least a negative aim in life. Somewhat as prisoners beguile their days by taming a spider, the reformed drunkard makes an interest out of abstaining from intoxicating drinks, and may live for that negation. There is something, at least, *not to be done* each day; and a cold triumph awaits him every evening.

We had one on board with us, whom I have already referred to under the name of Mackay, who seemed to me not only a good instance of this failure in life of which we have been speaking, but a good type of the intelligence which here surrounded me. Physically he was a small Scotsman, standing a little back as though he were already carrying the elements of a corporation, and his looks somewhat marred by the smallness of his eyes. Mentally, he was endowed above the average. There were but few subjects on which he could not converse with understanding and a dash of wit; (and from these he had voluntarily abstracted his intelligence. His style of talking was remarkable; his words were selected with great discretion and out of a full possession of the English language; and he delivered) himself slowly and with gusto, like a man who enjoyed his own sententiousness. He was a dry, quick, pertinent debater, speaking with a small voice, and swinging on his heels to launch and emphasise an argument. When he began a discussion, he could not bear to leave it off, but would pick the subject to the bone, without once relinquishing a point. An engineer by trade, Mackay believed in the unlimited perfectibility of all machines except the human machine. The latter he gave up with ridicule for a compound of carrion and perverse gases. He had an appetite for disconnected facts which I can only compare to the savage taste for beads. What is called information was indeed a passion with the man, and he not only delighted to receive it, but could pay you back in kind.

With all these capabilities, here was Mackay, already no

longer young, on his way to a new country, with no prospects, no money, and but little hope. He was almost tedious in the cynical disclosures of his despair. "The ship may go down for me," he would say, "now or to-morrow. I have nothing to lose and nothing to hope." And again: "I am sick of the whole damned performance." He was, like the kind little man already quoted, another so-called victim of the bottle. But Mackay was miles from publishing his weakness to the world; laid the blame of his failure on corrupt masters and a corrupt State policy; and after he had been one night overtaken and had played the buffoon in his cups, sternly, though not without tact, suppressed all reference to his escapade. It was a treat to see him manage this; the various jesters withered under his gaze, and you were forced to recognise in him a certain steely force, and a gift of command which might have ruled a senate.

In truth it was not whiskey that had ruined him; he was ruined long before for all good human purposes but conversation. His eyes were sealed by a cheap, school-book materialism. He could see nothing in the world but money and steam-engines. He did not know what you meant by the word happiness. He had forgotten the simple emotions of childhood, and perhaps never encountered the delights of youth. He believed in production, that useful figment of economy, as if it had been real like laughter; and production, without prejudice to liquor, was his god and guide. One day he took me to task — a novel cry to me — upon the over-payment of literature. Literary men, he said, were more highly paid than artisans; yet the artisan made threshing-machines and butter-churns, and the man of letters, except in the way of a few useful handbooks, made nothing worth the while. He produced a mere fancy article. Mackay's notion of a book was Hoppus's *Measurer.*[6] Now in my time I have possessed and even studied that work.

6. Edward Hoppus's *Practical Measuring Made Easy to the Meanest Capacity by a New Set of Tables, Which Shew, at Sight, the Solid Contents of Any Piece of Timber, Stone, &c.* was first published in 1738 and was later reissued with abbreviated titles, such as *Practical Measurer.*

⟨I found Hoppus a careful although scarce a stimulating writer; and I own he left something in my soul unsatisfied. If⟩ I were to be left to-morrow on Juan Fernandez, Hoppus's is not the book that I should choose for my companion volume.

I tried to fight the point with Mackay. I made him own that he had taken pleasure in reading books otherwise, to his view, insignificant; but he was too wary to advance a step beyond the admission. It was in vain for me to argue that here was pleasure ready-made and running from the spring, whereas his ploughs and butter-churns were but means and mechanisms to give men the necessary food and leisure before they start upon the search for pleasure; he jibbed and ran away from such conclusions. The thing was different, he declared, and nothing was serviceable but what had to do with food. "Eat, eat, eat!" he cried; "that's the bottom and the top." By an odd irony of circumstance, he grew so much interested in this discussion that he let the hour slip by unnoticed and had to go without his tea. He had enough sense and humour, indeed he had no lack of either, to have chuckled over this himself in private; and even to me he referred to it with the shadow of a smile. ⟨Here, at least, was my contention in a nutshell: his sentiments were saddening to me, yet it was with interest that I listened to him as he spoke; on his side, although he forgot the staff of life for the pleasure he had in continuing the dispute, he thought my views not only silly but wickedly wrong.⟩

Mackay was a hot bigot. He would not hear of religion. I have seen him waste hours of time in argument with all sorts of poor human creatures who understood neither him nor themselves, and he had had the boyishness to dissect and criticise even so small a matter as the riddler's definition of mind. He snorted aloud with zealotry and the lust for intellectual battle. Anything, whatever it was, that seemed to him likely to discourage the continued passionate production of corn and steam-engines he resented like a conspiracy against the people. Thus, when I put in the plea for literature, that it was only in good books, or in the society of the good, that a man could get help in his conduct, he declared I was in a different world from him. "Damn my conduct!" said he. "I have given it up for a bad job. My question is, Can I drive a nail?" And he plainly looked upon me as one who was insidiously seeking to reduce the people's annual bellyful of corn and steam-engines. ⟨I feel there is some mistake in this alarm, and that the people could get through life perhaps with less of either. But when I hinted something of that view, and that to spend less was, after all, as good a way out of the difficulty of life as to gain more, he accused me, in almost as many words, of the sin of aristocracy and a desire to grind the masses. Perhaps there was some indelicacy on my part in presenting him with such an argument; for it is not in his class that such a movement must be inaugurated; and we must see the rich honest, before we need look hopefully to see the poor considerate.

Mackay was the very man to be reclaimed by total abstinence; and if reclaimed, would present a typical instance of those useless successes and victorious defeats which are too often the only trophies of the movement. The sort of reformation that I care about must be of a more sweeping order. I have not the least aversion to the continued poverty of many tipplers; I am far more concerned about the continued prosperity and power of many unworthy capitalists. Although I am far from cherishing unfriendly feelings towards Mackay, for the man both interested and amused me, it seems still an open question whether, for the general interests of the race, he had not better remain poor and drink himself to death. There was nothing in him worth saving but his talents, which he would be sure to misapply. He had no hope but to make money and to squander it. As he is, you have a shiftless, tippling engineer; but let him be rich, and he will be an oppressor of men. Working man and master are but John and Jack; and when Mackay bewails the hard condition of his class, he is only rejecting the legitimate course of his own philosophy. "Damn my conduct!" is an agreeable and light hearted sentiment on a man's own lips; but it becomes practically inconvenient when it is adopted as a principle by others.)

It may be argued that these opinions spring from the defect of culture; that a narrow and pinching way of life not only exaggerates to a man the importance of material conditions, but indirectly, by denying him the necessary books and leisure, keeps his mind ignorant of larger thoughts; and that hence springs this overwhelming concern about diet, and hence the bald view of existence professed by Mackay. Had this been an English peasant the conclusion would be tenable. ⟨I was already a young man when I was first brought into contact with some of the heavy English labourers of Suffolk; and only those who have some acquaintance with the same class in Scotland, can conceive the astonishment and disgust with which I viewed the difference. To me, they seemed scarce human, but like a very gross and melancholy sort of ape; and though I may have been unfortunate in the examples that fell under my observation, the fact of my amazement is enough to my present purpose. The feeling was the more impressed on me after my return to Scotland, by a conversation with a labourer upon the shores of Fife. This man was cleaning a barge, in which I was driven to take refuge from a squall of rain; and he sat down by my side, fantastically, not to say disgustingly, bedaubed with liquid manure. But his mind was clean and vigorous and full of grave thoughts. He spoke with me of education, culture and the learned professions. "Aye," said he, "that's the thing for a man to be happy. *Ye see, he has aye something ayont.*" It would be hard to set forth more clearly the advantages of an intellectual life. You could not call this man uncultured; and yet his is no uncommon case among the field labourers of Scotland. A sound, sometimes even an ambitious education lays the basis; the metaphysical and sentimental turn of the race leads them, at their outdoor work, to hoard and improve on what they have learned; the *Bible* and even the *Shorter Catechism* (like it or not, as you please) are works of a high scope which stimulate the mind; and many a peasant has his own heresy or holds orthodoxy on some terms of his own. As a people, they are not ignorant, not uncultured and certainly, you would say, not materialistic.⟩ But Mackay had most of the elements of a liberal education. He had skirted metaphysical and mathematical studies. He had a thoughtful hold of what he knew, which would be exceptional among bankers. He had been brought up in the midst of hot-house piety, and told, with incongruous pride, the story of his own brother's deathbed ecstasies. Yet he had somehow failed to fulfil himself, and was adrift like a dead thing among external circumstances, without hope or lively preference or shaping aim. And further, there seemed a tendency among many of his fellows to fall into the same blank and unlovely opinions. One thing, indeed, is not to be learned in Scotland, and that is, the way to be happy. Yet that is the whole of culture, and perhaps two-thirds of morality. Can it be that the Puritan school, by divorcing a man from nature, by thinning out his instincts, and setting the stamp of its disapproval on whole fields of human activity and interest, leads at last directly to material greed? ⟨Not in Scotland alone, but in New England also, there are features that might justify the suspicion.⟩

Nature is a good guide through life, and the love of simple pleasures next, if not superior, to virtue; and we had on board an Irishman who based his claim to the widest and most affectionate popularity precisely upon these two qualities, that he was natural and happy. He boasted a fresh colour, a tight little figure, unquenchable gaiety, and indefatigable good-will. His clothes puzzled the diagnostic mind, until you heard he had been once a private coachman, when they became eloquent and seemed a part of his biography. His face contained the rest, and, I fear, a prophecy of the future; the hawk's nose above accorded so ill with the pink baby's mouth below. His spirit and his pride belonged, you might say, to the nose: while it was the general shiftlessness expressed by the other that had thrown him from situation to situation, and at length on board the emigrant ship. Barney ate, so to speak, nothing from the galley; his own tea, butter, and eggs supported him throughout the voyage; and about meal-time you might often find him up to the elbows in amateur cookery. His was the first voice heard singing among all the passengers; he was the first who fell to dancing. From Loch Foyle to Sandy Hook, there was not a piece of fun undertaken but there was Barney in the midst.

You ought to have seen him when he stood up to sing at our concerts — his tight little figure stepping to and fro, and his feet shuffling to the air, his eyes seeking and bestowing encouragement — and to have enjoyed the bow, so nicely calculated between jest and earnest, between grace and clumsiness, with which he brought each song to a conclusion. He was not only a great favourite among ourselves, but his songs attracted the lords of the saloon, who often leaned to hear him over the rails of the hurricane-deck. He was somewhat pleased but not at all abashed, by this attention; and one night, in the midst of his famous performance of "Billy Keogh," I saw him spin half round in a pirouette and throw an audacious wink to an old gentleman above.

This was the more characteristic, as, for all his daffing, he was a modest and very polite little fellow among ourselves. He would not have hurt the feelings of a fly, nor throughout the passage did he give a shadow of offence; yet he was always, by his innocent freedoms and love of fun, brought upon that narrow margin where politeness must be natural to walk without a fall. He was once seriously angry, and that in a grave, quiet manner, because they supplied no fish on Friday; for Barney was a conscientious Catholic. He had likewise strict notions of refinement; and when, late one evening, after the women had retired, a young Scotsman struck up an indecent song, Barney's drab clothes were immediately missing from the group. His taste was for the society of gentlemen, of whom, with the reader's permission, there was no lack in our five steerages and second cabin; and he avoided the rough and positive with a girlish shrinking. Mackay, partly from his superior powers of mind, which rendered him incomprehensible, partly from his extreme opinions, was especially distasteful to the Irishman. I have seen him slink off, with backward looks of terror and offended delicacy, while the other, in his witty, ugly way, had been professing hostility to God, and an extreme theatrical readiness to be shipwrecked on the spot. These utterances hurt the little coachman's modesty like a bad word. ⟨His love for music was inborn and generous; none had so ready an applause as Barney; I have seen the delight with which he was introduced to Scotch dance music and his silent contempt for the melodies of the Music Hall. And it is àpropos of Barney that I must relate the great change which overtook the organization of our nightly concerts. Barney had no distaste for whiskey; and he and the young Jack-of-all-Trades received many a stiff glass from enthusiastic hearers. The fiddler, on the other hand, being silent and almost morose, fiddled away nightly and received no invitations to the bar. This partiality began to prey upon his mind; and one evening he made a clean breast of it to Jones and threatened to strike work. Here was a bomb shell in our camp. Barney and the Jack-of-all-Trades were certainly our two most esteemed vocalists; we might have continued to run the concerts on their attraction only; but it was not to be thought of that a valued collaborator should retire under a sense of neglect. The fiddler, too, should have his whiskey. It was decided to collect money, and offer a little collation upon deck to the performers in a body.

I am afraid we were all a little thoughtless, and I in the front rank; upon meeting Barney, I opened the matter to him without preparation and in terms that were perhaps too naked. He flushed to his neck. "Well then," he said, "I do not sing at your concerts any more": adding he was glad enough to sing to amuse his friends, but would not sing at all for whiskey. I could only murmur that I thought he was right; and on that, he turned upon his heel and left me to my degradation. As everybody connected with the affair was now in a false position, and myself in the falsest, I retired to the cabin or, in so many words, hid myself.

What passed on deck, I never rightly knew. It appears, however, it was a scene of consternation for awhile; and Jones and
young O'Reilly were cursing me for my defection. I must own
I left them to bear the brunt that evening; but my time came
too; for as I was sitting below and making some pretence to
write my notes, I received a message that Barney wished to
speak with me on deck. I went up with the resignation of the
condemned criminal, feeling that if he wished my blood, it was
no less than due to him, and, generally, that I had been blunt,
inconsiderate and ungentlemanly. But there he was — bless his
heart! — waiting to load me with apologies. He had spoken
sharply; he had been impolite; he could not rest till he was
pardoned. "You have always been a good friend to me," was
his humble way of putting it, when the fact was that we had
been good friends together. I protested that it was I alone who
stood in need of pardon; but he would hear of no such thing;
and I daresay we walked half an hour about the deck, before
he consented to a compromise by which we were to pardon
one another.

Meantime the system of concerts had been permanently
destroyed, not at all, as Barney maintained, by his pride and ill-
temper, but by a general want of tact among the rest of us;
and instead, a select company moved by invitation into the
second cabin. It was a kind of high life below stairs, which
pleased me far less than our public and open air festivals of the
past. But in this small way, they were not unsuccessful and
offered some curious features. The fiddler combed his hair before appearing on this new and more select stage; and another
performer, the young bride of whom the reader has been told,
now lifted up a small and rather sweet pipe in little drawing-
room ditties, sometimes alone, sometimes accompanied by her
husband. But the point was the effect produced on Barney. In
this small, quiet and, so to speak, genteel society, he opened
like a rose. Pleasure looked out of his eyes. He seemed less
merry than on deck, but his manners grew more affectionate
and domestic; I have never seen a gallantry so kind as that with

which he treated the ladies of this small circle; and he would
have sung himself to death to give us pleasure. Nor can I find
words to tell you with what enthusiasm he greeted the singing
of the bride. These drawing room songs were exactly after his
heart; he delighted in that music-mistress style; I believe the
very smallness of the voice seemed to him a mark of refinement. Up to nearly midnight, he sat on deck declaring and
exaggerating his delight.

His Irishisms and merry simplicities of speech were our current money and went round the steerage like the day's news.
Once, he got two pills from the Doctor, took one, and brought
the other back with scorn. He was of Captain Burnaby's mind,
it appeared; nothing would please him but Corkle's pills and
not less than four of these. The Doctor protested he had but
one box, which he reserved for his own use and that of the
cabin passengers. "Sure, Doctor," said Barney, "am n't I not
the same Christian as yourself and the cabin passengers?" I
need hardly say, the pills were given. Indeed he had only to
spring the brogue on any one of us, and he could command
what we had.

One story more I must relate, as I have some notes of what
he said, and the incident besides completes the character of
Barney. I have spoken of a semi-official position, that of assistant to the Steerage steward, and how rapidly the semi-
officials grew disgusted and resigned the place. The second of
these had reigned, as I said, for a whole day. About noon on
the morrow, a good many of us were hanging round the hatchway at the foot of companion No. 2 and 3, when round came
the steerage steward, with his white sheet of loaves girt about
him, like a man going forth to sow; and behind, carrying with
both hands a huge tin dish of butter, who but Barney? He
was greeted with acclamation; passed among us, rosy and smiling, half amused, half gratified with the distinction; and followed his superior down one of the galleries, with an overdone
air of business, like a child helping to lay the table.

Perhaps ten minutes elapsed; and then Barney reappeared at

full speed out of the steerage, set the dish down upon the hatchway with a bang, and threw himself rolling on the tarpaulin.

"The divel in your butter!" he cried, and buried his face in his hands.

The sheeted steward now followed and looked distressfully on his assistant amid shouts of laughter. It was some time before he found anything to say, and even then his voice came hollow from a profound consciousness that he should exhort in vain.

"Come along!" he cried feebly. "Up with it, Johnny!"

"Sorry am I that iver you took Johnny in your mouth," retorted Barney.

And the steward, seeing all was over, departed in search of other help; Barney had concluded his career as a semi official; how the rations were finally served out upon that occasion is more than I can tell.

Meantime Barney picked himself up, a rueful looking Barney.

"I must go on deck," said he. "I'm sick wid their butter. I can feel the smell of it!"

"It's rotten," struck in an old woman.

"Rotten?" cried Barney, brightening up. "Well, I'll tell ye. I gave a Dutchman down there the full of me hat of it. He wouldn't be plased wid less!"

And so greatly comforted by having raised another laugh and callously unconcerned at his desertion, he departed upon deck and shall disappear from these pages.)

THE SICK MAN

One night Jones, the young O'Reilly, and myself were walking arm-in-arm and briskly up and down the deck. Six bells had rung; a head-wind blew chill and fitful, the fog was closing in with a sprinkle of rain, and the fog-whistle had been turned on, and now divided time with its unwelcome outcries, loud like a bull, thrilling and intense like a mosquito. ⟨The decks were deserted.⟩ Even the watch lay somewhere snugly out of sight. ⟨We passed the furnaces and through a blast of heat; and as we cleared the deck house, met the cold wind upon our cheek; and these alternations alone marked our promenade.⟩

For some time we observed something lying black and hud-dled in the scuppers, ⟨not far from where I was wakened by the fireman. At first we made light of it; but as we passed again and again, it began insensibly to occupy our minds; and as we reached the spot, the talk would languish, the pace would halt, and our three heads would all be inclined to that side. Almost unconsciously, we were beginning to grow in-terested in the black bundle; and before long by a natural process, we should have stopped of our own accord to satisfy our curiosity. But the matter was taken out of our hands; for the bundle⟩ heaved a little and moaned aloud. We ran to the rails. An elderly man, but whether passenger or seaman⟨, whether beautiful or the reverse, it⟩ was impossible in the darkness to determine, lay grovelling on his belly in the west scup-pers, and kicking feebly with his outspread toes. ⟨He had been sick and his head was in his vomit.⟩ We asked him what was amiss, and he replied incoherently, with a strange accent and in a voice unmanned by terror, that he had cramp in the stomach, that he had been ailing all day, had seen the doctor

twice, and had walked the deck against fatigue till he was
overmastered and had fallen where we found him.

Jones remained by his side, while O'Reilly and I hurried off
to seek the doctor. We knocked in vain at the doctor's cabin;
there came no reply; nor could we find any one to guide us.
It was no time for delicacy; so we ran once more forward;
and I, whipping up a ladder and touching my hat to the officer
of the watch, addressed him as politely as I could —

"I beg your pardon, sir; but there is a man lying bad with
cramp in the lee scuppers; and I can't find the doctor."

He looked at me peeringly in the darkness; and then, somewhat harshly, "Well, *I* can't leave the bridge, my man," said he.

"No, sir; but you can tell me what to do," I returned.

"Is it one of the crew?" he asked.

"I believe him to be a fireman," I replied⟨, going merely on
my last experience.⟩

I daresay officers are much annoyed by complaints and
alarmist information from their freight of human creatures; but
certainly, whether it was the idea that the sick man was one of
the crew, or from something conciliatory in my address, the
officer in question was immediately relieved and mollified;
and speaking in a voice much freer from constraint, advised me
to find a steward and despatch him in quest of the doctor, who
would now be in the smoking-room over his pipe.

One of the stewards was often enough to be found about
this hour down our companion, Steerage No. 2 and 3; that
was his smoking-room of a night. ⟨I have asked myself repeatedly whether I should give his exact rank, and I find my heart
fails me. If I call him Blackwood, I shall have a name answerable
enough to his appearance, and leave him to the enjoyment of
his privacy. I do not wish to bear tales out of school against an
individual.⟩

O'Reilly and I rattled down the companion, breathing hurry;
and in his shirt-sleeves and perched across the carpenter's
bench upon one thigh, found Blackwood; a neat, bright, dap-
per, Glasgow-looking man, with a bead of an eye and a rank

twang in his speech. I forget who was with him, but the pair were enjoying a deliberate talk over their pipes. I daresay he was tired with his day's work, and eminently comfortable at that moment; and the truth is I did not stop to consider his feelings, but told my story in a breath.

"Steward," said I, "there's a man lying bad with cramp, and I can't find the doctor."

He turned upon me as pert as a sparrow, but with a black look that is the prerogative of man; and taking his pipe out of his mouth —

"That's none of my business," said he. "I don't care."

⟨So far as I have gone, I have not often heard an uglier speech; the French, in their academical manner, would call it cynical; brutal and devilish must serve the turn of a homely English speaker.⟩ I could have strangled the little ruffian where he sat. The thought of his cabin civility and cabin tips filled me with indignation. I glanced at O'Reilly; he was pale and quivering, and looked like assault and battery every inch of him. But we had a better card than violence.

"You will have to make it your business," said I, "for I am sent to you by the officer on the bridge."

Blackwood was fairly tripped. He made no answer, but put out his pipe, gave me one murderous look, and set off upon his errand strolling. From that day forward, I should say, he improved to me in courtesy, as though he had repented his evil speech and were anxious to leave a better impression. ⟨But I cannot help it: I hate every button upon that man's jacket.⟩

When we got on deck again, Jones was still beside the sick man; and two or three late stragglers had gathered round and were offering suggestions. One proposed to give the patient water, which was promptly negatived. Another bade us hold him up; he himself prayed to be let lie; but as it was at least as well to keep him off the streaming decks, O'Reilly and I supported him between us. It was only by main force that we did so, and neither an easy nor an agreeable duty; for he fought in his paroxysms like a frightened child, and moaned miserably when he resigned himself to our control.

⟨"Take care of your knee," said I to O'Reilly. "I have got mine in the vomit."

I thought the patient too much occupied to mind our observations; but he heard me, relaxed his struggles, and began to twist in a new way with his arm across his body. I could not imagine what he was at; till suddenly forth came a coloured handkerchief; and he held it out to me, saying "Wipe your knee wi' that."

We all know about Sir Philip Sidney: here is a Roland for his Oliver. It is easier to say a fine thing on the field of honour than in such a scene of physical disgrace; and the number of persons is considerable who would be shorn of all romantic notions by having been dog-sick immediately before and on the very spot where the occasion rose. It was the unaffected courtliness of a good heart. You have wet your knee in my service; well then, here is my handkerchief! It is true the man thought he was come to his last hour: a thought to favour dignity. That was indeed his argument against our friendly violence.⟩ "O let me lie!" he pleaded. "I'll no' get better anyway." And then, with a moan that went to my heart, "O why did I come upon this miserable journey?"

I was reminded of the song which I had heard a little while before in the close, tossing steerage: "O why left I my hame?"

Meantime Jones, relieved of his immediate charge, had gone off to the galley, where we could see a light. There he found a belated cook scouring pans by the radiance of two lanterns, and one of these he sought to borrow. The scullion was backward. "Was it one of the crew?" he asked. And when Jones, smitten with my theory, had assured him that it was a fireman, he reluctantly left his scouring and came towards us at an easy pace, with one of the lanterns swinging from his finger. The light, as it reached the spot, showed us an elderly man, thickset, and grizzled with years; but the shifting and coarse shadows concealed from us the expression and even the design of his face.

So soon as the cook set eyes on him he gave a sort of whistle. "*It's only a passenger!*" said he; and turning about, made, lantern and all, for the galley.

"He's a man anyway," cried Jones in indignation.

"Nobody said he was a woman," said a gruff voice, which I recognised for that of the bo's'un. (But I think he must have made the remark to give himself a countenance, and because he lacked the courage of his qualities; for, far from joining against us, he helped Jones to get the lantern from the cook.)

All this while there was no word of Blackwood or the doctor; and now the officer came to our side of the ship and asked, over the hurricane-deck rails, if the doctor were not yet come. We told him not.

"No?" he repeated with a breathing of anger; and we saw him hurry aft in person.

Ten minutes after the doctor made his appearance deliberately enough and examined our patient with the lantern. He made little of the case, had the man brought aft to the dispensary, dosed him, and sent him forward to his bunk. Two of his neighbours in the steerage had now come to our assistance, expressing loud sorrow that such "a fine cheery body" should be sick; and these, claiming a sort of possession, took him entirely under their own care. The drug had probably relieved him, for he struggled no more, and was led along plaintive and patient, but protesting. His heart recoiled at the thought of the steerage. "O let me lie down upon the bieldy[1] side," he cried; "O dinna take me down!" And again: "O why did ever I come upon this miserable voyage?" And yet once more, with a gasp and a wailing prolongation of the fourth word: "I had no *call* to come." But there he was; and by the doctor's orders and the kind force of his two shipmates disappeared down the companion of Steerage No. 1 into the den allotted him.

At the foot of our own companion, just where I had found

1. Scottish word for "sheltering."

Blackwood, Jones and the bo's'un were now engaged in talk. This last was a gruff, cruel-looking seaman, who must have passed near half a century upon the seas; square-headed, goat-bearded, with heavy blonde eyebrows, and an eye without radiance, but inflexibly steady and hard. I had not forgotten his rough speech; but I remembered also that he had helped us about the lantern; and now seeing him in conversation with Jones, and being choked with indignation, I proceeded to blow off my steam.

"Well," said I, "I make you my compliments upon your steward," and furiously narrated what had happened.

"I've nothing to do with him," replied the bo's'un. "They're all alike. They wouldn't mind if they saw you all lying dead one upon the top of another." ⟨And he made a quaint gesture with his pipe, expressive, so far as my imagination served me to interpret, of someone going up in an explosion.⟩

This was enough. A very little humanity went a long way with me after the experience of the evening. A sympathy grew up at once between the bo's'un and myself; and that night, and during the next few days, I learned to appreciate him better. He was a remarkable type, and not at all the kind of man you find in books. He had been at Sebastopol under English colours; and again in a States ship, "after the *Alabama*,² and praying God we shouldn't find her." He was a high Tory and a high Englishman. No manufacturer could have held opinions more hostile to the working man and his strikes. "The workmen," he said, "think nothing of their country. They think of nothing but themselves. They're damned greedy, selfish fellows." He would not hear of the decadence of England. "They say they send us beef from America," he argued; "but who pays for it? All the money in the world's in England." The Royal Navy was the best of possible services, according to him. "Anyway the officers are gentlemen," said he; "and you can't get hazed to death by a damned non-commission —— as you

2. A Confederate ironclad battleship, which destroyed 57 ships of the United States before it was sunk in 1864.

can in the army." Among nations, England was the first; then came France. He respected the French navy and liked the French people; and if he were forced to make a new choice in life, "by God, he would try Frenchmen!" For all his looks and rough cold manners, I observed that children were never frightened by him; they divined him at once to be a friend; and one night when he had chalked his hand and went about stealthily setting his mark on people's clothes, it was incongruous to hear this formidable old salt chuckling over his boyish monkey trick.

In the morning, my first thought was of the sick man. I was afraid I should not recognize him, so baffling had been the light of the lantern; and found myself unable to decide if he were Scots, English, or Irish. He had certainly employed north-country words and elisions; but the accent and the pronunciation seemed unfamiliar and incongruous in my ear.

To descend on an empty stomach into Steerage No. 1 was an adventure that required some nerve. The stench was atrocious; each respiration tasted in the throat like some horrible kind of cheese; and the squalid aspect of the place was aggravated by so many people worming themselves into their clothes in the twilight of the bunks. You may guess if I was pleased, not only for him, but for myself also, when I heard that the sick man was better and had gone on deck.

The morning was raw and foggy, though the sun suffused the fog with pink and amber; the fog-horn still blew, stertorous and intermittent; and to add to the discomfort, the seamen were just beginning to wash down the decks. But for a sick man this was heaven compared to the steerage. I found him standing on the hot-water pipe, just forward of the saloon deck-house. He was smaller than I had fancied, and plain-looking; but his face was distinguished by strange and fascinating eyes, limpid grey from a distance, but, when looked into, full of changing colours and grains of gold. His manners were mild and uncompromisingly plain; and I soon saw that, when once started, he delighted to talk. His accent and language had been formed in the

most natural way, since he was born in Ireland, had lived a
quarter of a century on the banks of Tyne, and was married to
a Scots wife. A fisherman in the season, he had fished the east
coast from Fisherrow to Whitby. When the season was over,
and the great boats, which required extra hands, were once
drawn up on shore till the next spring, he worked as a labourer
about chemical furnaces, or along the wharves unloading vessels. In this comparatively humble way of life he had gathered
a competence, and could speak of his comfortable house, his
hayfield, and his garden. On this ship, where so many accomplished artisans were fleeing from starvation, he was present on a pleasure trip to visit a brother in New York.

Ere he started, he informed me he had been warned against
the steerage and the steerage fare, and recommended to bring
with him a ham and tea and a spice loaf. But he laughed to
scorn such counsels. "*I'm* not afraid," he had told his adviser,
"*I'll* get on for ten days. I've not been a fisherman for nothing."
For it is no light matter, as he reminded me, to be in an open
boat, perhaps waist-deep with herrings, day breaking with a
scowl, and for miles on every hand lee-shores, unbroken, iron-
bound, surf-beat, with only here and there an anchorage where
you dare not lie, or a harbour impossible to enter with the wind
that blows. The life of a North Sea fisher is one long chapter
of exposure and hard work and insufficient fare; and even if he
makes land at some bleak fisher port, perhaps the season is bad
or his boat has been unlucky, and after fifty hours' unsleeping
vigilance and toil, not a shop will give him credit for a loaf of
bread. Yet the steerage of the emigrant ship had been too vile
for the endurance of a man thus rudely trained. He had
scarce eaten since he came on board, until the day before, when
his appetite was tempted by some excellent pea-soup. We were
all much of the same mind on board, and beginning with myself, had dined upon pea-soup not wisely but too well; only
with him the excess had been punished, perhaps because he was
weakened by former abstinence, and his first meal had resulted
in a cramp. He had determined to live henceforth on biscuit;

and when, two months later, he should return to England, to make the passage by saloon. The second cabin, after due inquiry, he scouted as another edition of the steerage.

He spoke apologetically of his emotion when ill. "Ye see, I had no call to be here," said he; "and I thought it was by with me last night. I've a good house at home, and plenty to nurse me, and I had no real call to leave them." Speaking of the attentions he had received from his shipmates generally, "they were all so kind," he said, "that there's none to mention." And except in so far as I might share in this, he troubled me with no reference to my services. ⟨This was choice courtesy. I write with all measure, and except in the matter of bowing and scraping, I have never met a finer gentleman. He had the essentials of that business, in all senses of the expression, by heart.⟩

But what affected me in the most lively manner was the wealth of this day-labourer, paying a two months' pleasure visit to the States, and preparing to return in the saloon, and the new testimony rendered by his story, not so much to the horrors of the steerage as to the habitual comfort of the working classes. One foggy, frosty December evening, I encountered on Liberton Hill, near Edinburgh, an Irish labourer trudging homeward from the fields. Our roads lay together, and it was natural that we should fall into talk. He was covered with mud; an inoffensive, ignorant creature, who thought the Atlantic Cable was a secret contrivance of the masters the better to oppress labouring mankind; and I confess I was astonished to learn that he had nearly three hundred pounds in the bank. But this man had travelled over most of the world, and enjoyed wonderful opportunities on some American railroad, with two dollars a shift and double pay on Sunday and at night; whereas my fellow-passenger had never quitted Tyneside, and had made all that he possessed in that same accursed, down-falling England, whence skilled mechanics, engineers, millwrights, and carpenters were fleeing as from the native country of starvation.

Fitly enough, we slid off on the subject of strikes and wages and hard times. Being from the Tyne, and a man who had gained and lost in his own pocket by these fluctuations, he had much to say, and held strong opinions on the subject. He spoke sharply of the masters, and, when I led him on, of the men also. The masters had been selfish and obstructive; the men selfish, silly, and light-headed. He rehearsed to me the course of a meeting at which he had been present, and the somewhat long discourse which he had there pronounced, calling into question the wisdom and even the good faith of the Union delegates; and although he had escaped himself through flush times and starvation times with a handsomely provided purse, he had so little faith in either man or master, and so profound a terror for the unerring Nemesis of mercantile affairs, that he could think of no hope for our country outside of a sudden and complete political subversion. Down must go Lords and Church and Army; and capital, by some happy direction, must change hands from worse to better, or England stood condemned. Such principles, he said, were growing "like a seed."

From this mild, soft, domestic man, these words sounded unusually ominous and grave. I had heard enough revolutionary talk among my workmen fellow-passengers; but most of it was hot and turgid, and fell discredited from the lips of unsuccessful men. This man was calm; he had attained prosperity and ease; ⟨he was a gentleman;⟩ he disapproved the policy which had been pursued by labour in the past; and yet this was his panacea, — to rend the old country from end to end, and from top to bottom, and in clamour and civil discord remodel it with the hand of violence. ⟨I thought of the Bo'swain, and wondered how such men and measures would recommend themselves to him and his like, if he had any. I thought too of the blessings of emigration: that men sufficiently instructed, who had for long times together received wages greater than many a man of letters and who yet, from drunkenness, shiftlessness and lack of balance, had failed flatly in life's battle, could still escape and make a new beginning somewhere else. For if the polity is to be subverted and the state's pedestals thrown down, let it be by clear-seeing people strung up by inborn generosity to the task, and not by waifs and beggars exasperated by external and perhaps well deserved reverses.)

THE STOWAWAYS

On the Sunday, among a party of men who were talking in our companion, Steerage No. 2 and 3, we remarked a new figure. He wore tweed clothes, well enough made if not very fresh, and a plain smoking-cap. His face was pale, with pale eyes, and spiritedly enough designed; but though not yet thirty, a sort of blackguardly degeneration had already overtaken his features. The fine nose had grown fleshy towards the point, the pale eyes were sunk in fat. His hands were strong and elegant; his experience of life evidently varied; his speech full of pith and verve; his manners forward, but perfectly presentable. The lad who helped in the second cabin told me, in answer to a question, that he did not know who he was, but thought, "by his way of speaking, and because he was so polite, that he was some one from the saloon."

I was not so sure, for to me there was something equivocal in his air and bearing. He might have been, I thought, the son of some good family who had fallen early into dissipation and run from home(; though even then, he would have spoken with a clearer accent, and his pronunciation would either have respected orthography more thoroughly or slurred it in a different manner). But, making every allowance, how admirable was his talk! I wish you could have heard him tell his own stories. They were so swingingly set forth, in such dramatic language, and illustrated here and there by such luminous bits of acting, that they could only lose in any reproduction. There were tales of the P. and O. Company, where he had been an officer; of the East Indies, where in former years he had lived lavishly; of the Royal Engineers, where he had served for a period; and of a dozen other sides of life, each introducing some vigorous thumb-nail portrait. He had the talk to himself that night, we were all so glad to listen. The best talkers usually address themselves to some particular society; there they are kings, elsewhere camp-followers, as a man may know Russian and yet be ignorant of Spanish; but this fellow had a frank, headlong power of style, and a broad, human choice of subject, that would have turned any circle in the world into a circle of hearers. He was a Homeric talker, plain, strong, and cheerful; and the things and the people of which he spoke became readily and clearly present to the minds of those who heard him. This, with a certain added colouring of rhetoric and rodomontade, must have been the style of Burns, who equally charmed the ears of duchesses and hostlers.

Yet freely and personally as he spoke, many points remained obscure in his narration. The Engineers, for instance, was a service which he praised highly; it is true there would be trouble with the sergeants; but then the officers were gentlemen, and his own, in particular, one among ten thousand. It sounded so far exactly like an episode in the rakish, topsy-turvy life of such an one as I had imagined. But then there came incidents more doubtful, which showed an almost impudent greed after gratuities, and a truly impudent disregard for truth. And then there was the tale of his departure. He had wearied, it seems, of Woolwich, and one fine day, with a companion, slipped up to London for a spree. I have a suspicion that spree was meant to be a long one; but God disposes all things; and one morning, near Westminster Bridge, whom should he come across but the very sergeant who had recruited him at first! What followed? He himself indicated cavalierly that he had then resigned. Let us put it so. But these resignations are sometimes very trying.

At length, after having delighted us for hours, he took himself away from the companion; and I could ask Mackay who and what he was. "That?" said Mackay. "Why, that's one of the stowaways."

"No man," said the same authority, "who has had anything

to do with the sea, would ever think of paying for a passage."
I give the statement as Mackay's, without indorsement; yet I
am tempted to believe that it contains a grain of truth; and if
you add that the man shall be impudent and thievish, or else
dead-broke, it may even pass for a fair representation of the
facts. We gentlemen of England who live at home at ease have,
I suspect, very insufficient ideas on the subject. All the world
over, people are stowing away in coal-holes and dark corners,
and when ships are once out to sea, appearing again, begrimed
and bashful, upon deck. The career of these sea-tramps partakes largely of the adventurous. They may be poisoned by
coal-gas, or die by starvation in their place of concealment; or
when found they may be clapped at once and ignominiously
into irons, thus to be carried to their promised land, the port of
destination, and alas! brought back in the same way to that
from which they started, and there delivered over to the magis-
trates and the seclusion of a county jail. Since I crossed the Atlantic, one miserable stowaway was found in a dying state
among the fuel, uttered but a word or two, and departed for a
farther country than America. (On Jones's last passage before
that on which I met him, no fewer than eleven had presented
themselves from different quarters of the ship; and the captain
had them all in irons until two of their number fainted and the
passengers interposed to beg them off.

Just as the confraternity of beggars know and communicate
among themselves the generous or saving character of different
houses; just as, in the old days before the Prison Discipline
Act, many indigent persons might have been observed on the
approach of Christmas making for the neighbourhood of Wake-
field Jail, where, for a petty theft or an aggravated misdemean-
our, the best sort of criminal entertainment might be had till
the return of Spring; so, among the stowaway class, one line of
steamers is distinguished from another by the nature of the
treatment which they may expect on board. Thus the line on
which I sailed was said to be particularly favoured by stowaways with their faces towards the States; and thus such another,

greatly preferred by saloon passengers, is shunned like the plague by a sea-tramp. On this last, he would invariably be brought back and punished; on the former, he is half sure to make out the voyage and be landed, a free citizen and independent voter, at the harbour of New York.⟩

When the stowaway appears on deck, he has but one thing to pray for: that he be set to work, which is the price and sign of his forgiveness. After half an hour with a swab or a bucket, he feels himself as secure as if he had paid for his passage. It is not altogether a bad thing for the company, who get more or less efficient hands for nothing but a few plates of junk and duff; and every now and again find themselves better paid than by a whole family of cabin passengers. Not long ago, for instance, a packet was saved from nearly certain loss by the skill and courage of a stowaway engineer. As was no more than just, a handsome subscription rewarded him for his success; but even without such exceptional good fortune, as things stand in England and America, the stowaway will often make a good profit out of his adventure. Four engineers stowed away last summer on the same ship, the *Circassia*; and before two days after their arrival each of the four had found a comfortable berth. This was the most hopeful tale of emigration that I heard from first to last; and as you see, the luck was for stowaways.

My curiosity was much inflamed by what I heard; and the next morning, as I was making the round of the ship, I was delighted to find the ex-Royal Engineer engaged in washing down the white paint of a deck-house. There was another fellow at work beside him, a lad not more than twenty, in the most miraculous tatters, his handsome face sown with grains of beauty and lighted up by expressive eyes. Four stowaways had been found aboard our ship before she left the Clyde; but these two had alone escaped the ignominy of being put ashore. Alick, my acquaintance of last night, was Scots by birth, and by trade a practical engineer; the other was from Devonshire, and had been to sea before the mast. Two people more unlike by training, character, and habits, it would be hard to imagine; yet here they were together, scrubbing paint.

Alick had held all sorts of good situations, and wasted many opportunities in life. I have heard him end a story with these words: "That was in my golden days, when I used finger-glasses." [1] Situation after situation failed him; then followed the depression of trade, and for months he had hung round with other idlers, playing marbles all day in the West Park, and going home at night to tell his landlady how he had been seeking for a job. I believe this kind of existence was not unpleasant to Alick himself, and he might have long continued to enjoy idleness and a life on tick; but he had a comrade, let us call him Brown, who grew restive. This fellow was continually threatening to slip his cable for the States, and at last, one Wednesday, Glasgow was left widowed of her Brown. Some months afterwards, Alick met another old chum in Sauchiehall Street.

"By the by, Alick," said he, "I met a gentleman in New York who was asking for you."

"Who was that?" asked Alick.

"The new second engineer on board the *So-and-so*," was the reply.

"Well, and who is he?"

"Brown, to be sure."

For Brown had been one of the fortunate quartette aboard the *Circassia*. If that was the way of it in the States, Alick thought it was high time to follow Brown's example. He spent his last day, as he put it, "reviewing the yeomanry," and the next morning says he to his landlady, "Mrs. X., I'll not take porridge to-day, please; I'll take some eggs."

"Why, have you found a job?" she asked, delighted.

"Well, yes," returned the perfidious Alick; "I think I'll start to-day."

And so, well lined with eggs, start he did, but for America. I am afraid that landlady has seen the last of him.

It was easy enough to get on board in the confusion that at-

1. More commonly called finger bowls.

tends a vessel's departure; and in one of the dark corners of
Steerage No. 1, flat in a bunk and with an empty stomach,
Alick made the voyage from the Broomielaw to Greenock.
That night, the ship's yeoman pulled him out by the heels and
had him before the mate. Two other stowaways had already
been found and sent ashore; but by this time darkness had fallen, they were out in the middle of the estuary, and the last
steamer had left them till the morning.

"Take him to the forecastle and give him a meal," said the
mate, "and see and pack him off the first thing to-morrow."

In the forecastle he had supper, a good night's rest, and
breakfast; and was sitting placidly with a pipe, fancying all was
over and the game up for good with that ship, when one of
the sailors grumbled out an oath at him, with a "What are you
doing there?" and "Do you call that hiding, anyway?" There
was need of no more: Alick was in another bunk before the
day was older. Shortly before the passengers arrived, the ship
was cursorily inspected. He heard the round come down the
companion and look into one pen after another, until they
came within two of the one in which he lay concealed. Into
these last two they did not enter, but merely glanced from
without; and Alick had no doubt that he was personally favoured in this escape. It was the character of the man to at-
tribute nothing to luck and but little to kindness; whatever
happened to him he had earned in his own right amply; favours
came to him from his singular attraction and adroitness, and
misfortunes he had always accepted with his eyes open. Half
an hour after the searchers had departed, the steerage began to
fill with legitimate passengers, and the worst of Alick's troubles
was at an end. He was soon making himself popular, smoking
other people's tobacco, and politely sharing their private stock
of delicacies, and when night came, he retired to his bunk beside the others with composure.

Next day by afternoon, Lough Foyle being already far behind, and only the rough north-western hills of Ireland within
view, Alick appeared on deck to court inquiry and decide his

fate. As a matter of fact, he was known to several on board, and even intimate with one of the engineers; but it was plainly not the etiquette of such occasions for the authorities to avow their information. Every one professed surprise and anger on his appearance, and he was led prisoner before the captain.

"What have you got to say for yourself?" inquired the captain.

"Not much," said Alick; "but when a man has been a long time out of a job, he will do things he would not under other circumstances."

"Are you willing to work?"

Alick swore he was burning to be useful.

"And what can you do?" asked the captain.

He replied composedly that he was a brass-fitter by trade.

"I think you will be better at engineering?" suggested the officer, with a shrewd look.

"No, sir," says Alick simply. — "There's few can beat me at a lie," was his engaging commentary to me as he recounted the affair.

"Have you been to sea?" again asked the captain.

"I've had a trip on a Clyde steamboat, sir, but no more," replied the unabashed Alick.

"Well, we must try and find some work for you," concluded the officer.

And hence we behold Alick, clear of the hot engine-room, lazily scraping paint and now and then taking a pull upon a sheet. "You leave me alone," was his deduction. "When I get talking to a man, I can get round him." (For my own part, I should have drawn a different conclusion namely, that when a man is determined to be in a good business, nothing will put him out.)

The other stowaway, whom I will call the Devonian—it was noticeable that neither of them told his name — had both been brought up and seen the world in a much smaller way. His father, a confectioner, died and was closely followed by his mother. His sisters had taken, I think, to dressmaking. He himself had returned from sea about a year ago and gone to live with his brother, who kept the "George Hotel" — "it was not quite a real hotel," added the candid fellow — and had a hired man to mind the horses. At first the Devonian was very welcome; but as time went on his brother not unnaturally grew cool towards him, and he began to find himself one too many at the "George Hotel." "I don't think brothers care much for you," he said, as a general reflection upon life. Hurt at this change, nearly penniless, and too proud to ask for more, he set off on foot and walked eighty miles to Weymouth, living on the journey as he could. He would have enlisted, but he was too small for the army and too old for the navy; and thought himself fortunate at last to find a berth on board a trading dandy.[2] Somewhere in the Bristol Channel, the dandy sprung a leak and went down; and though the crew were picked up and brought ashore by fishermen, they found themselves with nothing but the clothes upon their back. His next engagement was scarcely better-starred; for the ship proved so leaky, and frightened them all so heartily during a short passage through the Irish Sea, that the entire crew deserted and remained behind upon the quays of Belfast.

Evil days were now coming thick on the Devonian. He could find no berth in Belfast, and had to work a passage to Glasgow on a steamer. She reached the Broomielaw on a Wednesday: the Devonian had a bellyful that morning, laying in breakfast manfully to provide against the future, and set off along the quays to seek employment. But he was now not only penniless, his clothes had begun to fall in tatters; he had begun to have the look of a street Arab; and captains will have nothing to say to a ragamuffin; for in that trade, as in all others, it is the coat that depicts the man. You may hand, reef, and steer like an angel, but if you have a hole in your trousers, it is like a millstone round your neck. The Devonian lost heart at so many refusals. He had not the impudence to beg; although, as he said, "when I had money of my own, I always gave it." It was only

2. A sloop or cutter with special rigging.

on Saturday morning, after three whole days of starvation, that he asked a scone from a milkwoman, who added of her own accord a glass of milk. He had now made up his mind to stow away, not from any desire to see America, but merely to obtain the comfort of a place in the forecastle and a supply of familiar sea-fare. He lived by begging, always from milk-women, and always scones and milk, and was not once refused. It was vile wet weather, and he could never have been dry. By night he walked the streets, and by day slept upon Glasgow Green, and heard, in the intervals of his dozing, the famous theologians of the spot clear up intricate points of doctrine and appraise the merits of the clergy. He had not much instruction; he could "read bills on the street," but was "main bad at writ-ing;" yet these theologians seem to have impressed him with a genuine sense of amusement. Why he did not go to the Sailors' Home I know not; I presume there is in Glasgow one of these institutions, which are by far the happiest and the wisest effort of contemporaneous charity; but I must stand to my author, as they say in old books, and relate the story as I heard it. In the meantime, he had tried four times to stow away in different vessels, and four times had been discovered and handed back to starvation. The fifth time was lucky; and you may judge if he were pleased to be aboard ship again, at his old work, and with duff twice a week. He was, said Alick, " a devil for the duff." Or if devil was not the word, it was one if anything stronger.

The difference in the conduct of the two was remarkable. The Devonian was as willing as any paid hand, swarmed aloft among the first, pulled his natural weight and firmly upon a rope, and found work for himself when there was none to show him. Alick, on the other hand, was not only a skulker in the grain, but took a humorous and fine-gentlemanly view of the transaction. He would speak to me by the hour in ostenta-tious idleness; and only if the bo's'un or a mate came by, fell-to languidly for just the necessary time till they were out of sight. "I'm not breaking my heart with it," he remarked. ⟨"So I observe," said I, with cordial adhesion.⟩

Once there was a hatch to be opened near where he was stationed; he watched the preparations for a second or so suspiciously, and then, "Hullo," said he, "here's some real work coming — I'm off," and he was gone that moment. Again, calculating the six guinea passage-money, and the probable duration of the passage, he remarked pleasantly that he was getting six shillings a day for this job, "and it's pretty dear to the company at that." "They are making nothing by me," was another of his observations; "they're making something by that fellow." And he pointed to the Devonian, who was just then busy to the eyes.

The more you saw of Alick, the more, it must be owned, you learned to despise him. His natural talents were of no use either to himself or others; for his character had degenerated like his face, and become pulpy and pretentious. Even his power of persuasion, which was certainly very surprising, stood in some danger of being lost or neutralised by overconfidence. He lied in an aggressive, brazen manner, like a pert criminal in the dock; and he was so vain of his own cleverness that he could not refrain from boasting, ten minutes after, of the very trick by which he had deceived you. "Why, now I have more money than when I came on board," he said one night, exhibiting a sixpence, "and yet I stood myself a bottle of beer before I went to bed yesterday. And as for tobacco, I have fifteen sticks of it." That was fairly successful indeed; yet a man of his superiority, and with a less obtrusive policy, might, who knows? have got the length of half a crown. ⟨I warn Alick as a sort of well wisher: if he persist, the days of finger glasses are gone by for him forever, and he may have to clean paint in earnest or do yet dirtier work before the end. For instance, he spent a whole evening recounting to Jones and me a series of very cheap and blackguardly exploits, in which poor women were his easy and unpitied victims. A man of his talent and habit of the world, should have perceived the effect he was producing.⟩ A man who prides himself upon persuasion should learn the persuasive faculty of silence, above all as to his own misdeeds. It is only in the farce and for dramatic purposes that Scapin enlarges on his peculiar talents to the world at large.

Scapin is perhaps a good name for this clever, unfortunate Alick; for at the bottom of all his misconduct there was a guiding sense of humour that moved you to forgive him. It was more than half as a jest that he conducted his existence. ⟨He was never entirely serious in a thought.⟩ "Oh, man," he said to me once with unusual emotion, like a man thinking of his mistress, "I would give up anything for a lark." ⟨And he stood for a while, smiling, with half shut eyes; and then proceeded to tell me how he would have passed the time on board, if he had been a passenger and free. It was fortunate for many that he had to mind his white paint, for his plan was unkind; yet I cannot deny that it was funny.⟩

It was in relation to his fellow-stowaway that Alick showed the best, or perhaps I should say, the only, good points of his nature. "Mind you," he said suddenly, changing his tone, "mind you, that's a good boy. He wouldn't tell you a lie. A lot of them think he is a scamp because his clothes are ragged, but he isn't; he's as good as gold." To hear him, you became aware that Alick himself had a taste for virtue. He thought his own idleness and the other's industry equally becoming. He was no more anxious to ensure his own reputation as a liar than to uphold the truthfulness of his companion; and he seemed unaware of what was incongruous in his attitude, and was plainly sincere in both characters. ⟨But he was one who looked largely upon life, and would have been equally ready to adjudge the Montyon prize for virtue[3] or to sit as umpire in a competition of liars.⟩

It was not surprising that he should take an interest in the Devonian, for the lad worshipped and served him in love and

---

3. Baron Montyon (1733–1820) willed a large sum to the Institut de France, part of whose income is distributed annually by the Académie française as a prize to a poor Frenchman judged to have performed the most virtuous action of the year.

wonder. Busy as he was, he would find time to warn Alick of
an approaching officer, or even to tell him that the coast was
clear, and he might slip off and smoke a pipe in safety. "Tom,"
he once said to him, for that was the name which Alick ordered him to use, "if you don't like going to the galley, I'll go
for you. You ain't used to this kind of thing, you ain't. But I'm
a sailor; and I can understand the feelings of any fellow, I
can." Again, he was hard up and casting about for some tobacco, for he was not so liberally used in this respect as others
perhaps less worthy, when Alick offered him the half of one
of his fifteen sticks. I think, for my part, he might have increased the offer to a whole one, or perhaps a pair of them, and
not lived to regret his liberality. But the Devonian refused.
"No," he said, "you're a stowaway like me; I won't take it
from you, I'll take it from some one who's not down on his
luck."

It was notable in this generous lad that he was strongly under the influence of sex. If a woman passed near where he was
working, his eyes lit up, his hand paused, and his mind wandered instantly to other thoughts. ⟨"*C'est Vénus tout entier.*"⟩ [4]
It was natural that he should exercise a fascination proportionally strong upon women. He begged, you will remember, from
women only, and was never refused. Without wishing to explain away the charity of those who helped him, I cannot but
fancy he may have owed a little to his handsome⟨, long nose,
to his attractive eyes, to the grains of beauty on his⟩ face, and
to that quick, responsive nature, formed for love, which speaks
eloquently through all disguises, and can stamp an impression in
ten minutes' talk or an exchange of glances. He was the more
dangerous in that he was far from bold, but seemed to woo in
spite of himself, and with a soft and pleading eye. Ragged as
he was, and many a scarecrow is in that respect more comfort-

4. The full line, correctly quoted from Racine, *Phèdre*, I, iii, 306, is:
"C'est Vénus toute entière à sa proie attachée" ("It is Venus wholly
attached to her prey").

ably furnished, even on board he was not without some curious admirers.

There was a girl among the passengers, a tall, blonde, handsome, strapping Irishwoman, with a wild, accommodating eye, whom Alick had dubbed Tommy, with that transcendental appropriateness that defies analysis. ⟨On her and her various admirers, and trusting implicitly in his own powers of talk, he based schemes of mystification that would have put a score of people by the ears in eight and forty hours and kept the rest of the ship's company in inextinguishable mirth. The Devonian, who always listened to him greedily as to a god, suggested some modification of the plan.

"You don't understand how to work these things," observed Alick loftily.

"I suppose I don't, I suppose you do," retorted the Devonian.

"God!" cried Alick with fervour, "I've had a career of experience at least!"⟩

One day the Devonian was lying for warmth in the upper stoke-hole, which stands open on the deck, when Irish Tommy came past, very neatly attired, as was her custom.

"Poor fellow," she said, stopping, "you haven't a vest."

"No," he said; "I wish I 'ad."

Then she stood and gazed on him in silence, until, in his embarrassment, for he knew not how to look under this scrutiny, he pulled out his pipe and began to fill it with tobacco.

"Do you want a match?" she asked. And before he had time to reply, she ran off and presently returned with more than one.

That was the beginning and the end, as far as our passage is concerned, of what I will make bold to call this love-affair. There are many relations which go on to marriage and last during a lifetime, in which less human feeling is engaged than in this scene of five minutes at the stoke-hole.

⟨It was perhaps because of this strong principle open in his character, that the Devonian's chief aspiration was after a clean shirt. That, and I hope many other things, have now been given him; for he worked so well and was so willing and pleasant on board, that he was offered a berth on the steamer into which he had crept unbidden.

I have already recommended the emigrant rather to go second cabin than steerage. Let me add, if he has the tact to carry it out and wisely to choose both his steamer and his hiding place on board, that he had better go as stowaway than either. The forecastle, I am told, is a far more desirable lodging than steerage No. 1; the fare is better and more cleanly served; and if his body be sound, the deck work will only benefit his health and keep his mind cheerful and disengaged. In point of economy, there is, of course, no comparison possible: the stowaway passage costing exactly nothing. At the same time, it is awkward to reach a foreign land with only sixpence, and that was all that the persuasive Alick had managed to scrape together on the passage. To be taken where you want to go and then brought back again for punishment in irons, is, to say the least of it, annoying. And to perish of hunger and bad air in a solitary coal hole, like a poisoned rat behind the skirting, is a tragical and ghastly death. There are the pro's and the con's, on which the reader may decide his own conduct for himself.)

Rigidly speaking, this would end the chapter of the stowaways; but in a larger sense of the word I have yet more to add. Jones had discovered and pointed out to me a young woman who was remarkable among her fellows for a pleasing and interesting air. She was poorly clad, to the verge, if not over the line, of disrespectability, with a ragged old jacket and a bit of a sealskin cap no bigger than your fist; but her eyes, her whole expression, and her manner, even in ordinary moments, told of a true womanly nature, capable of love, anger, and devotion. She had a look, too, of refinement, like one who might have been a better lady than most, had she been allowed the opportunity. When alone she seemed pre-occupied and sad; but she was not often alone; there was usually by her side a heavy, dull, gross man in rough clothes, chary of speech and gesture — not from caution, but poverty of disposition; a man like a ditcher, unlovely and uninteresting; whom she petted and tended and waited on with her eyes as if he had been Amadis of Gaul. It was strange to see this hulking fellow dog-sick, and this delicate, sad woman caring for him. He seemed, from first to last, insensible of her caresses and attentions, and she seemed unconscious of his insensibility. The Irish husband who sang his wife to sleep, and this Scottish girl serving her Orson,[5] were the two bits of human nature that most appealed to me throughout the voyage.

On the Thursday before we arrived, the tickets were collected; and soon a rumour began to go round the vessel; and this girl, with her bit of sealskin cap, became the centre of whispering and pointed fingers. She also, it was said, was a stowaway of a sort; for she was on board with neither ticket nor money; and the man with whom she travelled was the father of a family, who had left wife and children to be hers. The ship's officers discouraged the story, which may therefore have been a story and no more; but it was believed in the steerage, and the poor girl had to encounter many curious eyes from that day forth.

5. Stevenson probably had in mind the medieval French prose romance *Valentin et Orson,* describing these twin brothers, the latter suckled by a bear in a wood and growing up to be a gross, wild man; but he may also have thought of John Wolcott's *Orson and Ellen* (1798), a tale about a young farmer who makes love to and deserts a faithful village girl.

PERSONAL EXPERIENCE
AND REVIEW

Travel is of two kinds; and this voyage of mine across the ocean combined both. "Out of my country and myself I go," sings the old poet:[1] and I was not only travelling out of my country in latitude and longitude, but out of myself in diet, associates, and consideration. Part of the interest and a great deal of the amusement flowed, at least to me, from this novel situation in the world.

I found that I had what they call fallen in life with absolute success and verisimilitude. I was taken for a steerage passenger; no one seemed surprised that I should be so; and there was nothing but the brass plate between decks to remind me that I had once been a gentleman. In a former book, describing a former journey, I expressed some wonder that I could be readily and naturally taken for a pedlar,[2] and explained the accident by the difference of language and manners between England and France. I must now take a humbler view; for here I was among my own countrymen, somewhat roughly clad, to be sure, but with every advantage of speech and manner; and I am bound to confess that I passed for nearly anything you please except an educated gentleman. The sailors called me "mate," the officers addressed me as "my man," my comrades accepted me without hesitation for a person of their own character and experience, but with some curious information.

1. In idea and style this line might be by Stevenson, and it appears again in the chapter "At Compiègne" in *An Inland Voyage*. The reference to "the old poet" may be like the attribution in *Travels with a Donkey* to an "old play" of six lines of poetry actually written by Stevenson and later incorporated in his published poems.
2. See "We are Pedlars," Chap. VI of *An Inland Voyage*.

One, a mason himself, believed I was a mason; several, and among these at least one of the seamen, judged me to be a petty officer in the American navy; and I was so often set down for a practical engineer that at last I had not the heart to deny it. From all these guesses I drew one conclusion, which told against the insight of my companions. They might be close observers in their own way, and read the manners in the face; but it was plain that they did not extend their observation to the hands. ⟨There is nothing strange in the omission: the only marvel being that, where we are all as much interested about our neighbours, so few should have learned to look critically at a part of the body, uncovered like the face and nearly as eloquent and personal.⟩

To the saloon passengers also I sustained my part without a hitch. It is true I came little in their way; but when we did encounter, there was no recognition in their eye, although I confess I sometimes courted it in silence. All these, my inferiors and equals, took me, like the transformed monarch in the story, for a mere common, human man. They gave me a hard, dead look, with the flesh about the eye kept unrelaxed.

With the women this surprised me less, as I had already experimented on the sex by going abroad through a suburban part of London simply attired in a sleeve-waistcoat. The result was curious. I then learned for the first time, and by the exhaustive process, how much attention ladies are accustomed to bestow on all male creatures of their own station; for, in my humble rig, each one who went by me caused me a certain shock of surprise and a sense of something wanting. In my normal circumstances, it appeared, every young lady must have paid me some passing tribute of a glance; and though I had often been unconscious of it when given, I was well aware of its absence when it was withheld. My height seemed to decrease with every woman who passed me, for she passed me like a dog. This is one of my grounds for supposing that what are called the upper classes may sometimes produce a disagreeable impression in what are called the lower; and I wish some one would continue my experiment, and find out exactly at what stage of toilette a man becomes invisible to the well-regulated female eye.

Here on shipboard the matter was put to a more complete test; for, even with the addition of speech and manner, I passed among the ladies for precisely the average man of the steerage. It was one afternoon that I saw this demonstrated. A very plainly dressed woman was taken ill on deck. I think I had the luck to be present at every sudden seizure during all the passage; and on this occasion found myself in the place of importance, supporting the sufferer. There was not only a large crowd immediately around us, but a considerable knot of saloon passengers leaning over our heads from the hurricane-deck. One of these, an elderly managing woman, hailed me with counsels. Of course I had to reply; and as the talk went on, I began to discover that the whole group took me for the husband. I looked upon my new wife, poor creature, with mingled feelings; and I must own she had not even the appearance of the poorest class of city servant-maids, but looked more like a country wench who should have been employed at a roadside inn. (I confess openly, I was chagrined at this.) Now was the time for me to go and study the brass plate.

To such of the officers as knew about me — the doctor, the purser, and the stewards — I appeared in the light of a broad joke. The fact that I spent the better part of my day in writing had gone abroad over the ship and tickled them all prodigiously. Whenever they met me they referred to my absurd occupation with familiarity and breadth of humorous intention. Their manner was well calculated to remind me of my fallen fortunes. You may be sincerely amused by the amateur literary efforts of a gentleman, but you scarce publish the feeling to his face. "Well!" they would say: "still writing?" And the smile would widen into a laugh. The purser came one day into the cabin, and, touched to the heart by my misguided industry, offered me some other kind of writing, "for which," he added pointedly, "you will be paid." This was nothing else than to

copy out the list of passengers. ⟨It was odd how my feeling
of amusement was tempered by soreness. One of the sailors was
the only man on board, besides my particular friends, who
could be persuaded to take my literary character in earnest. I
discussed the subject with him one night until his watch was
over; he was much interested by all that I told him; and in
return recommended me a work called *Tom Holt's Log*, the
principal incidents of which he obligingly described. I hand
over the recommendation, fresh as I received it, to the reader;
for I have not yet had an opportunity to see the book in
question. But I will propose a wager, founding on a pretty
large induction, that it is either excellent or downright penny
trash. There seems to be no medium in the tastes of the un-
literary class; mediocrity must tremble for its judgment; either
strong, lively matter solidly handled, or mere ink and banditti,
forms its literary diet.⟩

Another trick of mine which told against my reputation was
my choice of roosting-place in an active draught upon the
cabin floor. I was openly jeered and flouted for this eccen-
tricity; and a considerable knot would sometimes gather at the
door to see my last dispositions for the night. This was em-
barassing, but I learned to support the trial with equanimity.

Indeed I may say that, upon the whole, my new position
sat lightly and naturally upon my spirits. I accepted the consequences with readiness, and found them far from difficult
to bear. The steerage conquered me; I conformed more and
more to the type of the place, not only in manner but at heart,
growing hostile to the officers and cabin passengers who looked
down upon me, and day by day greedier for small delicacies.
Such was the result, as I fancy, of a diet of bread and butter,
soup and porridge. We think we have no sweet tooth as long
as we are full to the brim of molasses; but a man must have
sojourned in the workhouse before he boasts himself indifferent to dainties. Every evening, for instance, I was more and
more pre-occupied about our doubtful fare at tea. If it was
delicate my heart was much lightened; if it was but broken

fish I was proportionally downcast. The offer of a little jelly from a fellow-passenger more provident than myself caused a marked elevation in my spirits. And I would have gone to the ship's end and back again for an oyster or a chipped fruit.

⟨Judge, then, of my delight, when a turn of events made me a sort of favoured inferior and welcome in the chief steward's office. It fell out thus. One day at dinner, the soup for the first time failed us. A despicable broth was followed by a piece of fresh meat no less despicable, and some salt horse racier than game. I left table, went off to the steward, told him I could eat nothing, and was at once supplied with bread and cheese for which he would not suffer me to pay. Meanwhile, during my absence, indignation had warmed up to the boiling point around the second cabin table. One of the company volunteered to write a letter of complaint, which he sealed, without showing it to any one, and handed over to the others to be laid before the captain in a deputation. The letter was brought and the plan explained to me on deck. As no one had seen the terms and the writer himself proposed to remain in the background, I discouraged the whole affair; the deputation fell through; and the missive was delivered single-handed by O'Reilly, who little imagined on what errand he had been dispatched. By three in the afternoon, the petard had burst; and the steward, the understewards and the whole second cabin were playing their parts in an absurd but most unpleasant tragi-comedy. The letter, on being opened, was found to be without a signature. With an odd alternation of dash and prudence, the man who hotly volunteered to lead the attack, had but given a run-away knock and disappeared, leaving O'Reilly in the breach. The prolonged consequences, the councils, the diplomacy, nay, the tears, which flowed from this ill-judged anonasume [?], are too many to be set down here. But as I found myself unpleasantly situated, having made a complaint that very day, I sent a note disclaiming the authorship of the letter. That, like the famous pin which the young gentleman picked up before the merchant's window, was the beginning of my fortune. Thenceforth, I found myself a welcome visitor in the steward's box. I could see the cabin passengers at table; I was shown the bill of fare for the day; and when I left, the steward would fill my pocket with greengages. I have not been in such a situation since I was a child and prowled upon the frontiers of a dinner party. But I found myself unchanged by time. I looked with the same envy on the good things passing by for others. The bill of fare was mine; I pored over it, whetted my appetite, made a dozen dinners in ten minutes and grovelled soul and body in Barmecide feasts; and when the talk was over, made my departure, happy like a tipped schoolboy, with my pocketful of fruit. I had regained the holy simplicity, the frank, piratical instincts of my youth; I was back in Eden and the glades of Arcady; and if I was still a gentleman on a brass plate, in relation to these greengages I may call myself a savage. Perhaps I understand in a more human manner than before, the tithes exacted by domestic servants.)

In other ways I was content with my position. It seemed no disgrace to be confounded with my company; for I may as well declare at once I found their manners as gentle and becoming as those of any other class. I do not mean that my friends could have sat down without embarrassment and laughable disaster at the table of a duke. That does not imply an inferiority of breeding, but a difference of usage. Thus I flatter myself that I conducted myself well among my fellow-passengers; yet my most ambitious hope is not to have avoided faults, but to have committed as few as possible. I know too well that my tact is not the same as their tact, and that my habit of a different society constituted, not only no qualification, but a positive disability to move easily and becomingly in this. When Jones complimented me — because I "managed to behave very pleasantly" to my fellow-passengers, was how he put it — I could follow the thought in his mind, and knew his compliment to be such as we pay foreigners on their proficiency in English. I daresay this praise was given me immediately on the back of some unpardonable solecism, which had led him to review my conduct as a whole. We are all ready to laugh at the ploughman among lords; we should consider also the case of a lord among the ploughmen. I have seen a lawyer in the house of a Hebridean fisherman; and I know, but nothing will induce me to disclose, which of these two was the better gentleman. Some of our finest behaviour, though it looks well enough from the boxes, may seem even brutal to the gallery. We boast too often manners that are parochial rather than universal; that, like a country wine, will not bear transportation for a hundred miles, nor from the parlour to the kitchen. To be a gentleman is to be one all the world over, and in every relation and grade of society. It is a high calling, to which a man must first be born, and then devote himself for life. And, unhappily, the manners of a certain so-called upper grade have a kind of currency, and meet with a certain external acceptation throughout all the others, and this tends to keep us well satisfied with slight acquirements and the amateurish accomplishments of a clique. But manners, like art, should be human and central.

Some of my fellow-passengers, as I now moved among them in a relation of equality, seemed to me excellent gentlemen. They were not rough, nor hasty, nor disputatious; debated pleasantly, differed kindly; were helpful, gentle, patient, and placid. The type of manners was plain, and even heavy; there was little to please the eye, but nothing to shock; and I thought gentleness lay more nearly at the spring of behaviour than in many more ornate and delicate societies. I say delicate, where I cannot say refined; a thing may be fine like ironwork, without being delicate like lace. There was here less delicacy; the skin supported more callously the natural surface of events, the mind received more bravely the crude facts of human existence; but I do not think that there was less effective refinement, less consideration for others, less polite suppression of self. ⟨Of Barney and the old fisher, for instance, I may hope the reader has now some notion of his own; let him ask himself if he meets gentlemen so accomplished at his club. Not every day by many, I am sure. And I know for my part, that I have had a great opportunity, and should have learned some better manners for the future.

It will be understood that) I speak of the best among my fellow-passengers; for in the steerage, as well as in the saloon, there is a mixture. (The women, in particular, too often displeased me by something hard and forward, by something alternately sullen and jeering both in speech and conduct. But, to begin with, this may have been my own fault, for the game of manners is more easily played with a good partner; and in the second place, it may have depended entirely on the difference of sex. I am led to fancy this, because it was in the younger women alone that I was thus displeased. The elder and the married women behaved to me in my capacity of steerage passenger and their co-equal, exactly as they would if I had come on horseback with a groom behind me. What, then, ailed the girls? May I not construe these taunts and tiffs and sulks, as so many challenges into the field of courtship? Many animals and the youth of even the most delicate classes, conduct their love dalliance under the similitude of a quarrel; and something of this modest subterfuge survives perhaps in every marriage or advanced flirtation. Now the girls of our company and perhaps the people of that class (among themselves) may prefer at least to open the campaign on these aggressive tactics. They are forward and backward to provoke the men, that the first kiss may be taken in a tussle and furiously resented. At least I was not amenable to these advances, if such they were; and I thought the women greatly and even surprisingly inferior to the men. It is true that the class of women who emigrate is not likely, for many reasons, to be the best. And I should add, what seems hardly necessary, for it is involved in every word that I have written on the subject, that these were all Scotch and Irish girls; not one from England.)

Those, then, with whom I found myself in sympathy, and

of whom I may therefore hope to write with a greater measure of truth, were not only as good in their manners, but endowed with very much the same natural capacities, and about as wise in deduction, as the bankers and barristers of what is called society. One and all were too much interested in disconnected facts, and loved information for its own sake with too rash a devotion; but people in all classes display the same appetite as they gorge themselves daily with the miscellaneous gossip of the newspaper. Newspaper reading, as far as I can make out, is often rather a sort of brown study than an act of culture. I have myself palmed off yesterday's issue on a friend, and seen him re-peruse it for a continuance of minutes with an air at once refreshed and solemn. Workmen, perhaps, pay more attention; but though they may be eager listeners, they have rarely seemed to me either willing or careful thinkers. Culture is not measured by the greatness of the field which is covered by our knowledge, but by the nicety with which we can perceive relations in that field, whether great or small. Workmen, certainly those who were on board with me, I found wanting in this quality or habit of the mind. They did not perceive relations, ⟨mutually reactive and conditioned by a million others;⟩ but leaped to a so-called cause, and thought the problem settled. Thus the cause of everything in England was the form of government, and the cure for all evils was, by consequence, a revolution. It is surprising how many of them said this, and that none should have had a definite thought in his head as he said it. Some hated the Church because they disagreed with it; some hated Lord Beaconsfield because of war and taxes; all hated the masters, possibly with reason. But these feelings were not at the root of the matter; the true reasoning of their souls ran thus — I have not got on; I ought to have got on; if there was a revolution I should get on. How? They had no idea. Why? Because — because — well, look at America!

To be politically blind is no distinction; we are all so, if you come to that. At bottom, as it seems to me, there is but one question in modern home politics, though it appears in many shapes, and that is the question of money; and but one political remedy, that the people should grow wiser and better. My workmen fellow-passengers were as impatient and dull of hearing on the second of these points as any member of Parliament; but they had some glimmerings of the first. They would not hear of improvement on their part, but wished the world made over again in a crack, so that they might remain improvident and idle and debauched, and yet enjoy the comfort and respect that should accompany the opposite virtues; and it was in this expectation, as far as I could see, that many of them were now on their way to America. But on the point of money they saw clearly enough that inland politics, so far as they were concerned, were reducible to the question of annual income; a question which should long ago have been settled by a revolution, they did not know how, and which they were now about to settle for themselves, once more they knew not how, by crossing the Atlantic in a steamship of considerable tonnage.

And yet it has been amply shown them that the second or income question is in itself nothing, and may as well be left undecided, if there be no wisdom and virtue to profit by the change. It is not by a man's purse, but by his character, that he is rich or poor. (What have the colliers done with their great earnings? My Irish labourer had his three hundred pounds in bank, and was still young. My old North Sea fisher took a pleasure trip to see the States, and had his house and hayfield by the Tyne. There come periods in every country when the struggle for existence grows too fierce to be endured, and a man will do well, if he is able, to escape where the forces are balanced more evenly and daily bread is an affair of course. But to travel after high wages, I have been told by workmen, is never the way to come to easy circumstances, even for the best. And as for those who have already had their opportunity, and lost it, and come out of the flush times in England as poor as they began, we may well wonder with what hope they take to emigration. Wages must fluctuate; work must come and go;

the power of manual labour is a gift so common that none but the exceptionally skilled can count upon employment; and when the evil days are here again, the rest shall emigrate once more and once more with empty pockets. I do not at all despise the relief of a time, however brief and passing, of comparative ease in money matters; for while any man can be poor for a month or two with equanimity and even merriment, it is the long continuous drag and the daily recurrence of the same small cares that weary patience and lead on despair. Let them follow high wages, by all means; but let them not suppose that either a change of country or a change of government will make those rich or contented who are without the virtues of the state.) Barney will be poor, Alick will be poor, Mackay will be poor, let them go where they will, and wreck all the governments under heaven; they will be poor until they die.

Nothing is perhaps more notable in the average workman than his surprising idleness, and the candour with which he confesses to the failing. It has to me been always something of a relief to find the poor, as a general rule, so little oppressed with work. I can in consequence enjoy my own more fortunate beginning with a better grace. The other day I was living with a farmer in America, an old frontiersman, who had worked and fought, hunted and farmed, from his childhood up. He excused himself for his defective education on the ground that he had been overworked from first to last. Even now, he said, anxious as he was, he had never the time to take up a book. In consequence of this, I observed him closely; he was occupied for four or, at the extreme outside, for five hours out of the twenty-four, and then principally in walking; and the remainder of the day he passed in sheer idleness, either eating fruit or standing with his back against a door. I have known men do hard literary work all morning, and then undergo quite as much physical fatigue by way of relief as satisfied this powerful frontiersman for the day. He, at least, like all the educated class, did so much homage to industry as to persuade himself he was industrious. But the average mechanic recognises his idleness with effrontery; he has even, as I am told, organised it.

I give the story as it was told me, and it was told me for a fact. A man fell from a housetop in the city of Aberdeen, and was brought into hospital with broken bones. He was asked what was his trade, and replied that he was a *tapper*. No one had ever heard of such a thing before; the officials were filled with curiosity; they besought an explanation. It appeared that when a party of slaters were engaged upon a roof, they would now and then be taken with a fancy for the public-house. Now a seamstress, for example, might slip away from her work and no one be the wiser; but if these fellows adjourned, the tapping of the mallets would cease, and thus the neighbourhood be advertised of their defection. Hence the career of the tapper. He has to do the tapping and keep up an industrious bustle on the housetop during the absence of the slaters. When he taps for only one or two the thing is child's-play, but when he has to represent a whole troop, it is then that he earns his money in the sweat of his brow. Then must he bound from spot to spot, reduplicate, triplicate, sextuplicate his single personality, and swell and hasten his blows, until he produce a perfect illusion for the ear, and you would swear that a crowd of emulous masons were continuing merrily to roof the house. It must be a strange sight from an upper window.

I heard nothing on board of the tapper; but I was astonished at the stories told by my companions. Skulking, shirking, malingering, were all established tactics, it appeared. They could see no dishonesty when a man who is paid for an hour's work gives half an hour's consistent idling in its place. Thus the tapper would refuse to watch for the police during a burglary, and call himself an honest man. It is not sufficiently recognised that our race detests to work. If I thought that I should have to work every day of my life as hard as I am working now, I should be tempted to give up the struggle. And the workman early begins on his career of toil. He has never had his fill of holidays in the past, and his prospect of holidays in the future is both distant and uncertain. In the circumstances, it would require a high degree of virtue not to snatch alleviations for the moment.

There were many good talkers on the ship; and I believe good talking of a certain sort is a common accomplishment among working men. Where books are comparatively scarce, a greater amount of information will be given and received by word of mouth; and this tends to produce good talkers, and, what is no less needful for conversation, good listeners. They could all tell a story with effect. I am sometimes tempted to think that the less literary class show always better in narration; they have so much more patience with detail, are so much less hurried to reach the points, and preserve so much juster a proportion among the facts. At the same time their talk is dry; they pursue a topic ploddingly, have not an agile fancy, do not throw sudden lights from unexpected quarters, and when the talk is over they often leave the matter where it was. They mark time instead of marching. They think only to argue, not to reach new conclusions, and use their reason rather as a weapon of offence than as a tool for self-improvement. Hence the talk of some of the cleverest was unprofitable in result, because there was no give and take; they would grant you as little as possible for premise, and begin to dispute under an oath to conquer or to die.

But the talk of a workman is apt to be more interesting than that of a wealthy merchant, because the thoughts, hopes, and fears of which the workman's life is built lie nearer to necessity and nature. They are more immediate to human life. An income calculated by the week is a far more human thing than one calculated by the year, and a small income, simply from its smallness, than a large one. I never wearied listening to the details of a workman's economy, because every item stood for some real pleasure. If he could afford pudding twice a week, you know that twice a week the man ate with genuine gusto and was physically happy; while if you learn that a rich man has seven courses a day, ten to one the half of them remain untasted, and the whole is but misspent money and a weariness to the flesh.

The difference between England and America to a working man was thus most humanly put to me by a fellow-passenger: "In America," said he, "you get pies and puddings." I do not hear enough, in economy books, of pies and pudding. A man lives in and for the delicacies, adornments, and accidental attributes of life, such as pudding to eat and pleasant books and theatres to occupy his leisure. The bare terms of existence would be rejected with contempt by all. If a man feeds on bread and butter, soup and porridge, his appetite grows wolfish after dainties. And the workman dwells in a borderland, and is always within sight of those cheerless regions where life is more difficult to sustain than worth sustaining. Every detail of our existence, where it is worth while to cross the ocean after pie and pudding, is made alive and enthralling by the presence of genuine desire; but it is all one to me whether Crœsus has a hundred or a thousand thousands in the bank. There is more adventure in the life of the working man who descends as a common soldier into the battle of life, than in that of the millionaire who sits apart in an office, like Von Moltke, and only directs the manœuvres by telegraph. Give me to hear about the career of him who is in the thick of the business; to whom one change of market means an empty belly, and another a copious and savoury meal. This is not the philosophical, but the human side of economics; it interests like a story; and the life of all who are thus situated partakes in a small way of the charm of *Robinson Crusoe*; for every step is critical, and human life is presented to you naked and verging to its lowest terms.

NEW YORK

As we drew near to New York I was at first amused, and
then somewhat staggered, by the cautions and the grisly tales
that went the round. You would have thought we were to
land upon a cannibal island. You must speak to no one in the
streets, as they would not leave you till you were rooked and
beaten. You must enter a hotel with military precautions; for
the least you had to apprehend was to awake next morning
without money or baggage, or necessary raiment, a lone forked
radish in a bed; and if the worst befell, you would instantly
and mysteriously disappear from the ranks of mankind.

I have usually found such stories correspond to the least
modicum of fact. Thus I was warned, I remember, against the
roadside inns of the Cevennes, and that by a learned professor;
and when I reached Pradelles the warning was explained; it
was but the far-away rumour and reduplication of a single
terrifying story already half a century old, and half forgotten
in the theatre of the events. So I was tempted to make light
of these reports against America. But we had on board with us
a man whose evidence it would not do to put aside. He had
come near these perils in the body; he had visited a robber inn.
The public has an old and well-grounded favour for this class
of incident, and shall be gratified to the best of my power.

My fellow-passenger, whom we shall call M'Naughten, had
come from New York to Boston with a comrade, seeking work.
They were a pair of rattling blades; and, leaving their baggage
at the station, passed the day in beer-saloons, and with congenial spirits, until midnight struck. Then they applied themselves to find a lodging, and walked the streets till two, knocking at houses of entertainment and being refused admittance, or

themselves declining the terms. By two the inspiration of their liquor had begun to wear off; they were weary and humble, and after a great circuit found themselves in the same street where they had begun their search, and in front of a French hotel where they had already sought accommodation. Seeing the house still open, they returned to the charge. A man in a white cap sat in an office by the door. He seemed to welcome them more warmly than when they had first presented themselves, and the charge for the night had somewhat unaccountably fallen from a dollar to a quarter. They thought him ill-looking, but paid their quarter apiece, and were shown upstairs to the top of the house. There, in a small room, the man in the white cap wished them pleasant slumbers.

The room was furnished with a bed, a chair, and some conveniences. The door did not lock on the inside; and the only sign of adornment was a couple of framed pictures, one close above the head of the bed, and the other opposite the foot, and both curtained, as we may sometimes see valuable water-colours, or the portraits of the dead, or works of art more than usually skittish in the subject. It was perhaps in the hope of finding something of this last description that M'Naughten's comrade pulled aside the curtain of the first. He was startlingly disappointed. There was no picture. The frame surrounded, and the curtain was designed to hide, an oblong aperture in the partition, through which they looked forth into the dark corridor. A person standing without could easily take a purse from under the pillow, or even strangle a sleeper as he lay abed. M'Naughten and his comrade stared at each other like Balboa and his men, "with a wild surmise;" and then the latter, catching up the lamp, ran to the other frame and roughly raised the curtain. There he stood, petrified; and M'Naughten, who had followed, grasped him by the wrist in terror. They could see into another room, larger in size than that which they occupied, where three men sat crouching and silent in the dark. For a second or so these five persons looked each other in the eyes, then the curtain was dropped, and M'Naughten and

his friend made but one bolt of it out of the room and down
the stairs. The man in the white cap said nothing as they
passed him; and they were so pleased to be once more in the
open night that they gave up all notion of a bed, and walked
the streets of Boston till the morning.

No one seemed much cast down by these stories, but all
inquired after the address of a respectable hotel; and I, for my
part, put myself under the conduct of Mr. Jones. Before noon
of the second Sunday we sighted the low shores outside of
New York harbour; the steerage passengers must remain on
board to pass through Castle Garden[1] on the following morning; but we of the second cabin made our escape along with the
lords of the saloon; and by six o'clock Jones and I issued into
West Street, sitting on some straw in the bottom of an open
baggage-waggon. It rained miraculously; and from that moment
till on the following night I left New York, there was scarce a
lull, and no cessation of the downpour. The roadways were
flooded; a loud strident noise of falling water filled the air; the
restaurants smelt heavily of wet people and wet clothing.

It took us but a few minutes, though it cost us a good deal
of money, to be rattled along West Street to our destination:
"Reunion House, No. 10 West Street, one minute's walk from
Castle Garden; convenient to Castle Garden, the Steamboat
Landings, California Steamers and Liverpool Ships; Board and
Lodging per day 1 dollar, single meals 25 cents, lodging per
night 25 cents; private rooms for families; no charge for storage
or baggage; satisfaction guaranteed to all persons; Michael
Mitchell, Proprietor." Reunion House was, I may go the length
of saying, a humble hostelry. You entered through a long bar-
room, thence passed into a little dining-room, and thence into
a still smaller kitchen. The furniture was of the plainest; but
the bar was hung in the American taste, with encouraging and
hospitable mottoes. ⟨There is something youthful in this fashion

1. Circular building on the southernmost point of Manhattan that
served as an immigrant receiving station before the establishment of
Ellis Island.

which pleases me; it runs into the advertisements; they do not merely offer you your money's worth of perfunctory attendance, but hold out golden prospects and welcome you with both hands; such a proprietor defies black care to follow you into his saloon; such another, touching the keynote with precision, invites you to his bar "to have a good time with the boys." So they not only insure their own attention but the wit and friendly spirit of their guests.)

Jones was well known; we were received warmly; and two minutes afterwards I had refused a drink from the proprietor, and was going on, in my plain European fashion, to refuse a cigar, when Mr. Mitchell sternly interposed, and explained the situation. He was offering to treat me, it appeared; whenever an American bar-keeper proposes anything, it must be borne in mind that he is offering to treat; and if I did not want a drink, I must at least take the cigar. I took it bashfully, feeling I had begun my American career on the wrong foot. I did not enjoy that cigar; but this may have been from a variety of reasons, even the best cigar often failing to please if you smoke three-quarters of it in a drenching rain.

For many years America was to me a sort of promised land. "Westward the march of empire holds its way;" [2] the race is for the moment to the young; what has been and what is we imperfectly and obscurely know; what is to be yet lies beyond the flight of our imaginations. Greece, Rome, and Judæa are gone by for ever, leaving to generations the legacy of their accomplished work; China still endures, an old inhabited house in the brand-new city of nations; England has already declined, since she has lost the States; and to these States, therefore, yet undeveloped, full of dark possibilities, and grown, like another Eve, from one rib out of the side of their own old land, the minds of young men in England turn naturally at a certain hopeful period of their age. It will be hard for an American to

2. Stevenson recalls incorrectly a line from Bishop George Berkeley's poem "On the Prospect of Planting Arts and Learning in America," which should read, "Westward the course of empire takes its way."

understand the spirit. But let him imagine a young man who shall have grown up in an old and rigid circle, following by-gone fashions and taught to distrust his own fresh instincts, and who now suddenly hears of a family of cousins, all about his own age, who keep house together by themselves and live far from restraint and tradition; let him imagine this, and he will have some imperfect notion of the sentiment with which spirited English youths turn to the thought of the American Republic. It seems to them as if, out west, the war of life was still conducted in the open air, and on free barbaric terms; as if it had not yet been narrowed into parlours, nor begun to be conducted, like some unjust and dreary arbitration, by com-promise, costume, forms of procedure, and sad, senseless self-denial. Which of these two he prefers, a man with any youth still left in him will decide rightly for himself. He would rather be houseless than denied a pass-key; rather go without food than partake of a stalled ox in stiff, respectable society; rather be shot out of hand than direct his life according to the dictates of the world.

He knows or thinks nothing of the Maine Laws,[3] the Puritan sourness, the fierce, sordid appetite for dollars, or the dreary existence of country towns. A few wild story-books which de-lighted his childhood form the imaginative basis of his picture of America. In course of time, there is added to this a great crowd of stimulating details — vast cities that grow up as by enchantment; the birds, that have gone south in autumn, re-turning with the spring to find thousands camped upon their marshes, and the lamps burning far and near along populous streets; forests that disappear like snow; countries larger than Britain that are cleared and settled, one man running forth with his household gods before another, while the bear and the Indian are yet scarce aware of their approach; oil that gushes from the earth; gold that is washed or quarried in the brooks or glens of the Sierras; and all that bustle, courage, action, and

3. Laws that prohibited the manufacture and sale of intoxicating liquors.

constant kaleidoscopic change that Walt Whitman has seized and set forth in his vigorous, cheerful, and loquacious verses. (Even the shot-gun, the navy revolver and the bowie knife, seem more connected with courage than with cruelty. I remember a while ago when Chicago was burned, hearing how a man, ere he began to rebuild his house, put up a board with some such inscription as the following: "All lost. Have a wife and three children. Have the world to begin again;" and then in large capitals the word: *"Energy."* The pluck and the expansion are alike youthful, and go straight to a young heart. Yes, it seemed to me, here was the country after all; here the undaunted stock of mankind, worthy to earn a new world.

I think Americans are scarce aware of this romantic attraction exercised by their land upon their cousins over sea. Perhaps they are unable to detect it under a certain jealousy and repentant soreness with which we regard a prosperity that might have been ours but for our own misconduct. Perhaps, too, we purposely conceal it; for we do not yet despair of the old ship. And perhaps the feeling flourishes more freely in the absence of any embodied and gently disappointing Uncle Sam. Europe is visited yearly by a crowd of preposterous fellows who, stung by some inattention or merely sick with patriotism, decline their titles of superiority in our ears and insult us with statistics by the page. From some such excursion, they return full of bitterness because the English show so small an interest and so modified a pleasure in the progress of the States. Truly; but perhaps we should please them better, if they would measure the growth of America on some different standard from the decline of England. That capital essayist, Mr. Lowell, suffered much from "a certain condescension in foreigners," [4] by which they made him feel that America was still young and incomplete; there is, I fear, a certain assumption in the American, by which he manages to taunt us with our age and

4. James Russell Lowell's "On a Certain Condescension in Foreigners" appeared first in the *Atlantic Monthly* of January 1869 and was collected in the third edition of *My Study Windows*.

debility. And since I am on this subject, let me courteously invite each American citizen who purposes travelling in Europe, either to hold his peace upon the subject of the Alabama claims; or if he must discuss the matter, to first refund from his own pocket the money which was paid by the one party and accepted by the other to conclude and definitively bury the dispute. The first American I ever encountered after I had begun to adore America, quarrelled with me, or else I quarrelled with him, about the Alabama claims. He has not been the last. Yet I never started the subject; indeed I know nothing about it, except that the money was paid; and fight for my flag in ignorance like a man before the mast.

It is possible that some people are always best at home, though the reverse is scandalously true of others. I have just been reading Mr. Charles Reade's *Woman Hater* (for which I wish to thank him), and I am reminded of Zoe Vizard's remark: "What does that matter? We are abroad." Sedentary, respectable people seem to leave some vital qualities behind them when they travel: *non omnia sua secum;* they are not themselves, and with all that mass of baggage, have forgotten to put up their human virtues. A Bohemian may not have much to recommend him, but what he has, is at least his own and indefeasible. You may rely as surely upon his virtues as upon his vices, for they are both bred in the bone. Neither have been assumed to suit the temper of society, or depend in any degree on the vicinity of Portman Square.[5] But respectable people, transplanted from their own particular zone of respectability, too often lose their manners, their good sense, and a considerable part of their religion. For instance I have not yet seen the Sabbatarian who did not visibly relax upon the continent. Hence perhaps the difference between the American abroad and the American at home. If one thing were deeply written on my mind, it was this: that the American dislikes England and the English; and yet I had no sooner crossed the

5. Fashionable residential area in London.

Atlantic, than I began to think it an unfounded notion. The old country — so they called it with an accent of true kindliness — was plainly not detested; they spoke of it with a certain emotion, as of a father from whom they had parted in anger and who was since dead; and wherever I went, I found my nationality an introduction. I am old-fashioned enough to be patriotic, particularly when away from home; and thus the change delighted and touched me. Up to the moment of my arrival, I had connected Americans with hostility, not to me indeed, but to my land; from that moment forward, I found that was a link which I had thought to be a barrier, and knew that I was among blood relations.

So much had I written some time ago, with great good sense, as I thought, and complete catholicity of view. But it began at first to dawn upon me slowly, and was then forced upon me in a thunderclap, that I had myself become one of those uncivil travellers whom I so heartily condemned: that while here I was, kindly received, I could not find a good word nor so much as a good thought for the land that harboured me; that I was eager to spy its faults and shrank from the sight of virtues as if they were injustices to England. Such was the case; explain it how you may. It was too like my home, and yet not like enough. It stood to me like a near relation who is scarce a friend, and who may disgrace us by his mis-conduct and yet cannot greatly please by his prosperity. I can bear to read the worst word of a Frenchman about England, and can do so smiling; but let an American take up the tale, and I am all quivering susceptibility from head to foot. There is still a sense of domestic treachery when we fall out, and a sense of unwarrantable coolness even when we agree.

Did you ever read the parable of the Prodigal Son? Or do you fancy, if things had been reversed and the prodigal come home in broadcloth and a chaise and four, that his brother who had stayed at home and stood by the old concern, would be better satisfied with the result? He might have been; not I. I have not enough justice in me for a case so trying. And then in one version of the parable, the prodigal was driven from home with barbarous usage; and O! what a bitterness is added to the cup! Your own Benjamin Franklin has foreseen my case. "Were it possible for *us* to forget and forgive," he wrote, "it is not possible for *you* (I mean the British nation) to forgive the people you have so heavily injured." [6] Incisive Franklin! Yours is the prophecy, mine the ill-feeling. I have all the faults of my forefathers on my stomach; I have historical remorse; I cannot see America but through the jaundiced spectacles of criminality.

And surely if jealousy be, as I believe it is, only the most radical, primeval and naked form of admiration — admiration in war paint, so to speak — then every word of my confession proves a delicate flattery like incense. Sail on, O mighty Union! God knows I wish you a noble career. Only somehow, when I was younger, I used to feel as if I had some portion in your future; but first I began to meet Americans in my own home, and they did not run to greet me as I hoped; and then I came myself into these states, and found my own heart not pure of ancient hatred. With that I knew I was a stranger, and you did but justice to refuse me copyright. Yet it is with disappointed tenderness that I behold you steaming off to glory in your new and elegant turret ship, while I remain behind to go down with the old three decker. We have feelings that will not be uttered in prose; and where poetry is absent, jingle must serve the turn.

> With half a heart I wander here
>   As from an age gone by,
> A brother — yet, though young in years,
>   An elder brother I!
>
> You speak another tongue from mine,
>   Though both were English born.
> I towards the night of time decline:
>   You mount into the morn.

6. From Franklin's letter of July 30, 1776, to Lord Howe.

Youth shall grow great and strong and free
    But age must still decay.
Tomorrow for the States — for me
    England and yesterday! [7]

Here I was at last in America, and was soon out upon New York streets, spying for things foreign. The place had to me an air of Liverpool; but such was the rain that not Paradise itself would have looked inviting. We were a party of four, under two umbrellas; Jones and I and two Scots lads, recent immigrants, and not indisposed to welcome a compatriot. They had been six weeks in New York, and neither of them had yet found a single job or earned a single halfpenny. Up to the present they were exactly out of pocket by the amount of the fare.

The lads soon left us. Now I had sworn by all my gods to have such a dinner as would rouse the dead; there was scarce any expense at which I should have hesitated; the devil was in it but Jones and I should dine like heathen emperors. I set to work, asking after a restaurant; and I chose the wealthiest and most gastronomical-looking passers-by to ask from. Yet, although I had told them I was willing to pay anything in reason, one and all sent me off to cheap, fixed-price houses, where I would not have eaten that night for the cost of twenty dinners. I do not know if this were characteristic of New York, or whether it was only Jones and I who looked un-dinerly and discouraged enterprising suggestions. But at length, by our own sagacity, we found a French restaurant, where there was a French waiter, some fair French cooking, some so-called French wine, and French coffee to conclude the whole. I never entered into the feelings of Jack on land so completely as when I tasted that coffee.

I suppose we had one of the "private rooms for families" at Reunion House. It was very small; furnished with a bed, a chair, and some clothes-pegs; and it derived all that was neces-

7. First published, with changes, in *Underwoods* (1887).

sary for the life of the human animal through two borrowed
lights; one, looking into the passage, and the second opening,
without sash, into another apartment, where three men fitfully
snored, or, in intervals of wakefulness, drearily mumbled to
each other all night long. It will be observed that this was
almost exactly the disposition of the room in M'Naughten's
story. Jones had the bed; I pitched my camp upon the floor;
he did not sleep until near morning, and I, for my part, never
closed an eye. ⟨Some of this wakefulness was due to the change
from shipboard; but the better part, in my case, to a certain
distressing malady which had been growing on me during the
last few days and of which more anon.⟩

At sunrise I heard a cannon fired; and shortly afterwards the
men in the next room gave over snoring for good, and began
to rustle over their toilettes. The sound of their voices as they
talked was low and moaning, like that of people watching by
the sick. Jones, who had at last begun to doze, tumbled and
murmured, and every now and then opened unconscious eyes
upon me where I lay. I found myself growing eerier and eerier,
for I daresay I was a little fevered by my restless night, and
hurried to dress and get down-stairs.

You had to pass through the rain, which still fell thick and
resonant, to reach a lavatory on the other side of the court.
There were three basin-stands, and a few crumpled towels and
pieces of wet soap, white and slippery like fish; nor should I
forget a looking-glass and a pair of questionable combs. Another Scots lad was here, scrubbing his face with a good will.
He had been three months in New York and had not yet found
a single job nor earned a single halfpenny. Up to the present,
he also was exactly out of pocket by the amount of the fare.
I began to grow sick at heart for my fellow-emigrants.

Of my nightmare wanderings in New York I spare to tell.
I had a thousand and one things to do; only the day to do them
in, and a journey across the continent before me in the evening.
It rained with patient fury; every now and then I had to get
under cover for a while in order, so to speak, to give my

mackintosh a rest; for under this continued drenching it began to grow damp on the inside. I went to banks, post-offices, railway-offices, restaurants, publishers, booksellers, money-changers, and wherever I went a pool would gather about my feet, and those who were careful of their floors would look on with an unfriendly eye. Wherever I went, too, the same traits struck me: the people were all surprisingly rude and surprisingly kind. The money-changer cross-questioned me like a French commissary, asking my age, my business, my average income, and my destination, beating down my attempts at evasion, and receiving my answers in silence; and yet when all was over, he shook hands with me up to the elbows, and sent his lad nearly a quarter of a mile in the rain to get me books at a reduction. Again, in a very large publishing and bookselling establishment, a man, who seemed to be the manager, received me as I had certainly never before been received in any human shop, indicated squarely that he put no faith in my honesty, and refused to look up the names of books or give me the slightest help or information, on the ground, like the steward, that it was none of his business. I lost my temper at last, said I was a stranger in America and not learned in their etiquette; but I would assure him, if he went to any bookseller in England, of more handsome usage. The boast was perhaps exaggerated; but like many a long shot, it struck the gold. The manager passed at once from one extreme to the other; I may say that from that moment he loaded me with kindness; he gave me all sorts of good advice, wrote me down addresses, and came bare-headed into the rain to point me out a restaurant where I might lunch, nor even then did he seem to think that he had done enough. These are (it is as well to be bold in statement) the manners of America. It is this same opposition that has most struck me in people of almost all classes and from east to west. By the time a man had about strung me up to be the death of him by his insulting behaviour, he himself would be just upon the point of melting into confidence and serviceable attentions. Yet I suspect, although I have met with the like in so many parts, that this must be the character of some particular State or group of States; for in America, and this again in all classes, you will find some of the softest-mannered gentlemen in the world.

⟨I returned to Mitchell's to write some letters, and then made the acquaintance of his stripling daughter. She was a slip of a girl at that attractive period of life when the girl just begins to put on the forms of the woman, and yet retains an accent and character of her own. Her looks were dark, strange and comely. Her eyes had a caressing fixity, which made you inclined to turn aside your own. She was what is called a reading girl, and it was because she saw books in my open knapsack as I sat writing at a table near the bar, that she plucked up courage to address me. Had I any songs? she asked me, touching a volume with her finger. I told her I had not; but she still hovered by, and again inquired, if any of the books were nice? I gave her a volume of my own, not because I thought it so nice, but because it had a likeness of myself in the frontispiece, which I thought it would amuse the child to recognise. She was delighted beyond measure, and read a good many pages aloud to her sister as I sat writing; the sister, I must confess, soon wearied and ran away; but the other child, with admirable courage, persevered till it was time for me to go. I wish her a kind husband who will have, without my wishing it, a most desirable wife, particularly for an author.

I went to a chemist's in Broadway, a great temple near the Post Office, where I was examined and prescribed for by a fine gentleman in fine linen and with the most insinuative manners. My wrists were a mass of sores; so were many other parts of my body. The itching was at times overwhelming; at times, too, it was succeeded by furious stinging pains, like so many cuts with a carriage whip. There were moments when even a stoic or an Indian Gymnosophist might have been excused for some demonstration of interest; and for my part, I was ready to roll upon the floor in my paroxysms. The gentleman in fine linen told me, with admirable gravity, that my liver was out of order, and presented me with a blue pill, a seidlitz powder and a little bottle of some salt and colourless fluid to take night and morning on the journey. He might as well have given me a cricket bat and a copy of Johnson's dictionary, I might have lived exclusively on blue pills and been none the better. But the diagnosis of the gentleman in fine linen was hopelessly at fault. Perhaps he had moved too exclusively in elegant circles; perhaps he was too noble-minded to suspect me of anything disgraceful. The true name of my complaint, I will never divulge, for I know what is due to the reader and to myself; but there is every reason to believe that I am not the only emigrant who has arrived in the Western world with similar symptoms. It is indeed a piece of emigrant experience, though one which I had not desired to share. Should any person be so intoxicated by my descriptions of an emigrant's career, as to desire to follow in my footsteps, here is a consideration which may modify if not eradicate the wish. But I have since been told that with a ring of red sublimate about the wrist, a man may plunge into the vilest company unfearing. I had no red sublimate: that is my story; hence these tears.)

I was so wet when I got back to Mitchell's towards the evening, that I had simply to divest myself of my shoes, socks, and trousers, and leave them behind for the benefit of New York city. No fire could have dried them ere I had to start; and to pack them in their present condition was to spread ruin among my other possessions. With a heavy heart I said farewell to them as they lay a pulp in the middle of a pool upon the floor of Mitchell's kitchen. I wonder if they are dry by now. Mitchell hired a man to carry my baggage to the station, which was hard by, accompanied me thither himself, and recommended me to the particular attention of the officials. No one could have been kinder. Those who are out of pocket may go safely to Reunion House, where they will get decent meals and find an honest and obliging landlord. I owed him this word of thanks, before I enter fairly on the second chapter of my emigrant experience.

PART II

Across the Plains

NOTES BY THE WAY
TO COUNCIL BLUFFS

Monday. — It was, if I remember rightly, five o'clock when we were all signalled to be present at the Ferry Depot of the railroad. An emigrant ship had arrived at New York on the Saturday night, another on the Sunday morning, our own on Sunday afternoon, a fourth early on Monday; and as there is no emigrant train on Sunday, a great part of the passengers from these four ships was concentrated on the train by which I was to travel. There was a Babel of bewildered men, women, and children. The wretched little booking-office, and the baggage-room, which was not much larger, were crowded thick with emigrants, and were heavy and rank with the atmosphere of dripping clothes. Open carts full of bedding stood by the half-hour in the rain. The officials loaded each other with recriminations. A bearded, mildewed little man, whom I take to have been an emigrant agent, was all over the place, his mouth full of brimstone, blustering and interfering. It was plain that the whole system, if system there was, had utterly broken down under the strain of so many passengers.

My own ticket was given me at once, and an oldish man, who preserved his head in the midst of this turmoil, got my baggage registered, and counselled me to stay quietly where I was till he should give me the word to move. I had taken along with me a small valise, a knapsack, which I carried on my shoulders, and in the bag of my railway rug the whole of Bancroft's *History of the United States*, in six fat volumes. It was as much as I could carry with convenience even for short distances, but it ensured me plenty of clothing, and the valise was at that moment, and often after, useful for a stool. I am sure I sat for an hour in the baggage-room, and wretched enough it was; yet, when at last the word was passed to me, and I picked up my bundles and got under way, it was only to exchange discomfort for downright misery and danger.

I followed the porters into a long shed reaching downhill from West Street to the river. It was dark, the wind blew clean through it from end to end; and here I found a great block of passengers and baggage, hundreds of one and tons of the other. I feel I shall have a difficulty to make myself believed; and certainly the scene must have been exceptional, for it was too dangerous for daily repetition. It was a tight jam; there was no fair way through the mingled mass of brute and living obstruction. Into the upper skirts of the crowd, porters, infuriated by hurry and overwork, clove their way with shouts. I may say that we stood like sheep, and that the porters charged among us like so many maddened sheep-dogs; and I believe these men were no longer answerable for their acts. It mattered not what they were carrying, they drove straight into the press, and when they could get no farther, blindly discharged their barrowful. With my own hand, for instance, I saved the life of a child as it sat upon its mother's knee, she sitting on a box; and since I heard of no accident, I must suppose that there were many similar interpositions in the course of the evening. It will give some idea of the state of mind to which we were reduced if I tell you that neither the porter nor the mother of the child paid the least attention to my act. It was not till some time after that I understood what I had done myself, for to ward off heavy boxes seemed at the moment a natural incident of human life. Cold, wet, clamour, dead opposition to progress, such as one encounters in an evil dream, had utterly daunted the spirits. We had accepted this

purgatory as a child accepts the conditions of the world. For
my part, I shivered a little, and my back ached wearily; but I
believe I had neither a hope nor a fear, and all the activities of
my nature had become tributary to one massive sensation of
discomfort.

At length, and after how long an interval I hesitate to guess,
the crowd began to move, heavily straining through itself.
About the same time some lamps were lighted, and threw a sudden flare over the shed. We were being filtered out into the
river boat for Jersey City. You may imagine how slowly this
filtering proceeded, through the dense, choking crush, every
one overladen with packages or children, and yet under the
necessity of fishing out his ticket by the way; but it ended at
length for me, and I found myself on deck, under a flimsy
awning, and with a trifle of elbow-room to stretch and breathe
in. This was on the starboard; for the bulk of the emigrants
stuck hopelessly on the port side, by which we had entered.
In vain the seamen shouted to them to move on, and threatened them with shipwreck. These poor people were under a
spell of stupor, and did not stir a foot. It rained as heavily as
ever, but the wind now came in sudden claps and capfuls, not
without danger to a boat so badly ballasted as ours; and we
crept over the river in the darkness, trailing one paddle in the
water like a wounded duck, and passed ever and again by
huge, illuminated steamers running many knots, and heralding
their approach by strains of music. The contrast between these
pleasure embarkations and our own grim vessel, with her list
to port and her freight of wet and silent emigrants, was of
that glaring description which we count too obvious for the
purposes of art.

The landing at Jersey City was done in a stampede. I had a
fixed sense of calamity, and, to judge by conduct, the same
persuasion was common to us all. A panic selfishness, like that
produced by fear, presided over the disorder of our landing.
People pushed, and elbowed and ran, their families following
how they could. Children fell, and were picked up, to be re-

warded by a blow. One child, who had lost her parents, screamed steadily and with increasing shrillness, as though verging towards a fit; an official kept her by him, but no one else seemed so much as to remark her distress; and I am ashamed to say that I ran among the rest. I was so weary that I had twice to make a halt and set down my bundles in the hundred yards or so between the pier and the railway station, so that I was quite wet by the time that I got under cover. There was no waiting-room, no refreshment-room; the cars were locked; and for at least another hour, or so it seemed, we had to camp upon the draughty, gas-lit platform. I sat on my valise, too crushed to observe my neighbours; but as they were all cold, and wet, and weary, and driven stupidly crazy by the mismanagement to which we had been subjected, I believe they can have been no happier than myself. I bought half a dozen oranges from a boy, for oranges and nuts were the only refection to be had. As only two of them had even a pretence of juice, I threw the other four under the cars, and beheld, as in a dream, grown people and children groping on the track after my leavings. ⟨God knows they would get little comfort from these balls of yellow fibre. But the touch completes the misery of the picture.

You will tell me, perhaps, that people are jostled, driven, and condemned to wait in the cold and rain, to get upon an excursion train or to see a new piece in a theatre; and that these discomforts are constantly, if not always cheerfully supported. I cannot deny it; but whether it was because the trial lasted so long, or because we were here whole families together, carrying all their worldly goods and bent upon a serious end, I know only that I have never seen fellow creatures so stricken down, nor suffered, in my own person, such complete paralysis of mind. The whole business was a nightmare while it lasted, and is still a nightmare to remember. If the railway company cared — but then it does not, and I should address the winds. The officials, who are to blame for this unnecessary suffering, are without doubt humane men and subscribe to public char-

ities; but when all hands are piped, they may find their duty
lay some other way. Kindness is the first of virtues; and capacity in a man's own business the greatest kindness in his
reach.)

At last we were admitted into the cars, utterly dejected, and
far from dry. For my own part, I got out a clothes-brush, and
brushed my trousers as hard as I could, till I had dried them
and warmed my blood into the bargain; but no one else, except my next neighbour, to whom I lent the brush, appeared
to take the least precaution. As they were, they composed
themselves to sleep. I had seen the lights of Philadelphia, and
been twice ordered to change carriages and twice counter-
manded, before I allowed myself to follow their example.

Tuesday. — When I awoke it was already day; the train was
standing idle; I was in the last carriage, and, seeing some others
strolling to and fro about the lines, I opened the door and
stepped forth, as from a caravan by the wayside. We were
near no station, nor even, as far as I could see, within reach of
any signal. A green, open, undulating country stretched away
upon all sides. Locust-trees and a single field of Indian corn
gave it a foreign grace and interest; but the contours of the
land were soft and English. It was not quite England, neither
was it quite France; yet like enough either to seem natural in
my eyes. And it was in the sky, and not upon the earth, that I
was surprised to find a change. Explain it how you may, and
for my part I cannot explain it at all, the sun rises with a different splendour in America and Europe. There is more clear
gold and scarlet in our old-country mornings; more purple,
brown, and smoky orange in those of the new. It may be from
habit, but to me the coming of day is less fresh and inspiriting
in the latter; it has a duskier glory, and more nearly resembles
sunset; it seems to fit some subsequential, evening epoch of the
world, as though America were in fact, and not merely in
fancy, farther from the orient of Aurora and the springs of
day. I thought so then, by the railroad-side in Pennsylvania,
and I have thought so a dozen times since in far distant parts

of the continent. If it be an illusion, it is one very deeply rooted, and in which my eyesight is accomplice.

Soon after a train whisked by, announcing and accompanying its passage by the swift beating of a sort of chapel-bell upon the engine; and as it was for this we had been waiting, we were summoned by the cry of "All aboard!" and went on again upon our way. The whole line, it appeared, was topsy-turvy; an accident at midnight having thrown all the traffic hours into arrear. We paid for this in the flesh, for we had no meals all that day. Fruit we could buy upon the cars; and now and then we had a few minutes at some station with a meagre show of rolls and sandwiches for sale; but we were so many and so ravenous that, though I tried at every opportunity, the coffee was always exhausted before I could elbow my way to the counter.

Our American sunrise had ushered in a noble summer's day. There was not a cloud; the sunshine was baking; yet in the woody river-valleys among which we wound our way the atmosphere preserved a sparkling freshness till late in the afternoon. It had an inland sweetness and variety to one newly from the sea; it smelt of woods, rivers, and the delved earth. These, though in so far a country, were airs from home. I stood on the platform by the hour; and as I saw, one after another, pleasant villages, carts upon the highway and fishers by the stream, and heard cockcrows and cheery voices in the distance, and beheld the sun no longer shining blankly on the plains of ocean, but striking among shapely hills, and his light dispersed and coloured by a thousand accidents of form and surface, I began to exult with myself upon this rise in life like a man who had come into a rich estate. ⟨For we are creatures of the shore; and it is only on shore that our senses are supplied with a variety of matter, or that the heart can find her proper business. There is water enough for one by the coasts of any running stream; or if I must indeed look upon the ocean, let it be from along the seaboard, surf-bent, strewn with wreck and dotted at sundown with the clear lights that pilot home bound vessels. The revolution in my surroundings was certainly joyful and complete.⟩ And when I had asked the name of a river from the brakesman, ⟨the least surly of his class whom I encountered,⟩ and heard that it was called the Susquehanna, the beauty of the name seemed to be part and parcel of the beauty of the land. As when Adam with divine fitness named the creatures, so this word Susquehanna was at once accepted by the fancy. That was the name, as no other could be, for that shining river and desirable valley.[1]

None can care for literature in itself who do not take a special pleasure in the sound of names; and there is no part of the world where nomenclature is so rich, poetical, humorous, and picturesque as the United States of America. All times, races, and languages have brought their contribution. Pekin is in the same State with Euclid, with Bellefontaine, and with Sandusky. Chelsea, with its London associations of red brick, Sloane Square, and the King's Road, is own suburb to stately and primeval Memphis; there they have their seat, translated names of cities, where the Mississippi runs by Tennessee and Arkansas;[2] and both, while I was crossing the continent, lay watched by armed men, in the horror and isolation of a plague. Old, red Manhattan lies, like an Indian arrowhead under a steam factory, below Anglified New York. The names of the States and Territories themselves form a chorus of sweet and most romantic vocables: Delaware, Ohio, Indiana, Florida, Dakota, Iowa, Wyoming, Minnesota, and the Carolinas; there

1. The name so delighted Stevenson that from the train he wrote a letter to Sidney Colvin (published in Colvin's *The Letters of Robert Louis Stevenson to Family and Friends* [London, 1899], I, 145), whose first stanza reads:

"Of where or how, I nothing know;
    And why, I do not care;
    Enough if, even so,
My travelling eyes, my travelling mind can go
By flood and field and hill, by wood and meadow fair,
Beside the Susquehannah and along the Delaware."

2. Please pronounce *Arkansaw*, with the accent on the first. [Note by R. L. S.]

are few poems with a nobler music for the ear: a songful, tuneful land; and if the new Homer shall arise from the Western continent, his verse will be enriched, his pages sing spontaneously, with the names of states and cities that would strike the fancy in a business circular.

Late in the evening we were landed in a waiting-room at Pittsburg. I had now under my charge a young and sprightly Dutch widow with her children; these I was to watch over providentially for a certain distance farther on the way; but as I found she was furnished with a basket of eatables, I left her in the waiting-room to seek a dinner for myself.

I mention this meal, not only because it was the first of which I had partaken for about thirty hours, but because it was the means of my first introduction to a coloured gentleman. He did me the honour to wait upon me after a fashion, while I was eating; and with every word, look, and gesture marched me farther into the country of surprise. He was indeed strikingly unlike the negroes of Mrs. Beecher Stowe, or the Christy Minstrels of my youth. Imagine a gentleman, certainly somewhat dark, but of a pleasant warm hue, speaking English with a slight and rather odd foreign accent, every inch a man of the world, and armed with manners so patronisingly superior that I am at a loss to name their parallel in England. A butler perhaps rides as high over the unbutlered, but then he sets you right with a reserve and a sort of sighing patience which one is often moved to admire. And again, the abstract butler never stoops to familiarity. But the coloured gentleman will pass you a wink at a time; he is familiar like an upper-form boy to a fag; he unbends to you like Prince Hal with Poins and Falstaff. He makes himself at home and welcome. Indeed, I may say, this waiter behaved himself to me throughout that supper much as, with us, a young, free, and not very self-respecting master might behave to a good-looking chambermaid. I had come prepared to pity the poor negro, to put him at his ease, to prove in a thousand condescensions that I was no sharer in the prejudice of race; but I assure you I put my patronage away for another occasion, and had the grace to be pleased with that result.

Seeing he was a very honest fellow, I consulted him upon a point of etiquette: if one should offer to tip the American waiter? Certainly not, he told me. Never. It would not do. They considered themselves too highly to accept. They would even resent the offer. As for him and me, we had enjoyed a very pleasant conversation; he, in particular, had found much pleasure in my society; I was a stranger; this was exactly one of those rare conjunctures. . . . Without being very clear-seeing, I can still perceive the sun at noonday; and the coloured gentleman deftly pocketed a quarter.

Wednesday. — A little after midnight I convoyed my widow and orphans on board the train; and morning found us far into Ohio. This had early been a favourite home of my imagination; I have played at being in Ohio by the week, and enjoyed some capital sport there with a dummy gun, my person being still unbreeched. My preference was founded on a work which appeared in *Cassell's Family Paper*, and was read aloud to me by my nurse. It narrated the doings of one Custaloga, an Indian brave, who, in the last chapter, very obligingly washed the paint off his face and became Sir Reginald Somebody-or-other; a trick I never forgave him. The idea of a man being an Indian brave, and then giving that up to be a baronet, was one which my mind rejected. It offended verisimilitude, like the pretended anxiety of Robinson Crusoe and others to escape from unin-habited islands. ⟨Just you put me on an uninhabited island, I thought, and then we'll see!⟩

But Ohio was not at all as I had pictured it. We were now on those great plains which stretch unbroken to the Rocky Mountains. The country was flat like Holland, but far from being dull. All through Ohio, Indiana, Illinois, and Iowa, or for as much as I saw of them from the train and in my waking moments, it was rich and various, and breathed an elegance peculiar to itself. The tall corn pleased the eye; the trees were graceful in themselves, and framed the plain into long, aerial vistas; and the clean, bright, gardened townships spoke of country fare and pleasant summer evenings on the stoop. It was a sort of flat paradise; but, I am afraid, not unfrequented by the devil. That morning dawned with such a freezing chill as I have rarely felt; a chill that was not perhaps so measurable by instrument, as it struck home upon the heart and seemed to travel with the blood. Day came in with a shudder. White mists lay thinly over the surface of the plain, as we see them more often on a lake; and though the sun had soon dispersed and drunk them up, leaving an atmosphere of fever-heat and crystal pureness from horizon to horizon, the mists had still been there, and we knew that this paradise was haunted by killing damps and foul malaria. The fences along the line bore but two descriptions of advertisement; one to recommend tobaccos, and the other to vaunt remedies against the ague. At the point of day, and while we were all in the grasp of that first chill, a native of the State, who had got in at some way-station, pronounced it, with a doctoral air, "a fever-and-ague morning."

The Dutch widow was a person of some character. She had conceived at first sight a great aversion for the present writer, which she was at no pains to conceal. But, being a woman of a practical spirit, she made no difficulty about accepting my attentions, and encouraged me to buy her children fruits and candies, to carry all her parcels, and even to sleep upon the floor that she might profit by my empty seat. Nay, she was such a rattle by nature, and so powerfully moved to autobiographical talk, that she was forced, for want of a better, to take me into confidence and tell me the story of her life. I heard about her late husband, who seemed to have made his chief impression by taking her out pleasuring on Sundays. I could tell you her prospects, her hopes, the amount of her fortune, the cost of her house-keeping by the week, and a variety of particular matters that are not usually disclosed except to friends. At one station she shook up her children to look at a man on the platform and say if he were not like Mr.

Z.; while to me she explained how she had been keeping company with this Mr. Z., how far matters had proceeded, and how it was because of his desistance that she was now travelling to the west. Then, when I was thus put in possession of the facts, she asked my judgment on that type of manly beauty. I admired it to her heart's content. She was not, I think, remarkably veracious in talk, but broidered as fancy prompted, and built castles in the air out of her past; yet she had that sort of candour, to keep me, in spite of all these confidences, steadily aware of her aversion. Her parting words were ingeniously honest. "I am sure," said she, "we all *ought* to be very much obliged to you." I cannot pretend that she put me at my ease; but I had a certain respect for such a genuine dislike. A poor nature would have slipped, in the course of these familiarities, into a sort of worthless toleration for me.

We reached Chicago in the evening. I was turned out of the cars, bundled into an omnibus, and driven off through the streets to the station of a different railroad. Chicago seemed a great and gloomy city. I remember having subscribed, let us say sixpence, towards its restoration at the period of the fire; and now when I beheld street after street of ponderous houses and crowds of comfortable burghers, I thought it would be a graceful act for the corporation to refund that sixpence, or, at the least, to entertain me to a cheerful dinner. But there was no word of restitution. I was that city's benefactor, yet I was received in a third-class waiting-room, and the best dinner I could get was a dish of ham and eggs at my own expense.

I can safely say, I have never been so dog-tired as that night in Chicago. ⟨I sat, or rather lay, on some steps in the station, and was gratefully conscious of every point of contact between my body and the boards. My one ideal of pleasure was to stretch myself flat on my back with arms extended, like a dying hermit in a picture, and to move no more. I bought a newspaper, but could not summon up the energy to read it; I debated with myself if it were worth while to make a cigarette, and unanimously decided that it was not.⟩ When it was time to start, I descended the platform like a man in a dream. It was a long train, lighted from end to end; and car after car, as I came up with it, was not only filled, but overflowing. My valise, my knapsack, my rug, with those six ponderous tomes of Bancroft, weighed me double; I was hot, feverish, painfully athirst; and there was a great darkness over me, an internal darkness, not to be dispelled by gas. When at last I found an empty bench, I sank into it like a bundle of rags, the world seemed to swim away into the distance, and my consciousness dwindled within me to a mere pin's head, like a taper on a foggy night.

When I came a little more to myself, I found that there had sat down beside me a very cheerful, rosy little German gentleman, somewhat gone in drink, who was talking away to me, nineteen to the dozen, as they say. I did my best to keep up the conversation; for it seemed to me dimly as if something depended upon that. I heard him relate, among many other things, that there were pickpockets on the train, who had already robbed a man of forty dollars and a return ticket; but though I caught the words, I do not think I properly understood the sense until next morning; and I believe I replied at the time that I was very glad to hear it. What else he talked about I have no guess; I remember a gabbling sound of words, his profuse gesticulation, and his smile, which was highly explanatory; but no more. And I suppose I must have shown my confusion very plainly; for, first, I saw him knit his brows at me like one who has conceived a doubt; next, he tried me in German, supposing perhaps that I was unfamiliar with the English tongue; and finally, in despair, he rose and left me. I felt chagrined; but my fatigue was too crushing for delay, and, stretching myself as far as that was possible upon the bench, I was received at once into a dreamless stupor.

The little German gentleman was only going a little way into the suburbs after a *diner fin*, and was bent on entertainment while the journey lasted. Having failed with me, he pitched next upon another emigrant, who had come through from Canada, and was not one jot less weary than myself. Nay, even in a natural state, as I found next morning when we scraped acquaintance, he was a heavy, uncommunicative man. After trying him on different topics, it appears that the little German gentleman flounced into a temper, swore an oath or two, and departed from that car in quest of livelier society. Poor little gentleman! I suppose he thought an emigrant should be a rollicking, free-hearted blade, with a flask of foreign brandy and a long, comical story to beguile the moments of digestion. ⟨He should have met Alick; Alick and he would have been like brothers.⟩

Thursday. — I suppose there must be a cycle in the fatigue of travelling, for when I awoke next morning I was entirely renewed in spirits, and ate a hearty breakfast of porridge, with sweet milk, and coffee and hot cakes, at Burlington upon the Mississippi. Another long day's ride followed, with but one feature worthy of remark. At a place called Creston, a drunken man got in. He was aggressively friendly, but, according to English notions, not at all unpresentable upon a train. For one stage he eluded the notice of the officials; but just as we were beginning to move out of the next station, Cromwell by name, by came the conductor. There was a word or two of talk; and then the official had the man by the shoulders, twitched him from his seat, marched him through the car, and sent him flying on to the track. It was done in three motions, as exact as a piece of drill. The train was still moving slowly, although beginning to mend her pace, and the drunkard got his feet without a fall. He carried a red bundle, though not so red as his cheeks; and he shook this menacingly in the air with one hand, while the other stole behind him to the region of the kidneys. It was the first indication that I had come among revolvers, and I observed it with some emotion. The conductor stood on the steps with one hand on his hip, looking back at him; and perhaps this attitude imposed upon the creature, for he turned without further ado, and went off staggering along the track towards Cromwell, followed by a peal of laughter from the cars. They were speaking English all about me, but I knew I was in a foreign land.

Twenty minutes before nine that night we were deposited at the Pacific Transfer Station near Council Bluffs, on the eastern bank of the Missouri river. Here we were to stay the night at a kind of caravanserai, set apart for emigrants. But I gave way to a thirst for luxury, separated myself from my companions, and marched with my effects into the Union Pacific Hotel. A white clerk and a coloured gentleman, whom, in my plain European way, I should call the boots, were installed behind a counter like bank tellers. They took my name, assigned me a number, and proceeded to deal with my packages. And here came the tug of war. I wished to give up my packages into safe keeping; but I did not wish to go to bed. And this, it appeared, was impossible in an American hotel.

It was, of course, some inane misunderstanding, and sprang from my unfamiliarity with the language. For although two nations use the same words and read the same books, intercourse is not conducted by the dictionary. The business of life is not carried on by words, but in set phrases, each with a special and almost a slang signification. ⟨Thus every difference of habit modifies the spoken tongue, and even to send off a telegram or order a dish of oysters without some foreign indirectness, an Englishman must have partly learned to be an American. I speak of oysters, because that was the last example that I came across: in San Francisco, if you ask to have your oysters opened, it means they are to be taken from the shell.⟩ Some international obscurity prevailed between me and the coloured gentleman at Council Bluffs; so that what I was asking, which seemed very natural to me, appeared to him a monstrous exigency. He refused, and that with the plainness of the West. This American manner of conducting matters of business is, at first, highly unpalatable to the European. When we approach a man in the way of his calling, and for those services by which he earns his bread, we consider him for the time being our hired servant. But in the American opinion, two gentlemen meet and have a friendly talk with a view to exchanging favours if they shall agree to please. I know not which is the more convenient, nor even which is the more truly courteous. The English stiffness unfortunately tends to be continued after the particular transaction is at an end, and thus favours class separations. But on the other hand, these equalitarian plainnesses leave an open field for the insolence of Jack-in-office.

I was nettled by the coloured gentleman's refusal, and unbuttoned my wrath under the similitude of ironical submission. I knew nothing, I said, of the ways of American hotels; but I had no desire to give trouble. If there was nothing for it but to get to bed immediately, let him say the word, and though it was not my habit, I should cheerfully obey.

He burst into a shout of laughter. "Ah!" said he, "you do not know about America. They are fine people in America. Oh! you will like them very well. But you mustn't get mad. I know what you want. You come along with me."

And issuing from behind the counter, and taking me by the arm like an old acquaintance, he led me to the bar of the hotel.

"There," said he, pushing me from him by the shoulder, "go and have a drink!"

THE EMIGRANT TRAIN

All this while I had been travelling by mixed trains, where I might meet with Dutch widows and little German gentry fresh from table. I had been but a latent emigrant; now I was to be branded once more, and put apart with my fellows. It was about two in the afternoon of Friday that I found myself in front of the Emigrant House, with more than a hundred others, to be sorted and boxed for the journey. A white-haired official, with a stick under one arm, and a list in the other hand, stood apart in front of us, and called name after name in the tone of a command. At each name you would see a family gather up its brats and bundles and run for the hindmost of the three cars that stood awaiting us, and I soon concluded that this was to be set apart for the women and children. The second or central car, it turned out, was devoted to men travelling alone, and the third to the Chinese. The official was easily moved to anger at the least delay; but the emigrants were both quick at answering their names, and speedy in getting themselves and their effects on board.

The families once housed, we men carried the second car without ceremony by simultaneous assault. I suppose the reader has some notion of an American railroad-car, that long, narrow wooden box, like a flat-roofed Noah's ark, with a stove and a convenience, one at either end, a passage down the middle, and transverse benches upon either hand. Those destined for emigrants on the Union Pacific are only remarkable for their extreme plainness, nothing but wood entering in any part into their constitution, and for the usual inefficacy of the lamps, which often went out and shed but a dying glimmer even while they burned. The benches are too short for anything

but a young child. Where there is scarce elbow-room for two
to sit, there will not be space enough for one to lie. Hence the
company, or rather, as it appears from certain bills about the
Transfer Station, the company's servants, have conceived a
plan for the better accommodation of travellers. They prevail
on every two to chum together. To each of the chums they sell
a board and three square cushions stuffed with straw and covered with thin cotton. The benches can be made to face each
other in pairs, for the backs are reversible. On the approach of
night the boards are laid from bench to bench, making a couch
wide enough for two, and long enough for a man of the middle height; and the chums lie down side by side upon the
cushions with the head to the conductor's van and the feet to
the engine. When the train is full, of course this plan is impossible, for there must not be more than one to every bench,
neither can it be carried out unless the chums agree. It was to
bring about this last condition that our white-haired official
now bestirred himself. He made a most active master of cere-
monies, introducing likely couples, and even guaranteeing the
amiability and honesty of each. The greater the number of
happy couples the better for his pocket, for it was he who
sold the raw material of the beds. His price for one board and
three straw cushions began with two dollars and a half; but
before the train left, and I am sorry to say long after I had
purchased mine, it had fallen to one dollar and a half. ⟨I cannot
suppose that emigrants are thus befooled and robbed with the
connivance of the Company; yet this was the Company's servant. It is never pleasant to bear tales; but this is a system; the
emigrants are many of them foreigners and therefore easy to
cheat, and they are all so poor that it is unmanly to cheat them;
and if the white-haired leach is not contumeliously discharged
in this world, I leave him with all confidence to the devil in
the next. As for the emigrant, I have better news for him. Let
him quietly agree with a chum, but bid the official harpy from
his sight; and if he will read a few pages farther, he shall see
the profit of his reticence.⟩

The match-maker had a difficulty with me; perhaps, like some ladies, I showed myself too eager for union at any price; but certainly the first who was picked out to be my bedfellow declined the honour without thanks. He was an old, heavy, slow-spoken man, I think from Yankeeland, looked me all over with great timidity, and then began to excuse himself in broken phrases. He didn't know the young man, he said. The young man might be very honest, but how was he to know that? There was another young man whom he had met already in the train; he guessed *he* was honest, and would prefer to chum with *him* upon the whole. All this without any sort of excuse, as though I had been inanimate or absent. I began to tremble lest every one should refuse my company, and I be left rejected. But the next in turn was a tall, strapping, long-limbed, small-headed, curly-haired Pennsylvania Dutchman, with a soldierly smartness in his manner. To be exact, he had acquired it in the navy. But that was all one; he had at least been trained to desperate resolves, so he accepted the match, and the white-haired swindler pronounced the connubial benediction, and pocketed his fees.

The rest of the afternoon was spent in making up the train. I am afraid to say how many baggage-waggons followed the engine — certainly a score; then came the Chinese, then we, then the families, and the rear was brought up by the conductor in what, if I have it rightly, is called his caboose. The class to which I belonged was of course far the largest, and we ran over, so to speak, to both sides; so that there were some Caucasians among the Chinamen and some bachelors among the families. But our own car was pure from admixture, save for one little boy of eight or nine who had the whooping-cough. At last, about six, the long train crawled out of the Transfer Station and across the wide Missouri river to Omaha, westward bound.

It was a troubled, uncomfortable evening in the cars. There was thunder in the air, which helped to keep us restless. A man played many airs upon the cornet, and none of them were much attended to, until he came to "Home, Sweet Home." It was truly strange to note how the talk ceased at that, and the faces began to lengthen. I have no idea whether musically this air is to be considered good or bad; but it belongs to that class of art which may be best described as a brutal assault upon the feelings. Pathos must be relieved by dignity of treatment. If you wallow naked in the pathetic, like the author of "Home, Sweet Home," you make your hearers weep in an unmanly fashion; and even while yet they are moved, they despise themselves and hate the occasion of their weakness. It did not come to tears that night, for the experiment was interrupted. An elderly, hard-looking man, with a goatee beard, and about as much appearance of sentiment as you would expect from a retired slaver, turned with a start and bade the performer stop that "damned thing." "I've heard about enough of that," he added; "give us something about the good country we're going to." A murmur of adhesion ran round the car; the performer took the instrument from his lips, laughed and nodded, and then struck into a dancing measure; and, like a new Timotheus, stilled immediately the emotion he had raised.

The day faded; the lamps were lit; a party of wild young men, who got off next evening at North Platte, stood together on the stern platform, singing "The Sweet By-and-Bye" with very tuneful voices; the chums began to put up their beds; and it seemed as if the business of the day were at an end. But it was not so; for, the train stopping at some station, the cars were instantly thronged with the natives, wives and fathers, young men and maidens, some of them in little more than nightgear, some with stable-lanterns, and all offering beds for sale. Their charge began with twenty-five cents a cushion, but fell, before the train went on again, to fifteen, with the bedboard gratis, or less than one-fifth of what I had paid for mine at the Transfer. This is my contribution to the economy of future emigrants.

A great personage on an American train is the newsboy. He sells books (such books!), papers, fruit, lollipops, and cigars;

and on emigrant journeys, soap, towels, tin washing-dishes, tin coffee pitchers, coffee, tea, sugar, and tinned eatables, mostly hash or beans and bacon. Early next morning the newsboy went around the cars, and chumming on a more extended principle became the order of the hour. It requires but a co-partnery of two to manage beds; but washing and eating can be carried on most economically by a syndicate of three. I myself entered a little after sunrise into articles of agreement, and became one of the firm of Pennsylvania, Shakespeare, and Dubuque. Shakespeare was my own nickname on the cars; Pennsylvania that of my bedfellow; and Dubuque, the name of a place in the State of Iowa, that of an amiable young fellow going west to cure an asthma, and retarding his recovery by incessantly chewing or smoking, and sometimes chewing and smoking together. I have never seen tobacco so sillily abused. Shakespeare bought a tin washing-dish, Dubuque a towel, and Pennsylvania a brick of soap. The partners used these instruments, one after another, according to the order of their first awaking; and when the firm had finished there was no want of borrowers. Each filled the tin dish at the water filter opposite the stove, and retired with the whole stock in trade to the platform of the car. There he knelt down, supporting himself by a shoulder against the woodwork, or one elbow crooked about the railing, and made a shift to wash his face and neck and hands, — a cold, an insufficient, and, if the train is moving rapidly, a somewhat dangerous toilet.

On a similar division of expense, the firm of Pennsylvania, Shakespeare, and Dubuque supplied themselves with coffee, sugar, and necessary vessels; and their operations are a type of what went on through all the cars. Before the sun was up the stove would be brightly burning; at the first station the natives would come on board with milk and eggs and coffee cakes; and soon from end to end the car would be filled with little parties breakfasting upon the bed-boards. It was the pleasantest hour of the day.

There were meals to be had, however, by the wayside; a

breakfast in the morning, a dinner somewhere between eleven and two, and supper from five to eight or nine at night. We had rarely less than twenty minutes for each; and if we had not spent many another twenty minutes waiting for some express upon a side track among miles of desert, we might have taken an hour to each repast and arrived at San Francisco up to time. For haste is not the foible of an emigrant train. It gets through on sufferance, running the gauntlet among its more considerable brethren; should there be a block, it is unhesitatingly sacrificed; and they cannot, in consequence, predict the length of the passage within a day or so. ⟨The meals, taken overland, were palateable; and they were not dear, at least for us. I had the pleasure, at one station, of dining in the same room, with express passengers eastward bound, getting dish for dish the identical same dinner, and paying exactly half the charge. It was an experience in which I delighted, and I began to see the advantages of a state of Emigrancy.⟩ Civility is the main comfort that you miss. Equality, though conceived very largely in America, does not extend so low down as to an emigrant. Thus in all other trains a warning cry of "All aboard!" recalls the passengers to take their seats; but as soon as I was alone with emigrants, and from the Transfer all the way to San Francisco, I found this ceremony was pretermitted; the train stole from the station without note of warning, and you had to keep an eye upon it even while you ate. The annoyance is considerable, and the disrespect both wanton and petty.

Many conductors, again, will hold no communication with an emigrant. I asked a conductor one day at what time the train would stop for dinner; as he made no answer I repeated the question, with a like result; a third time I returned to the charge, and then Jack-in-office looked me coolly in the face for several seconds and turned ostentatiously away. I believe he was half-ashamed of his brutality; for when another person made the same inquiry, although he still refused the information, he condescended to answer, and even to justify his reticence in a voice loud enough for me to hear. It was, he said, his principle not to tell people where they were to dine; for one answer led to many other questions, as, what o'clock it was; or, how soon should we be there? and he could not afford to be eternally worried.

As you are thus cut off from the superior authorities, a great deal of your comfort depends on the character of the newsboy. He has it in his power indefinitely to better and brighten the emigrant's lot. The newsboy with whom we started from the Transfer was a dark, bullying, contemptuous, insolent scoundrel, who treated us like dogs. Indeed, in his case, matters came nearly to a fight. It happened thus: he was going his rounds through the cars with some commodities for sale, and coming to a party who were at Seven-up or Cascino (our two games) upon a bed-board, slung down a cigar-box in the middle of the cards, knocking one man's hand to the floor. It was the last straw. In a moment the whole party were upon their feet, the cigars were upset, and he was ordered to "get out of that directly, or he would get more than he reckoned for." The fellow grumbled and muttered, but ended by making off, and was less openly insulting in the future. On the other hand, the lad who rode with us in this capacity from Ogden to Sacramento made himself the friend of all, and helped us with information, attention, assistance, and a kind countenance. He told us where and when we should have our meals, and how long the train would stop; kept seats at table for those who were delayed, and watched that we should neither be left behind nor yet unnecessarily hurried. You, who live at home at ease, can hardly realise the greatness of this service, even had it stood alone. When I think of that lad coming and going, train after train, with his bright face and civil words, I see how easily a good man may become the benefactor of his kind. Perhaps he is discontented with himself, perhaps troubled with ambitions; why, if he but knew it, he is a hero of the old Greek stamp; and while he thinks he is only earning a profit of a few cents, and that perhaps exorbitant, he is doing a man's work and bettering the world.

I must tell here an experience of mine with another news-boy. I tell it because it gives so good an example of that uncivil kindness of the American, which is perhaps their most be-wildering character to one newly landed. It was immediately after I had left the emigrant train; and I am told I looked like a man at death's door, so much had this long journey shaken me. I sat at the end of a car, and the catch being broken, and myself feverish and sick, I had to hold the door open with my foot for the sake of air. In this attitude my leg debarred the newsboy from his box of merchandise. I made haste to let him pass when I observed that he was coming; but I was busy with a book, and so once or twice he came upon me unawares. On these occasions he most rudely struck my foot aside; and though I myself apologised, as if to show him the way, he answered me never a word. ⟨I conceive I had a right to do as I was doing; it was no fault of mine if the car was out of repair; he must have seen, besides, my willingness to spare him trou-ble; and had I been Obstruction in person, it would not have justified either his violence or his silence.⟩ I chafed furiously, and I fear the next time it would have come to words. But suddenly I felt a touch upon my shoulder, and a large juicy pear was put into my hand. It was the newsboy, who had ob-served that I was looking ill, and so made me this present out of a tender heart. For the rest of the journey I was petted like a sick child; he lent me newspapers, thus depriving him-self of his legitimate profit on their sale, and came repeatedly to sit by me and cheer me up. ⟨I hate myself now, to think how little I encouraged him; but as was said by one of the best of men, taciturnity is another word for selfishness.⟩

THE PLAINS OF NEBRASKA

It had thundered on the Friday night, but the sun rose on Saturday without a cloud. We were at sea — there is no other adequate expression — on the plains of Nebraska. I made my observatory on the top of a fruit-waggon, and sat by the hour upon that perch to spy about me, and to spy in vain for something new. It was a world almost without a feature; an empty sky, an empty earth; front and back, the line of railway stretched from horizon to horizon, like a cue across a billiard-board; on either hand, the green plain ran till it touched the skirts of heaven. Along the track innumerable wild sunflowers, no bigger than a crown-piece, bloomed in a continuous flower-bed; grazing beasts were seen upon the prairie at all degrees of distance and diminution; and now and again we might perceive a few dots beside the railroad, which grew more and more distinct as we drew nearer, till they turned into wooden cabins, and then dwindled and dwindled in our wake until they melted into their surroundings, and we were once more alone upon the billiard-board. The train toiled over this infinity like a snail; and being the one thing moving, it was wonderful what huge proportions it began to assume in our regard. It seemed miles in length, and either end of it within but a step of the horizon. Even my own body or my own head seemed a great thing in that emptiness. I note the feeling the more readily as it is the contrary of what I have read of in the experience of others. Day and night, above the roar of the train, our ears were kept busy with the incessant chirp of grass-hoppers — a noise like the winding up of countless clocks and watches, which began after a while to seem proper to that land.

To one hurrying through by steam there was a certain exhilaration in this spacious vacancy, this greatness of the air, this discovery of the whole arch of heaven, this straight, unbroken, prison-line of the horizon. Yet one could not but reflect upon the weariness of those who passed by there in old days, at the foot's pace of oxen, painfully urging their teams, and with no landmark but that unattainable evening sun for which they steered, and which daily fled them by an equal stride. They had nothing, it would seem, to overtake; nothing by which to reckon their advance; no sight for repose or for encouragement; but stage after stage, only the dead green waste under foot, and the mocking, fugitive horizon. But the eye, as I have been told, found differences even here; and at the worst the emigrant came, by perseverance, to the end of his toil. It is the settlers, after all, at whom we have a right to marvel. Our consciousness, by which we live, is itself but the creature of variety. Upon what food does it subsist in such a land? What livelihood can repay a human creature for a life spent in this huge sameness? He is cut off from books, from news, from company, from all that can relieve existence but the prosecution of his affairs. A sky full of stars is the most varied spectacle that he can hope for. He may walk five miles and see nothing; ten, and it is as though he had not moved; twenty, and still he is in the midst of the same great level, and has approached no nearer to the one object within view, the flat horizon which keeps pace with his advance. We are full at home of the question of agreeable wall-papers, and wise people are of opinion that the temper may be quieted by sedative surroundings. But what is to be said of the Nebraskan settler? His is a wall-paper with a vengeance — one quarter of the universe laid bare in all its gauntness. His eye must embrace at every glance the whole seeming concave of the visible world; it quails before so vast an outlook, it is tortured by distance; yet there is no rest or shelter, till the man runs into his cabin, and can repose his sight upon things near at hand. Hence, I am told, a sickness of the vision peculiar to these empty plains.

Yet perhaps with sunflowers and cicadæ, summer and winter, cattle, wife and family, the settler may create a full and various existence. (We exaggerate the difficulties of a situation when we conceive and criticise it in fancy; for we forget that people live in this world by the day or week. Theory shows us an unbroken tenor to the last sickness; but the actual man lives it in pieces, and begins afresh with every morning. The blind can comfortably exist while seeing nothing; but there is this difference that they are not blind by choice. A man who is married is no longer master of his destiny, and carries a compensation along with him wherever he may go. But what can bring to Nebraska a lone, unfettered bachelor, who has all the world before him and might starve, if he preferred, in London or New York?)

One person at least I saw upon the plains who seemed in every way superior to her lot. This was a woman who boarded us at a way-station, selling milk. She was largely formed; her features were more than comely; she had that great rarity — a fine complexion which became her; and her eyes were kind, dark, and steady. She sold milk with patriarchal grace. There was not a line in her countenance, not a note in her soft and sleepy voice, but spoke of an entire contentment with her life. It would have been fatuous arrogance to pity such a woman. Yet the place where she lived was to me almost ghastly. Less than a dozen wooden houses, all of a shape and all nearly of a size, stood planted along the railway lines. Each stood apart in its own lot. Each opened direct off the billiard-board, as if it were a billiard-board indeed, and these only models that had been set down upon it ready-made. Her own, into which I looked, was clean but very empty, and showed nothing home-like but the burning fire. This extreme newness, above all in so naked and flat a country, gives a strong impression of artificiality. With none of the litter and discoloration of human life; with the paths unworn, and the houses still sweating from the axe, such a settlement as this seems purely scenic. The mind is loth to accept it for a piece of reality; and it seems incredible that life can go on with so few properties, or the great child, man, find entertainment in so bare a playroom.

And truly it is as yet an incomplete society in some points; or at least it contained, as I passed through, one person incompletely civilised. At North Platte, where we supped that evening, one man asked another to pass the milk-jug. This other was well dressed, and of what we should call a respectable appearance; a darkish man, high-spoken, eating as though he had some usage of society; but he turned upon the first speaker with extraordinary vehemence of tone —

"There's a waiter here!" he cried.

"I only asked you to pass the milk," explained the first.

Here is the retort verbatim —

"Pass? Hell! I'm not paid for that business; the waiter's paid for it. You should use civility at table, and, by God, I'll show you how!"

⟨He would show him how! I wonder what would be his charge for the twelve lessons. And this explosion, you will not forget, was to save himself the trouble of moving a milk jug a distance of perhaps thirty inches.⟩

The other man very wisely made no answer, and the bully went on with his supper as though nothing had occurred. It pleases me to think that some day soon he will meet with one of his own kidney; and that perhaps both may fall.

THE DESERT OF WYOMING

To cross such a plain is to grow home-sick for the mountains. I longed for the Black Hills of Wyoming, which I knew we were soon to enter, like an ice-bound whaler for the spring. Alas! and it was a worse country than the other. All Sunday and Monday we travelled through these sad mountains, or over the main ridge of the Rockies, which is a fair match to them for misery of aspect. Hour after hour it was the same unhomely and unkindly world about our onward path; tumbled boulders, cliffs that drearily imitate the shape of monuments and fortifications — how drearily, how tamely, none can tell who has not seen them; not a tree, not a patch of sward, not one shapely or commanding mountain form; sage-brush, eternal sage-brush; over all, the same weariful and gloomy colouring, greys warming into brown, greys darkening towards black; and for sole sign of life, here and there a few fleeing antelopes; here and there, but at incredible intervals, a creek running in a cañon. The plains have a grandeur of their own; but here there is nothing but a contorted smallness. Except for the air, which was light and stimulating, there was not one good circumstance in that God-forsaken land.

(I had, as I must tell you, been suffering a good deal all the way, from what the gentleman at New York was pleased to call my liver. The hot weather and the fever put into my blood by so much continuous travel, had aggravated these symptoms till they were strangely difficult to bear. When the fit was on me, I grew almost light headed. I had to make a second cigarette before the first was smoked, for tobacco alone gave me self command under these paroxysms of irritation. Fancy will give you no clew to what I endured; the basis was, as you might say, a mere annoyance; but when an annoyance is continued day and night and assumes by starts an absolute control upon your mind, not much remains to distinguish it from pain. I am obliged to touch upon this, but with a delicacy which the reader will appreciate, not only because it is a part of emigrant experience, but because it must stand as my excuse for many sins of omission in this chronicle.)

I had been suffering in my health a good deal all the way; and at last, whether I was exhausted by my complaint or poisoned in some wayside eating-house, the evening we left Laramie I fell sick outright. That was a night which I shall not readily forget. The lamps did not go out; each made a faint shining in its own neighbourhood, and the shadows were confounded together in the long, hollow box of the car. The sleepers lay in uneasy attitudes; here two chums alongside, flat upon their backs like dead folk; there a man sprawling on the floor, with his face upon his arm; there another half-seated with his head and shoulders on the bench. The most passive were continually and roughly shaken by the movement of the train; others stirred, turned, or stretched out their arms like children; it was surprising how many groaned and murmured in their sleep; and as I passed to and fro, stepping across the prostrate, and caught now a snore, now a gasp, now a half-formed word, it gave me a measure of the worthlessness of rest in that unresting vehicle. Although it was chill, I was obliged to open my window, for the degradation of the air soon became intolerable to one who was awake and using the full supply of life. Outside, in a glimmering night, I saw the black, amorphous hills shoot by unweariedly into our wake. They that long for morning have never longed for it more earnestly than I.

And yet when day came, it was to shine upon the same broken and unsightly quarter of the world. Mile upon mile, and not a tree, a bird, or a river. Only down the long, sterile cañons, the train shot hooting, and awoke the resting echo. That train was the one piece of life in all the deadly land; it was the one actor, the one spectacle fit to be observed in this paralysis of man and nature. And when I think how the railroad has been pushed through this unwatered wilderness and haunt of savage tribes, and now will bear an emigrant for some twelve pounds from the Atlantic to the Golden Gates; how at each stage of the construction, roaring, impromptu cities, full of gold and lust and death, sprang up and then died away again, and are now but wayside stations in the desert; how in these uncouth places pig-tailed Chinese pirates worked side by side with border ruffians and broken men from Europe, talking together in a mixed dialect, mostly oaths, gambling, drinking, quarrelling, and murdering like wolves; how the plumed hereditary lord of all America heard, in this last fastness, the scream of the "bad medicine-waggon" charioting his foes; and then when I go on to remember that all this epical turmoil was conducted by gentlemen in frock-coats, and with a view to nothing more extraordinary than a fortune and a subsequent visit to Paris, it seems to me, I own, as if this railway were the one typical achievement of the age in which we live, as if it brought together into one plot all the ends of the world and all the degrees of social rank, and offered to some great writer the busiest, the most extended, and the most varied subject for an enduring literary work. If it be romance, if it be contrast, if it be heroism that we require, what was Troy town to this? But, alas! it is not these things that are necessary — it is only Homer.

Here also we are grateful to the train, as to some god who conducts us swiftly through these shades and by so many hidden perils. Thirst, hunger, the sleight and ferocity of Indians, are all no more feared, so lightly do we skim these horrible lands; as the gull, who wings safely through the hurricane and past the shark. Yet we should not be forgetful of these hardships of the past; and to keep the balance true, since I have complained of the trifling discomforts of my journey perhaps more than was enough, let me add an original document. It was not written by Homer, but by a boy of eleven, long since dead, and is dated only twenty years ago.[1] I shall punctuate, to make things clearer, but not change the spelling: —

"My dear Sister Mary, — I am afraid you will go nearly crazy when you read my letter. If Jerry" (the writer's eldest brother) *"has not written to you before now, you will be surprised to heare that we are in California, and that poor Thomas"* (another brother, of fifteen) *"is dead. We started from —— in July, with plenty of provisions and too yoke oxen. We went along very well till we got within six or seven hundred miles of California, when the Indians attacked us. We found places where they had killed the emigrants. We had one passenger with us, too guns, and one revolver; so we ran all the lead We had into bullets (and) hung the guns up in the wagon so that we could get at them in a minit. It was about two o'clock in the afternoon; droave the cattel a little way; when a prairie chicken alited a little way from the wagon.*

"Jerry took out one of the guns to shoot it, and told Tom drive the oxen. Tom and I drove the oxen, and Jerry and the passenger went on. Then, after a little, I left Tom and caught up with Jerry and the other man. Jerry stopped for Tom to come up; me and the man went on and sit down by a little stream. In a few minutes we heard some noise; then three shots (they all struck poor Tom, I suppose); then they gave the war hoop, and as many as twenty of the red skins came down upon us. The three that shot Tom was hid by the side of the road in the bushes.

"I thought the Tom and Jerry were shot; so I told the other man that Tom and Jerry were dead, and that we had better try to escape, if possible. I had no shoes on; having a sore foot, I thought I would not put them on. The man and me run down the road, but We was soon stopt by an Indian on a pony. We then turend the other way, and run up the side of the Mountain,

1. The writer was Martin Mahoney, brother of Mrs. Mary Carson, Stevenson's landlady in San Francisco, from whom he obtained the letter.

and hid behind some cedar trees, and stayed there till dark. The Indians hunted all over after us, and verry close to us, so close that we could here there tomyhawks Jingle. At dark the man and me started on, I stubing my toes against sticks and stones. We traveld on all night; and next morning, Just as it was getting gray, we saw something in the shape of a man. It layed Down in the grass. We went up to it, and it was Jerry. He thought we ware Indians. You can imagine how glad he was to see me. He thought we was all dead but him, and we thought him and Tom was dead. He had the gun that he took out of the wagon to shoot the prairie Chicken; all he had was the load that was in it.

"We traveld on till about eight o'clock, We caught up with one wagon with too men with it. We had traveld with them before one day; we stopt and they Drove on; we knew that they was ahead of us, unless they had been killed to. My feet was so sore when we caught up with them that I had to ride; I could not step. We traveld on for too days, when the men that owned the cattle said they would (could) not drive them another inch. We unyoked the oxen; we had about seventy pounds of flour; we took it out and divided it into four packs. Each of the men took about 18 pounds apiece and a blanket. I carried a little bacon, dried meat, and little quilt; I had in all about twelve pounds. We had one pint of flour a day for our alloyance. Sometimes we made soup of it; sometimes we (made) pancakes; and sometimes mixed it up with cold water and eat it that way. We traveld twelve or fourteen days. The time came at last when we should have to reach some place or starve. We saw fresh horse and cattle tracks. The morning came, we scraped all the flour out of the sack, mixed it up, and baked it into bread, and made some soup, and eat everything we had. We traveld on all day without anything to eat, and that evening we Caught up with a sheep train of eight wagons. We traveld with them till we arrived at the settlements; and know I am safe in California, and got to good home, and going to school.

"Jerry is working in ——. It is a good country. You can get from 50 to 60 and 75 Dollars for cooking. Tell me all about the affairs in the States, and how all the folks get along."

And so ends this artless narrative. The little man was at school again, God bless him! while his brother lay scalped upon the deserts.

FELLOW-PASSENGERS

At Ogden we changed cars from the Union Pacific to the Central Pacific line of railroad. The change was doubly welcome; for, first we had better cars on the new line; and, second, those in which we had been cooped for more than ninety hours had begun to stink abominably. Several yards away, as we returned, let us say from dinner, our nostrils were assailed by air. I have stood on a platform while the whole train was shunting; and as the dwelling-cars drew near, there would come a whiff of pure menagerie, only a little sourer, as from men instead of monkeys. I think we are human only in virtue of open windows. Without fresh air, you only require a bad heart, and a remarkable command of the Queen's English, to become such another as Dean Swift; a kind of leering, human goat, leaping and wagging your scut on mountains of offence. I do my best to keep my head the other way, and look for the human rather than the bestial in this Yahoo-like business of the emigrant train. But one thing I must say: the car of the Chinese was notably the least offensive⟨, and that of the women and children by a good way the worst. A stroke of nature's satire⟩.

The cars on the Central Pacific were nearly twice as high, and so proportionally airier; they were freshly varnished, which gave us all a sense of cleanliness as though we had bathed; the seats drew out and joined in the centre, so that there was no more need for bed-boards; and there was an upper tier of berths which could be closed by day and opened at night. ⟨Thus in every way the accommodation was more cheerful and comfortable, and every one might have a bed to lie on if he pleased. The company deserve our thanks. It was the first sign I could observe of any kindly purpose towards the emigrant.

For myself it was, in some ways, a fatal change; for it fell to me to sleep in one of the lofts; and that I found to be impossible. The air was always bad enough at the level of the floor. But my bed was four feet higher, immediately under the roof, and shut into a kind of Saratoga trunk with one side partly open. And there, unless you were the Prince of Camby, it were madness to attempt to sleep.[1] Though the fumes were narcotic and weighed upon the eyelids, yet they so smartly irritated the lungs that I could only lie and cough. I spent the better part of one night walking to and fro and envying my neighbors.⟩

I had by this time some opportunity of seeing the people whom I was among. They were in rather marked contrast to the emigrants I had met on board ship while crossing the Atlantic. ⟨There was both less talent and less good manners; I believe I should add less good feeling, though that is implied. Kindness will out; and a man who is gentle will contrive to be a gentleman.⟩ They were mostly lumpish fellows, silent and noisy, a common combination; somewhat sad, I should say, with an extraordinary poor taste in humour, and little interest in their fellow-creatures beyond that of a cheap and merely external curiosity. If they heard a man's name and business, they seemed to think they had the heart of that mystery; but they were as eager to know that much as they were indifferent to the rest. Some of them were on nettles till they learned your name was Dickson and you a journeyman baker; but beyond that, whether you were Catholic or Mormon, dull or clever, fierce or friendly, was all one to them. Others who were not so stupid gossiped a little, and, I am bound to say, unkindly. A favourite witticism was for some lout to raise the alarm of "All aboard!" while the rest of us were dining, thus contribut-

1. Stevenson was probably thinking of King Cambyuskan in *The Squire's Tale* by Chaucer, for after a feast the ruler and his companions have their heads so "full of fumositee" from wine and are so tired from labor that they sleep soundly and dream for a long time.

ing his mite to the general discomfort. Such a one was always much applauded for his high spirits. When I was ill coming through Wyoming, I was astonished — fresh from the eager humanity on board ship — to meet with little but laughter. One of the young men even amused himself by incommoding me, as was then very easy; and that not from ill-nature, but mere clod-like incapacity to think, for he expected me to join the laugh. I did so, but it was phantom merriment. Later on, a man from Kansas had three violent epileptic fits, and though, of course, there were not wanting some to help him, it was rather superstitious terror than sympathy that his case evoked among his fellow-passengers. "Oh, I hope he's not going to die!" cried a woman; "it would be terrible to have a dead body!" And there was a very general movement to leave the man behind at the next station. This, by good fortune, the conductor neg-atived.

There was a good deal of story-telling in some quarters; in others, little but silence. In this society, more than any other that ever I was in, it was the narrator alone who seemed to enjoy the narrative. It was rarely that any one listened for the listening. If he lent an ear to another man's story, it was because he was in immediate want of a hearer for one of his own. Food and the progress of the train were the subjects most generally treated; many joined to discuss these who otherwise would hold their tongues. One small knot had no better occupation than to worm out of me my name; and the more they tried, the more obstinately fixed I grew to baffle them. They assailed me with artful questions and insidious offers of correspondence in the future; but I was perpetually on my guard, and parried their assaults with inward laughter. I am sure Dubuque would have given me ten dollars for the secret. He owed me far more, had he understood life, for thus preserving him a lively interest throughout the journey. I met one of my fellow-passengers months after, driving a street tramway car in San Francisco; and, as the joke was now out of season, told him my name without subterfuge. You never saw a man more chapfallen. But had my name been Demogorgon, after so prolonged a mystery he had still been disappointed.

There were no emigrants direct from Europe — save one German family and a knot of Cornish miners who kept grimly by themselves, one reading the New Testament all day long through steel spectacles, the rest discussing privately the secrets of their old-world, mysterious race. Lady Hester Stanhope believed she could make something great of the Cornish;[2] for my part, I can make nothing of them at all. A division of races, older and more original than that of Babel, keeps this close, esoteric family apart from neighbouring Englishmen. Not even a Red Indian seems more foreign in my eyes. This is one of the lessons of travel — that some of the strangest races dwell next door to you at home.

The rest were all American born, but they came from almost every quarter of that continent. All the States of the North had sent out a fugitive to cross the plains with me. From Virginia, from Pennsylvania, from New York, from far western Iowa and Kansas, from Maine that borders on the Canadas, and from the Canadas themselves — some one or two were fleeing in quest of a better land and better wages. The talk in the train, like the talk I heard on the steamer, ran upon hard times, short commons, and hope that moves ever westward. I thought of my shipful from Great Britain with a feeling of despair. They had come 3000 miles, and yet not far enough. Hard times bowed them out of the Clyde, and stood to welcome them at Sandy Hook. Where were they to go? Pennsylvania, Maine, Iowa, Kansas? These were not places for immigration, but for emigration, it appeared; not one of them, but I knew a man who had lifted up his heel and left it for an ungrateful country.

2. At least a quarter and perhaps a third of the miners of Cornwall emigrated to the Far West between 1871 and 1881, when their homeland suffered a severe depression. A good deal earlier the eccentric Lady Hester Stanhope lived in Wales (1808–10), assisting poor Welshmen, including miners, and Stevenson seems to have confused the subjects of her philanthropic interest.

And it was still westward that they ran. Hunger, you would have thought, came out of the east like the sun, and the evening was made of edible gold. And, meantime, in the car in front of me, were there not half a hundred emigrants from the opposite quarter? Hungry Europe and hungry China, each pouring from their gates in search of provender, had here come face to face. The two waves had met; east and west had alike failed; the whole round world had been prospected and condemned; there was no El Dorado anywhere; and till one could emigrate to the moon, it seemed as well to stay patiently at home. Nor was there wanting another sign, at once more picturesque and more disheartening; for as we continued to steam westward toward the land of gold, we were continually passing other emigrant trains upon the journey east; and these were as crowded as our own. Had all these return voyagers made a fortune in the mines? Were they all bound for Paris, and to be in Rome by Easter? It would seem not, for, whenever we met them, the passengers ran on the platform and cried to us through the windows, in a kind of wailing chorus, to "come back." On the plains of Nebraska, in the mountains of Wyoming, it was still the same cry, and dismal to my heart, "Come back!" That was what we heard by the way "about the good country we were going to." And at that very hour the Sand-lot of San Francisco was crowded with the unemployed, and the echo from the other side of Market Street was repeating the rant of demagogues.[3]

If in truth it were only for the sake of wages that men emigrate, how many thousands would regret the bargain! But wages, indeed, are only one consideration out of many; for we are a race of gipsies, and love change and travel for themselves.

3. The empty sandlots of San Francisco were the sites of Dennis Kearney's inflammatory speeches against rich landholders and Chinese laborers, as Stevenson describes more fully in "Monterey," pp. 151–167.

DESPISED RACES

Of all stupid ill-feelings, the sentiment of my fellow-Cau-
casians towards our companions in the Chinese car was the
most stupid and the worst. They seemed never to have looked
at them, listened to them, or thought of them, but hated them
a priori. The Mongols were their enemies in that cruel and
treacherous battle-field of money. They could work better
and cheaper in half a hundred industries, and hence there was
no calumny too idle for the Caucasians to repeat and even to
believe. They declared them hideous vermin, and affected a
kind of choking in the throat when they beheld them. Now,
as a matter of fact, the young Chinese man is so like a large
class of European women, that on raising my head and suddenly catching sight of one at a considerable distance, I have
for an instant been deceived by the resemblance. I do not say
it is the most attractive class of our women, but for all that
many a man's wife is less pleasantly favoured. Again, my
emigrants declared that the Chinese were dirty. I cannot say
they were clean, for that was impossible upon the journey; but
in their efforts after cleanliness they put the rest of us to shame.
We all pigged and stewed in one infamy, wet our hands and
faces for half a minute daily on the platform, and were un-
ashamed. But the Chinese never lost an opportunity, and you
would see them washing their feet — an act not dreamed of
among ourselves — and going as far as decency permitted to
wash their whole bodies. I may remark by the way that the
dirtier people are in their persons the more delicate is their
sense of modesty. A clean man strips in a crowded boathouse;
but he who is unwashed slinks in and out of bed without un-
covering an inch of skin. Lastly, these very foul and malo-

dorous Caucasians entertained the surprising illusion that it was the Chinese waggon, and that alone, which stank. I have said already that it was the exception, and notably the freshest of the three.

These judgments are typical of the feeling in all Western America. The Chinese are considered stupid because they are imperfectly acquainted with English. They are held to be base because their dexterity and frugality enable them to underbid the lazy, luxurious Caucasian. They are said to be thieves; I am sure they have no monopoly of that. They are called cruel; the Anglo-Saxon and the cheerful Irishman may each reflect before he bears the accusation.[1] I am told, again, that they are of the race of river pirates, and belong to the most despised and dangerous class in the Celestial Empire. But if this be so, what remarkable pirates have we here! and what must be the virtues, the industry, the education, and the intelligence of their superiors at home!

A while ago it was the Irish, now it is the Chinese that must go. Such is the cry. It seems, after all, that no country is bound to submit to immigration any more than to invasion: each is war to the knife, and resistance to either but legitimate defence. Yet we may regret the free tradition of the republic,

1. In the first printing in *Longman's Magazine* (August 1883) there follows here a sentence that reads: "It comes amiss from John Bull, who the other day forced that unhappy Zazel, all bruised and tottering from a dangerous escape, to come forth again upon the theatre, and continue to risk her life for his amusement; or from Pat, who makes it his pastime to shoot down the compliant farmer from behind a wall in Europe, or to stone the solitary Chinaman in California." One reason for the deletion may be the complexity of the references. The comment about John Bull alludes to England's policy under Disraeli in 1876–79 to support Turkey as a buffer against Russia and as a result to force the Christians of the recently liberated Crete — the unhappy Zazel, or scapegoat — to come again under the rule of the Moslems of Turkey. The comment about Pat alludes to the Land League of 1879, an Irish reform organization that used terrorist means against farmers in Ireland and England willing to become tenants of landlords who earlier had callously evicted less compliant workers of their lands. The comment about the solitary Chinaman is once again an allusion to the actions of Dennis Kearney and his followers.

which loved to depict herself with open arms, welcoming all unfortunates. And certainly, as a man who believes that he loves freedom, I may be excused some bitterness when I find her sacred name misused in the contention. It was but the other day that I heard a vulgar fellow in the Sand-lot, the popular tribune of San Francisco, roaring for arms and butchery. "At the call of Abreham Lincoln," said the orator, "ye rose in the name of freedom to set free the negroes; can ye not rise and liberate yourselves from a few dhirty Mongolians?" [2]

For my own part I could not look but with wonder and respect on the Chinese. Their forefathers watched the stars before mine had begun to keep pigs. Gunpowder and printing, which the other day we imitated, and a school of manners which we never had the delicacy so much as to desire to imitate, were theirs in a long-past antiquity. They walk the earth with us, but it seems they must be of different clay. They hear the clock strike the same hour, yet surely of a different epoch. They travel by steam conveyance, yet with such a baggage of old Asiatic thoughts and superstitions as might check the locomotive in its course. Whatever is thought within the circuit of the Great Wall; what the wry-eyed, spectacled schoolmaster teaches in the hamlets round Pekin; religions so old that our language looks a halfling boy alongside; philosophy so wise that our best philosophers find things therein to wonder at; all this travelled alongside of me for thousands of miles over plain and mountain. Heaven knows if we had one common thought or fancy all that way, or whether our eyes, which yet were formed upon the same design, beheld the same world out of the railway windows. And when either of us turned his thoughts to home and childhood, what a strange dissimilarity must there not have been in these pictures of the

2. In the first printing in *Longman's Magazine* (August 1883) there follows here a passage that reads: "It exceeds the license of an Irishman to rebaptise our selfish interests by the name of virtue. Defend your bellies, if you must; I, who do not suffer, am no judge in your affairs; but let me defend language, which is the dialect and one of the ramparts of virtue."

mind — when I beheld that old, grey, castled city, high throned above the firth, with the flag of Britain flying, and the red-coat sentry pacing over all; and the man in the next car to me would conjure up some junks and a pagoda and a fort of porcelain, and call it, with the same affection, home.

Another race shared among my fellow-passengers in the disfavour of the Chinese; and that, it is hardly necessary to say, was the noble red man of old story — he over whose own hereditary continent we had been steaming all these days. I saw no wild or independent Indian; indeed, I hear that such avoid the neighbourhood of the train; but now and again at way-stations, a husband and wife and a few children, disgracefully dressed out with the sweepings of civilisation, came forth and stared upon the emigrants. The silent stoicism of their conduct, and the pathetic degradation of their appearance, would have touched any thinking creature, but my fellow-passengers danced and jested round them with a truly Cockney baseness. I was ashamed for the thing we call civilisation. We should carry upon our consciences so much, at least, of our fore-fathers' misconduct as we continue to profit by ourselves.

If oppression drives a wise man mad, what should be raging in the hearts of these poor tribes, who have been driven back and back, step after step, their promised reservations torn from them one after another as the States extended westward, un-til at length they are shut up into these hideous mountain deserts of the centre — and even there find themselves in-vaded, insulted, and hunted out by ruffianly diggers? The evic-tion of the Cherokees (to name but an instance), the extortion of Indian agents, the outrages of the wicked, the ill-faith of all, nay, down to the ridicule of such poor beings as were here with me upon the train, make up a chapter of injustice and indignity such as a man must be in some ways base if his heart will suffer him to pardon or forget. These old, well-founded, historical hatreds have a savour of nobility for the independent. That the Jew should not love the Christian, nor the Irishman love the English, nor the Indian brave tolerate the

thought of the American, is not disgraceful to the nature of
man; rather, indeed, honourable, since it depends on wrongs
ancient like the race, and not personal to him who cherishes
the indignation.[3]

3. In the first printing in *Longman's Magazine* (August 1883) there
appears a final paragraph, presumably not printed in book form
because it is so similar to a passage in "Monterey." It reads: "As for
the Indians, there are of course many unteachable and wedded to war
and their wild habits; but many also who, with fairer usage, might
learn the virtues of the peaceful state. You will find a valley in the
county of Monterey, drained by the river of Carmel: a true Californian
valley, bare, dotted with chaparral, overlooked by quaint, unfinished
hills. The Carmel runs by many pleasant farms, a clear and shallow
river, loved by wading kine; and at last, as it is falling towards a quicksand and the great Pacific, passes a ruined mission on a hill. From the
church the eye embraces a great field of ocean, and the ear is filled with
a continuous sound of distant breakers on the shore. The roof has fallen;
the ground squirrel scampers on the graves; the holy bell of St. Charles
is long dismounted; yet one day in every year the church awakes from
silence, and the Indians return to worship in the church of their converted fathers. I have seen them trooping thither, young and old, in
their clean print dresses, with those strange, handsome, melancholy
features, which seem predestined to a national calamity and it was
notable to hear the old Latin words and old Gregorian music sung, with
nasal fervour, and in a swift, staccato style, by a trained chorus of Red
Indian men and women. In the huts of the Rancherie they have ancient
European Mass-books, in which they study together to be perfect. An
old blind man was their leader. With his eyes bandaged, and leaning
on a staff, he was led into his place in church by a little grandchild. He
had seen changes in the world since first he sang that music sixty years
ago, when there was no gold and no Yankees, and he and his people
lived in plenty under the wing of the kind priests. The mission church
is in ruins; the Rancherie, they tell me, encroached upon by Yankee
newcomers; the little age of gold is over for the Indian; but he has had
a breathing-space in Carmel valley before he goes down to the dust with
his red fathers."

TO THE GOLDEN GATES[1]

A little corner of Utah is soon traversed, and leaves no particular impressions on the mind. By an early hour on Wednesday morning we stopped to breakfast at Toano, a little station on a bleak, high-lying plateau in Nevada. The man who kept the station eating-house was a Scot, and learning that I was the same, he grew very friendly, and gave me some advice on the country I was now entering. "You see," said he, "I tell you this, because I come from your country." Hail, brither Scots!

His most important hint was on the moneys of this part of the world. There is something in the simplicity of a decimal coinage which is revolting to the human mind; thus the French, in small affairs, reckon strictly by halfpence; and you have to solve, by a spasm of mental arithmetic, such posers as thirty-two, forty-five, or even a hundred halfpence. In the Pacific States they have made a bolder push for complexity, and settle their affairs by a coin that no longer exists — the *bit*, or old Mexican real. The supposed value of the bit is twelve and a half cents, eight to the dollar. When it comes to two bits, the quarter-dollar stands for the required amount. But how about an odd bit? The nearest coin to it is a dime, which is short by a fifth. That, then, is called a *short bit*. If you have one, you lay it triumphantly down, and save two and a half cents. But if you have not, and lay down a quarter, the bar-keeper or shopman calmly tenders you a dime by way of change; and thus you have paid what is called a *long bit*, and lost two and a half cents, or even, by comparison with a short bit, five cents. In

1. Although the proper form is singular, Stevenson always uses the plural "Gates," as in the second paragraph of "San Francisco" and the opening chapter of *The Silverado Squatters*.

country places all over the Pacific coast, nothing lower than a bit is ever asked or taken, which vastly increases the cost of life; as even for a glass of beer you must pay fivepence or sevenpence-halfpenny, as the case may be. You would say that this system of mutual robbery was as broad as it was long; but I have discovered a plan to make it broader, with which I here endow the public. It is brief and simple — radiantly simple. There is one place where five cents are recognised, and that is the post-office. A quarter is only worth two bits, a short and a long. Whenever you have a quarter, go to the post-office and buy five cents' worth of postage-stamps; you will receive in change two dimes, that is, two short bits. The purchasing power of your money is undiminished. You can go and have your two glasses of beer all the same; and you have made yourself a present of five cents' worth of postage-stamps into the bargain. Benjamin Franklin would have patted me on the head for this discovery.

From Toano we travelled all day through deserts of alkali and sand, horrible to man, and bare sage-brush country that seemed little kindlier, and came by supper-time to Elko. As we were standing, after our manner, outside the station, I saw two men whip suddenly from underneath the cars, and take to their heels across country. They were tramps, it appeared, who had been riding on the beams since eleven of the night before; and several of my fellow-passengers had already seen and conversed with them while we broke our fast at Toano. These land stowaways play a great part over here in America, and I should have liked dearly to become acquainted with them.

At Elko an odd circumstance befell me. I was coming out from supper, when I was stopped by a small, stout, ruddy man, followed by two others taller and ruddier than himself.

"Ex-cuse me, sir," he said, "but do you happen to be going on?"

I said I was, whereupon he said he hoped to persuade me to desist from that intention. He had a situation to offer me, and if we could come to terms, why, good and well. "You see," he continued, "I'm running a theatre here, and we're a little short in the orchestra. You're a musician, I guess?"

I assured him that, beyond a rudimentary acquaintance with "Auld Lang Syne" and "The Wearing of the Green," I had no pretension whatever to that style. He seemed much put out of countenance; and one of his taller companions asked him, on the nail, for five dollars.

"You see, sir," added the latter to me, "he bet you were a musician; I bet you weren't. No offence, I hope?"

"None whatever," I said, and the two withdrew to the bar, where I presume the debt was liquidated.

This little adventure woke bright hopes in my fellow-travellers, who thought they had now come to a country where situations went a-begging. But I am not so sure that the offer was in good faith. Indeed, I am more than half persuaded it was but a feeler to decide the bet.

Of all the next day I will tell you nothing, for the best of all reasons, that I remember no more than that we continued through desolate and desert scenes, fiery hot and deadly weary. But some time after I had fallen asleep that night, I was awakened by one of my companions. It was in vain that I resisted. A fire of enthusiasm and whisky burned in his eyes; and he declared we were in a new country, and I must come forth upon the platform and see with my own eyes. The train was then, in its patient way, standing halted in a by-track. It was a clear, moonlit night; but the valley was too narrow to admit the moonshine direct, and only a diffused glimmer whitened the tall rocks and relieved the blackness of the pines. A hoarse clamour filled the air; it was the continuous plunge of a cascade somewhere near at hand among the mountains. The air struck chill, but tasted good and vigorous in the nostrils — a fine, dry, old mountain atmosphere. I was dead sleepy, but I returned to roost with a grateful mountain feeling at my heart.

When I awoke next morning, I was puzzled for a while to know if it were day or night, for the illumination was unusual. I sat up at last, and found we were grading slowly downward through a long snowshed; and suddenly we shot into an open; and before we were swallowed into the next length of wooden tunnel, I had one glimpse of a huge pine-forested ravine upon my left, a foaming river, and a sky already coloured with the fires of dawn. I am usually very calm over the displays of nature; but you will scarce believe how my heart leaped at this. It was like meeting one's wife. I had come home again — home from unsightly deserts to the green and habitable corners of the earth. Every spire of pine along the hill-top, every trouty pool along that mountain river, was more dear to me than a blood-relation. Few people have praised God more happily than I did. And thenceforward, down by Blue Cañon, Alta, Dutch Flat, and all the old mining camps, through a sea of mountain forests, dropping thousands of feet toward the far sea-level as we went, not I only, but all the passengers on board, threw off their sense of dirt and heat and weariness, and bawled like schoolboys, and thronged with shining eyes upon the platform, and became new creatures within and without. The sun no longer oppressed us with heat, it only shone laughingly along the mountain-side, until we were fain to laugh ourselves for glee. At every turn we could see farther into the land and our own happy futures. At every town the cocks were tossing their clear notes into the golden air, and crowing for the new day and the new country. For this was indeed our destination; this was "the good country" we had been going to so long.

By afternoon we were at Sacramento, the city of gardens in a plain of corn; and the next day before the dawn we were lying-to upon the Oakland side of San Francisco Bay. The day was breaking as we crossed the ferry; the fog was rising over the citied hills of San Francisco; the bay was perfect — not a ripple, scarce a stain, upon its blue expanse; everything was waiting, breathless, for the sun. A spot of cloudy gold lit first upon the head of Tamalpais, and then widened downward on its shapely shoulder; the air seemed to awaken, and began to sparkle; and suddenly

"The tall hills Titan discovered," [2]

and the city of San Francisco, and the bay of gold and corn, were lit from end to end with summer daylight.

2. Stevenson is recalling a line from Spenser's *The Faerie Queene,* I, ii, 7: "And the high hils Titan discoured."

The Old and New Pacific Capitals

MONTEREY

The Bay of Monterey has been compared by no less a person than General Sherman to a bent fishing-hook;[1] and the comparison, if less important than the march through Georgia, still shows the eye of a soldier for topography. Santa Cruz sits exposed at the shank; the mouth of the Salinas river is at the middle of the bend; and Monterey itself is cosily ensconced beside the barb. Thus the ancient capital of California faces across the bay, while the Pacific Ocean, though hidden by low hills and forest, bombards her left flank and rear with never-dying surf. In front of the town, the long line of sea-beach trends north and north-west, and then westward to enclose the bay. The waves which lap so quietly about the jetties of Monterey grow louder and larger in the distance; you can see the breakers leaping high and white by day; at night, the outline of the shore is traced in transparent silver by the moonlight and the flying foam; and from all round, even in quiet weather, the low, distant, thrilling roar of the Pacific hangs over the coast and the adjacent country like smoke above a battle.

These long beaches are enticing to the idle man. It would be hard to find a walk more solitary and at the same time more exciting to the mind. Crowds of ducks and sea-gulls hover over the sea. Sand-pipers trot in and out by troops after the retiring waves, trilling together in a chorus of infinitesimal song. Strange sea-tangles, new to the European eye, the bones of whales, or sometimes a whole whale's carcase, white with

1. This initial view of Monterey upon William Tecumseh Sherman's arrival in 1847 to serve as adjutant of the military governor of California is recalled by him in his *Memoirs* (1875), I, 17.

carrion-gulls and poisoning the wind, lie scattered here and there along the sands. The waves come in slowly, vast and green, curve their translucent necks, and burst with a surprising uproar, that runs, waxing and waning, up and down the long key-board of the beach. The foam of these great ruins mounts in an instant to the ridge of the sand glacis, swiftly fleets back again, and is met and buried by the next breaker. The interest is perpetually fresh. On no other coast that I know shall you enjoy, in calm, sunny weather, such a spectacle of Ocean's greatness, such beauty of changing colour, or such degrees of thunder in the sound. The very air is more than usually salt by this Homeric deep.

Inshore, a tract of sand-hills borders on the beach. Here and there a lagoon, more or less brackish, attracts the birds and hunters. A rough, spotty undergrowth partially conceals the sand. The crouching, hardy, live oaks flourish singly or in thickets — the kind of wood for murderers to crawl among — and here and there the skirts of the forest extend downward from the hills with a floor of turf and long aisles of pine-trees hung with Spaniard's Beard. Through this quaint desert the railway cars drew near to Monterey from the junction at Salinas City — though that and so many other things are now for ever altered — and it was from here that you had the first view of the old township lying in the sands, its white windmills bickering in the chill, perpetual wind, and the first fogs of the evening drawing drearily around it from the sea.

The one common note of all this country is the haunting presence of the ocean. A great faint sound of breakers follow you high up into the inland cañons; the roar of water dwells in the clean, empty rooms of Monterey as in a shell upon the chimney; go where you will, you have but to pause and listen to hear the voice of the Pacific. You pass out of the town to the south-west, and mount the hill among pine woods. Glade, thicket, and grove surround you. You follow winding sandy tracks that lead nowhither. You see a deer; a multitude of quail arises. But the sound of the sea still follows you as you advance, like that of wind among the trees, only harsher and stranger to the ear; and when at length you gain the summit, out breaks on every hand and with freshened vigour that same unending, distant, whispering rumble of the ocean; for now you are on the top of Monterey peninsula, and the noise no longer only mounts to you from behind along the beach towards Santa Cruz, but from your right also, round by China-town and Pinos lighthouse, and from down before you to the mouth of the Carmello river. The whole woodland is be-girt with thundering surges. The silence that immediately surrounds you where you stand is not so much broken as it is haunted by this distant, circling rumour. It sets your senses upon edge; you strain your attention; you are clearly and unusually conscious of small sounds near at hand; you walk listening like an Indian hunter; and that voice of the Pacific is a sort of disquieting company to you in your walk.

When once I was in these woods I found it difficult to turn homeward. All woods lure a rambler onward; but in those of Monterey it was the surf that particularly invited me to pro-long my walks. I would push straight for the shore where I thought it to be nearest. Indeed, there was scarce a direction that would not, sooner or later, have brought me forth on the Pacific. The emptiness of the woods gave me a sense of freedom and discovery in these excursions. I never in all my visits met but one man. He was a Mexican, very dark of hue, but smiling and fat, and he carried an axe, though his true business at that moment was to seek for straying cattle. I asked him what o'clock it was, but he seemed neither to know nor care; and when he in his turn asked me for news of his cattle, I showed myself equally indifferent. We stood and smiled upon each other for a few seconds, and then turned without a word and took our several ways across the forest.

One day — I shall never forget it — I had taken a trail that was new to me. After a while the woods began to open, the sea to sound nearer hand. I came upon a road, and, to my surprise, a stile. A step or two farther, and, without leaving the woods,

I found myself among trim houses. I walked through street after street, parallel and at right angles, paved with sward and dotted with trees, but still undeniable streets, and each with its name posted at the corner, as in a real town. Facing down the main thoroughfare — "Central Avenue," as it was ticketed — I saw an open-air temple, with benches and sounding-board, as though for an orchestra. The houses were all tightly shuttered; there was no smoke, no sound but of the waves, no moving thing. I have never been in any place that seemed so dream-like. Pompeii is all in a bustle with visitors, and its antiquity and strangeness deceive the imagination; but this town had plainly not been built above a year or two, and perhaps had been deserted overnight. Indeed it was not so much like a deserted town as like a scene upon the stage by daylight, and with no one on the boards. The barking of a dog led me at last to the only house still occupied, where a Scots pastor and his wife pass the winter alone in this empty theatre. The place was "The Pacific Camp Grounds, the Christian Seaside Resort." Thither, in the warm season, crowds come to enjoy a life of teetotalism, religion, and flirtation, which I am willing to think blameless and agreeable. The neighbourhood at least is well selected. The Pacific booms in front. Westward is Point Pinos, with the lighthouse in a wilderness of sand, where you will find the lightkeeper playing the piano, making models and bows and arrows, studying dawn and sunrise in amateur oil-painting, and with a dozen other elegant pursuits and interests to surprise his brave, old-country rivals. To the east, and still nearer, you will come upon a space of open down, a hamlet, a haven among rocks, a world of surge and screaming sea-gulls. Such scenes are very similar in different climates; they appear homely to the eyes of all; to me this was like a dozen spots in Scotland. And yet the boats that ride in the haven are of strange outlandish design; and, if you walk into the hamlet you will behold costumes and faces, and hear a tongue, that are unfamiliar to the memory. The joss-stick burns, the opium-pipe is smoked, the floors are strewn with slips of coloured paper — prayers, you would say, that had somehow missed their destination — and a man guiding his upright pencil from right to left across the sheet writes home the news of Monterey to the Celestial Empire.

The woods and the Pacific rule between them the climate of this seaboard region. On the streets of Monterey, when the air does not smell salt from the one, it will be blowing perfumed from the resinous tree-tops of the other. For days together a hot, dry air will overhang the town, close as from an oven, yet healthful and aromatic in the nostrils. The cause is not far to seek, for the woods are afire, and the hot wind is blowing from the hills. These fires are one of the great dangers of California. I have seen from Monterey as many as three at the same time, by day a cloud of smoke, by night a red coal of conflagration in the distance. A little thing will start them, and, if the wind be favourable, they gallop over miles of country faster than a horse. The inhabitants must turn out and work like demons, for it is not only the pleasant groves that are destroyed; the climate and the soil are equally at stake, and these fires prevent the rains of the next winter and dry up perennial fountains. California has been a land of promise in its time, like Palestine; but if the woods continue so swiftly to perish, it may become, like Palestine, a land of desolation.

To visit the woods while they are languidly burning is a strange piece of experience. The fire passes through the under-brush at a run. Every here and there a tree flares up in-stantaneously from root to summit, scattering tufts of flame, and is quenched, it seems, as quickly. But this last is only in semblance. For after this first squib-like conflagration of the dry moss and twigs, there remains behind a deep-rooted and consuming fire in the very entrails of the tree. The resin of the pitch-pine is principally condensed at the base of the bole and in the spreading roots. Thus, after the light, showy, skir-mishing flames, which are only as the match to the explosion, have already scampered down the wind into the distance, the true harm is but beginning for this giant of the woods. You may approach the tree from one side, and see it, scorched indeed from top to bottom, but apparently survivor of the peril. Make the circuit, and there, on the other side of the column, is a clear mass of living coal, spreading like an ulcer; while underground, to their most extended fibre, the roots are being eaten out by fire, and the smoke is rising through the fissures to the surface. A little while and, without a nod of warning, the huge pine-tree snaps off short across the ground, and falls prostrate with a crash. Meanwhile the fire continues its silent business; the roots are reduced to a fine ash; and long afterwards, if you pass by, you will find the earth pierced with radiating galleries, and preserving the design of all these subterranean spurs, as though it were the mould for a new tree instead of the print of an old one. These pitch-pines of Monterey are, with the single exception of the Monterey cypress, the most fantastic of forest trees. No words can give an idea of the contortion of their growth; they might figure without change in a circle of the nether hell as Dante pictured it; and at the rate at which trees grow, and at which forest fires spring up and gallop through the hills of California, we may look forward to a time when there will not be one of them left standing in that land of their nativity. At least they have not so much to fear from the axe, but perish by what may be called a natural although a violent death; while it is man in his short-sighted greed that robs the country of the nobler redwood. Yet a little while and perhaps all the hills of seaboard California may be as bald as Tamalpais.

I have an interest of my own in these forest fires, for I came so near to lynching on one occasion, that a braver man might have retained a thrill from the experience. I wished to be certain whether it was the moss, that quaint funereal ornament of Californian forests, which blazed up so rapidly when the flame first touched the tree. I suppose I must have been under the influence of Satan, for instead of plucking off a piece for my experiment, what should I do but walk up to a great pine tree in a portion of the wood which had escaped so much as scorching, strike a match, and apply the flame gingerly to one of the tassels. The tree went off simply like a rocket; in three seconds it was a roaring pillar of fire. Close by I could hear the shouts of those who were at work combating the original conflagration. I could see the waggon that had brought them tied to a live oak in a piece of open; I could even catch the flash of an axe as it swung up through the underwood into the sunlight. Had any one observed the result of my experiment my neck was literally not worth a pinch of snuff; after a few minutes of passionate expostulation I should have been run up to a convenient bough.

> "To die for faction is a common evil;
> But to be hanged for nonsense is the devil." [2]

I have run repeatedly, but never as I ran that day. At night I went out of town, and there was my own particular fire, quite distinct from the other, and burning, as I thought, with even greater vigour.

But it is the Pacific that exercises the most direct and obvious power upon the climate. At sunset, for months together, vast, wet, melancholy fogs arise and come shoreward from the ocean. From the hill-top above Monterey the scene is often noble, although it is always sad. The upper air is still bright with sunlight; a glow still rests upon the Gabelano Peak;[3] but the fogs are in possession of the lower levels; they crawl in scarves among the sandhills; they float, a little higher, in clouds of a gigantic size and often of a wild configuration; to the south, where they have struck the seaward shoulder of the mountains of Santa Lucia, they double back and spire up skyward like smoke. Where their shadow touches, colour dies out of the world. The air grows chill and deadly as they advance. The trade-wind freshens, the trees begin to sigh, and all the windmills in Monterey are whirling and creaking and filling their cisterns with the brackish water of the sands. It

2. Dryden, *Absalom and Achitophel*, II, 498–499.
3. Properly Gabilan Peak.

takes but a little while till the invasion is complete. The sea, in its lighter order, has submerged the earth. Monterey is curtained in for the night in thick, wet, salt, and frigid clouds, so to remain till day returns; and before the sun's rays they slowly disperse and retreat in broken squadrons to the bosom of the sea. And yet often when the fog is thickest and most chill, a few steps out of the town and up the slope, the night will be dry and warm and full of inland perfume.

MEXICANS, AMERICANS, AND INDIANS

The history of Monterey has yet to be written. Founded by Catholic missionaries, a place of wise beneficence to Indians, a place of arms, a Mexican capital continually wrested by one faction from another, an American capital when the first House of Representatives held its deliberations, and then falling lower and lower from the capital of the State to the capital of a county, and from that again, by the loss of its charter and town lands, to a mere bankrupt village, its rise and decline is typical of that of all Mexican institutions and even Mexican families in California.

Nothing is stranger in that strange State than the rapidity with which the soil has changed hands. The Mexicans, you may say, are all poor and landless, like their former capital; and yet both it and they hold themselves apart, and preserve their ancient customs and something of their ancient air.

The town, when I was there, was a place of two or three streets, economically paved with sea-sand, and two or three lanes, which were water-courses in the rainy reason, and at all times were rent up by fissures four or five feet deep. There were no street lights. Short sections of wooden sidewalk only added to the dangers of the night, for they were often high above the level of the roadway, and no one could tell where they would be likely to begin or end. The houses were for the most part built of unbaked adobe brick, many of them old for so new a country, some of very elegant proportions, with low, spacious, shapely rooms, and walls so thick that the heat of summer never dried them to the heart. At the approach of the rainy season a deathly chill and a graveyard smell began to hang about the lower floors; and diseases of the chest are common and fatal among house-keeping people of either sex. There was no activity but in and around the saloons, where people sat almost all day long playing cards. The smallest excursion was made on horseback. You would scarcely ever see the main street without a horse or two tied to posts, and making a fine figure with their Mexican housings. It struck me oddly to come across some of the *Cornhill* illustrations to Mr. Blackmore's *Erema*,[1] and see all the characters astride on English saddles. As a matter of fact, an English saddle is a rarity even in San Francisco, and you may say a thing unknown in all the rest of California. In a place so exclusively Mexican as Monterey, you saw not only Mexican saddles but true Vaquero riding — men always at the hand-gallop up hill and down dale, and round the sharpest corner, urging their horses with cries and gesticulations and cruel rotatory spurs, checking them dead with a touch, or wheeling them right-about-face in a square yard. The type of face and character of bearing are surprisingly un-American. The first ranged from something like the pure Spanish, to something, in its sad fixity, not unlike the pure Indian, although I do not suppose there was one pure blood of either race in all the country. As for the second, it was a matter of perpetual surprise to find, in that world of absolutely mannerless Americans, a people full of deportment, solemnly courteous, and doing all things with grace and decorum. In dress they ran to colour and bright sashes. Not even the most Americanised could always resist the temptation to stick a red rose into his hatband. Not even the most Americanised would descend to wear the vile dress-hat of civilisa-

1. Richard Doddridge Blackmore's *Erema; or, My Father's Sin*, published in *Cornhill Magazine* (Nov. 1876 — Nov. 1877), with illustrations by Frank Dicksee, deals with the wanderings to California of an English girl, the titular heroine, and her father, who has been falsely accused of murder.

tion. Spanish was the language of the streets. It was difficult to get along without a word or two of that language for an occasion. The only communications in which the population joined were with a view to amusement. A weekly public ball took place with great etiquette, in addition to the numerous fandangoes in private houses. There was a really fair amateur brass band. Night after night serenaders would be going about the street, sometimes in a company and with several instruments and voices together, sometimes severally, each guitar before a different window. It was a strange thing to lie awake in nineteenth-century America, and hear the guitar accompany, and one of these old, heart-breaking Spanish love-songs mount into the night air, perhaps in a deep baritone, perhaps in that high-pitched, pathetic, womanish alto which is so common among Mexican men, and which strikes on the unaccustomed ear as something not entirely human, but altogether sad.

The town, then, was essentially and wholly Mexican; and yet almost all the land in the neighbourhood was held by Americans, and it was from the same class, numerically so small, that the principal officials were selected. This Mexican and that Mexican would describe to you his old family estates, not one rood of which remained to him. You would ask him how that came about, and elicit some tangled story back-foremost, from which you gathered that the Americans had been greedy like designing men, and the Mexicans greedy like children, but no other certain fact. Their merits and their faults contributed alike to the ruin of the former landholders. It is true they were improvident, and easily dazzled with the sight of ready money; but they were gentlefolk besides, and that in a way which curiously unfitted them to combat Yankee craft. Suppose they have a paper to sign, they would think it a reflection on the other party to examine the terms with any great minuteness; nay, suppose them to observe some doubtful clause, it is ten to one they would refuse from delicacy to object to it. I know I am speaking within the mark, for I have seen such a case occur, and the Mexican, in spite of the advice of his lawyer, has signed the imperfect paper like a lamb. To have spoken in the matter, he said, above all to have let the other party guess that he had seen a lawyer, would have "been like doubting his word." The scruple sounds oddly to one of ourselves, who have been brought up to understand all business as a competition in fraud, and honesty itself to be a virtue which regards the carrying out, but not the creation, of agreements. This single unworldly trait will account for much of that revolution of which we are speaking. The Mexicans have the name of being great swindlers, but certainly the accusation cuts both ways. In a contest of this sort, the entire booty would scarcely have passed into the hands of the more scrupulous race.

Physically the Americans have triumphed; but it is not entirely seen how far they have themselves been morally conquered. This is, of course, but a part of a part of an extraordinary problem now in the course of being solved in the various States of the American Union. I am reminded of an anecdote. Some years ago, at a great sale of wine, all the odd lots were purchased by a grocer in a small way in the old town of Edinburgh. The agent had the curiosity to visit him some time after and inquire what possible use he could have for such material. He was shown, by way of answer, a huge vat where all the liquors, from humble Gladstone to imperial Tokay, were fermenting together. "And what," he asked, "do you propose to call this?" "I'm no' very sure," replied the grocer, "but I think it's going to turn out port." In the older Eastern States, I think we may say that this hotch-potch of races is going to turn out English, or thereabout. But the problem is indefinitely varied in other zones. The elements are differently mingled in the south, in what we may call the Territorial belt, and in the group of States on the Pacific coast. Above all, in these last we may look to see some singular hybrid — whether good or evil, who shall forecast? but certainly original and all their own. In my little restaurant at Monterey, we have sat down to table, day after day, a Frenchman, two Portuguese, an

Italian, a Mexican, and a Scotsman: we had for common visitors an American from Illinois, a nearly pure-blood Indian woman, and a naturalised Chinese; and from time to time a Switzer and a German came down from country ranches for the night. No wonder that the Pacific coast is a foreign land to visitors from the Eastern States, for each race contributes something of its own. Even the despised Chinese have taught the youth of California, none indeed of their virtues, but the debasing use of opium. And chief among these influences is that of the Mexicans.

The Mexicans, although in the State, are out of it. They still preserve a sort of international independence, and keep their affairs snug to themselves. Only four or five years ago, Vasquez the bandit, his troops being dispersed and the hunt too hot for him in other parts of California, returned to his native Monterey, and was seen publicly in her streets and saloons, fearing no man.[2] The year that I was there there occurred two reputed murders. As the Montereyans are exceptionally vile speakers of each other and of every one behind his back, it is not possible for me to judge how much truth there may have been in these reports; but in the one case every one believed, and in the other some suspected, that there had been foul play; and nobody dreamed for an instant of taking the authorities into their counsel. Now this is, of course, characteristic enough of the Mexicans; but it is a noteworthy feature that all the Americans in Monterey acquiesced without a word in this inaction. Even when I spoke to them upon the subject, they seemed not to understand my surprise; they had forgotten the traditions of their own race and upbringing, and become, in a word, wholly Mexicanised.

Again, the Mexicans, having no ready money to speak of,

2. Tiburcio Vasquez, who had a long career of crime, ranging from robberies to murder, had been hanged just four years before Stevenson arrived in Monterey, but he had already become a legend as a romantic leader of a band of highwaymen and a kind of local Robin Hood. Although he may have had a few followers, Vasquez did not command any troops.

rely almost entirely in their business transactions upon each other's worthless paper. Pedro the penniless pays you with an I O U from the equally penniless Miguel. It is a sort of local currency by courtesy. Credit in these parts has passed into a superstition. I have seen a strong, violent man struggling for months to recover a debt, and getting nothing but an exchange of waste paper. The very storekeepers are averse to asking for cash payments, and are more surprised than pleased when they are offered. They fear there must be something under it, and that you mean to withdraw your custom from them. I have seen the enterprising chemist and stationer begging me with fervour to let my account run on, although I had my purse open in my hand; and partly from the commonness of the case, partly from some remains of that generous old Mexican tradition which made all men welcome to their tables, a person may be notoriously both unwilling and unable to pay, and still find credit for the necessaries of life in the stores of Monterey. Now this villainous habit of living upon "tick" has grown into Californian nature. I do not mean that the American and European storekeepers of Monterey are as lax as Mexicans; I mean that American farmers in many parts of the State expect unlimited credit, and profit by it in the meanwhile without a thought for consequences. Jew storekeepers have already learned the advantage to be gained from this; they lead on the farmer into irretrievable indebtedness, and keep him ever after as their bond-slave hopelessly grinding in the mill. So the whirligig of time brings in its revenges, and except that the Jew knows better than to foreclose, you may see Americans bound in the same chains with which they themselves had formerly bound the Mexican. It seems as if certain sorts of follies, like certain sorts of grain, were natural to the soil rather than to the race that holds and tills it for the moment.

In the meantime, however, the Americans rule in Monterey County. The new county seat, Salinas City, in the bald, corn-bearing plain under the Gabelano Peak, is a town of a purely American character. The land is held, for the most part, in those enormous tracts which are another legacy of Mexican days, and form the present chief danger and disgrace of California; and the holders are mostly of American or British birth. We have here in England no idea of the troubles and inconveniences which flow from the existence of these large landholders — land-thieves, land-sharks, or land-grabbers, they are more commonly and plainly called. Thus the townlands of Monterey are all in the hands of a single man. How they came there is an obscure, vexatious question, and rightly or wrongly the man is hated with a great hatred. His life has been repeatedly in danger. Not very long ago, I was told, the stage was stopped and examined three evenings in succession by disguised horsemen thirsting for his blood. A certain house on the Salinas road, they say, he always passes in his buggy at full speed, for the squatter sent him warning long ago. But a year since he was publicly pointed out for death by no less a man than Mr. Dennis Kearney. Kearney is a man too well known in California, but a word of explanation is required for English readers. Originally an Irish drayman, he rose, by his command of bad language, to almost dictatorial authority in the State; throned it there for six months or so, his mouth full of oaths, gallowses, and conflagrations; was first snuffed out last winter by Mr. Coleman, backed by his San Francisco Vigilantes and three Gatling guns; completed his own ruin by throwing in his lot with the grotesque Greenbacker party; and had at last to be rescued by his old enemies, the police, out of the hands of his rebellious followers. It was while he was at the top of his fortune that Kearney visited Monterey with his battle-cry against Chinese labour, the railroad monopolists, and the land-thieves; and his one articulate counsel to the Montereyans was to "hang David Jacks." [3] Had the town been

3. At twenty-one, Dennis Kearney emigrated to San Francisco from his native Ireland and quickly became a demagogic leader, inveighing against the local railroad magnates, bankers, hack politicians, and particularly the competition from cheap Chinese labor. As founder of the Workingmen's party of California, he established temporary but substantial power. His inflammatory threats were kept from realization

American, in my private opinion, this would have been done years ago. Land is a subject on which there is no jesting in the West, and I have seen my friend the lawyer drive out of Monterey to adjust a competition of titles with the face of a captain going into battle, and his Smith-and-Wesson convenient to his hand.

On the ranche of another of these landholders you may find our old friend, the Truck system, in full operation.[4] Men live there, year in year out, to cut timber for a nominal wage, which is all consumed in supplies. The longer they remain in this desirable service the deeper they will fall in debt — a burlesque injustice in a new country, where labour should be precious, and one of those typical instances which explains the prevailing discontent and the success of the demagogue Kearney.

In a comparison between what was and what is in California, the praisers of times past will fix upon the Indians of Carmel. The valley drained by the river so named is a true Californian valley, bare, dotted with chaparral, overlooked by quaint, unfinished hills. The Carmel runs by many pleasant farms, a clear and shallow river, loved by wading kine; and at last, as it is falling towards a quicksand and the great Pacific, passes a ruined mission on a hill. From the mission church the eye embraces a great field of ocean, and the ear is filled with a continuous sound of distant breakers on the shore. But the day of the Jesuit[5] has gone by, the day of the Yankee has succeeded, and there is no one left to care for the converted savage. The church is roofless and ruinous, sea-breezes and sea-fogs, and

---

by the armed patrols led by William T. Coleman. David Jacks, a wealthy Scot who had accumulated some 60,000 acres of land since coming to Monterey in 1850, was a natural target for Kearney's attacks on land monopoly as being detrimental to the interest of workingmen.

4. A system of payments that amounted to barter (not uncommon in contemporary Scotland and England), by which employees on the sometimes remote ranches had to spend all their wages at the company store, often notorious for high prices.

5. Stevenson should have written "Franciscan," for this was the founding order.

the alternation of the rain and sunshine, daily widening the breaches and casting the crockets from the wall. As an antiquity in this new land, a quaint specimen of missionary architecture, and a memorial of good deeds, it had a triple claim to preservation from all thinking people; but neglect and abuse have been its portion. There is no sign of American interference, save where a head-board has been torn from a grave to be a mark for pistol-bullets. So it is with the Indians for whom it was erected. Their lands, I was told, are being yearly encroached upon by the neighbouring American proprietor, and with that exception no man troubles his head for the Indians of Carmel. Only one day in the year, the day before our Guy Fawkes,[6] the *padre* drives over the hill from Monterey; the little sacristy, which is the only covered portion of the church, is filled with seats and decorated for the service; the Indians troop together, their bright dresses contrasting with their dark and melancholy faces; and there, among a crowd of unsympathetic holiday-makers, you may hear God served with perhaps more touching circumstances than in any other temple under heaven. An Indian, stone-blind and about eighty years of age, conducts the singing; other Indians compose the choir; yet they have the Gregorian music at their finger-ends, and pronounce the Latin so correctly that I could follow the meaning as they sang. The pronunciation was odd and nasal, the singing hurried and staccato. "In sæcula sæculo-ho-horum," they went, with a vigorous aspirate to every additional syllable. I have never seen faces more vividly lit up with joy than the faces of these Indian singers. It was to them not only the worship of God, nor an act by which they recalled and commemorated better days, but was besides an exercise of culture, where all they knew of art and letters was united and expressed. And it made a man's heart sorry for the good fathers of yore who had taught them to dig and to reap, to read and to sing, who had given them European mass-books which they

6. Since the mission was named for San Carlos Borromeo, it celebrated St. Charles' Day, November 4.

still preserve and study in their cottages, and who had now passed away from all authority and influence in that land — to be succeeded by greedy land-thieves and sacrilegious pistol-shots. So ugly a thing may our Anglo-Saxon Protestantism appear beside the doings of the Society of Jesus.

But revolution in this world succeeds to revolution. All that I say in this paper is in a paulo-past tense. The Monterey of last year[7] exists no longer. A huge hotel has sprung up in the desert by the railway.[8] Three sets of diners sit down successively to table. Invaluable toilettes figure along the beach and between the live oaks; and Monterey is advertised in the newspapers, and posted in the waiting-rooms at railway stations, as a resort for wealth and fashion. Alas for the little town! it is not strong enough to resist the influence of the flaunting caravanserai, and the poor, quaint, penniless native gentlemen of Monterey must perish, like a lower race, before the millionaire vulgarians of the Big Bonanza.

7. 1879. [Note in Edinburgh Edition.]
8. In June 1880 the Hotel Del Monte, one of the most elegant spas in the United States, was opened to accommodate 750 guests.

SAN CARLOS DAY

A BARBARIAN AT THE CARMELLO MISSION

MY DEAR BRONSON[1]: —

You have asked me to give you something of what I saw upon Saint Carlos Day,[2] and being of a biddable disposition, I comply herewith.

I fancy everyone must play the part of a Barbarian some time or other in the course of his life, just as each, according to the proverb, must eat his peck of dust. We have a number of gentlemen here, all, oddly enough, answering to the name of John; very courteous and obliging I find them, though a little indistinct in the matter of English pronunciation, and all these gentlemen, with their charming wives and families, have become Barbarians by the simple process of crossing the sea. So it it with me: I am like a lost child on the Pacific Coast; and can only speak "as it strikes the stranger," and from a Barbarian standpoint.

Well, sir, I went to Carmello in a Buggy from Wolter's over a road which would be an extravagant farce in the country from which I came; I beheld a considerable concourse of people in their best, some firing guns — one standing up in a wagon and unweariedly beating a drum, just as though something were about to happen. I ate for the first time in my life (I began by saying that I was a barbarian) some *cara asada en las brassas*,[3] for which I m indebted to the Rev. Mr. Murphy,

1. The persons mentioned in this article were all local figures with whom Stevenson was acquainted, such as Crevole Bronson, the newspaper editor; Manuel Wolter, a Monterey drayman; and Adulpho Sanchez, soon to marry Fanny Osbourne's sister, Nellie Van de Grift. Mr. Graves presumably was a local schoolteacher.

2. This day is November 4 and is dedicated to San Carlos Borromeo, the saint for whom the Carmel mission was named. The day was also a subject in "Monterey" and the magazine version of "Across the Plains."

3. Calf's head roasted in hot coals.

and washed down my repast with my part of two bottles of wine — one from Simoneau and the other furnished and, I am bound to say, shared by Adulpho Sanchez. I am not the man (barbarian though I be) to draw comparisons; but I bore myself, I hope, like one who does not fear a bottle and a glass, and I had no cause to regret my daring.

All this touched me. I cannot remain unmoved when it comes to eating and drinking. But please, Bronson, why did that man beat the drum? I am on live coals, as the saying is, till I know what he had in view. It is pleasant, of course to play the drum; but people usually have some ulterior purpose when they indulge publicly and for hours together in that exercise. I dare say, I should like to play the drum, too; but then, I should go off somewhere by myself into a desert, and have it out alone with my maker; I shouldn't stand up in a wagon as if I were going to sell pills. Besides, I marked that man, and he had something on his mind. Let us know in the next issue. I cannot have been alone; others must have observed his little game and be still wondering like me.

But, sir, all this is not the matter in hand. I made two remarks upon St. Charles' Day, and first: you have there a church of extreme interest which is going the way of all roofless and neglected buildings. Every year with its summer drouth and winter rain, is hurrying that church into the number of things that are no more. Every year it becomes less easy and more expensive to save what remains. Believe me, it will not be lost money for the inhabitants of Monterey county, if they not only put their heads but their purses together to preserve this speaking relic of the past. In England some great noble or cotton spinner would purchase it, repair it and charge so much entry money to curious visitors. In France, still better, the government would take it in hand and make it one of the "Historical Monuments" of the nation. So piously, in these old countries, do people cherish what unites them to the past. Here, in America, on this beautiful Pacific Coast, you cannot afford to lose what you have. When I think how that bell first sounded from that Mission Church among the Indians of Carmello, and the echoes of the hills of Monterey first learned the unaccustomed note, I am moved, by sentiment, to pray for restitution or at least repair. And when I think how, as time goes on, visitors will flock to such a curiosity, as they flock to similar curiosities in Europe by the hundred and the thousand, and how the managers of our hotels, or their successors, may have cause to bless the man who put a roof on Carmel Church, I see that not only sentiment but the merest business prudence should lead you, and me, and all who take an interest in Monterey, to do our little best for that good end.

And second: I heard the old Indians singing mass. That was a new experience and one, I think, well worth hearing. There was the old man who led, and the women who so worthily followed. It was like a voice out of the past. They sang by tradition, from the teaching of early missionaries long since turned to clay:

> "King Pandion he is dead,
> All your friends are lapped in lead." [4]

And still in the roofless church, you may hear the old music. Padre Casanove will, I am sure, be the first to pardon and understand me, when I say that the old Gregorian singing preached a sermon more eloquent than his own. Peace on earth, good will to men so it seemed to me to say; and to me, as a Barbarian, who hears on all sides evil speech and the roughest bywords about the Indian race, to hear Carmel Indians sing their Latin words with so good a pronunciation and give out these ancient European chants with familiarity and fervor, suggested new and pleasant reflections. Here was an old, mediæval civilization, and your old primeval barbarian, hand-in-hand, the one devoutly following the other. And I could not help thinking that if there had been more priests and fewer land sharks and Indian agents, there would have

4. Richard Barnfield, "The Address to the Nightingale," slightly misquoted.

been happier days for a considerable number of human bipeds in your American continent.

I began by admitting that I was a Barbarian. Now, that I have proved it, I had better pause. That was how it struck "the stranger." A fine old church, a fine old race, both brutally neglected; a survival, a memory and a ruin. The United States Mint can coin many million more dollar pieces, but not make a single Indian; and when Carmel Church is in the dust, not all the wealth of all the States and Territories can replace what has been lost. No man's word can save the Indians from the ruin that awaits them; but the church? How, my dear Bronson, if you and I put together our little mites and, through the columns of your paper, wrought upon all hands to interest others in this useful work of protection? I feel sure that the money would be forthcoming before long; and the future little ones of Monterey would clap their hands to see the old Church, and learn by the sight of it more history than even Mr. Graves and all his successors can manage to teach them out of history books. I remain,

Yours,

THE MONTEREY BARBARIAN.[5]

5. The article was well received, for not only was its purpose endorsed by the rival Monterey *Democrat* on November 25, but the next weekly issue of the *Californian* on November 18 declared: "Since the publication last week of the communication of The Monterey Barbarian, praying that something may be done for the preservation of the old Carmel Church which is fast following the footsteps of all neglected things, we have been interviewed by different parties who have expressed a willingness to subscribe means within their power to help on the good work of restoration. A little energy displayed at this time by some of our influential citizens would save this old historical monument for generations to come, and add much of interest to engage the attention of tourists. The expense will not be great and then, it is but casting our bread upon the waters." These pleas seem to have been effective, for the restoration of the Mission San Carlos Borromeo del Rio Carmelo (Stevenson added the extra "l") was begun in the 1880's under the auspices of the resident pastor of Monterey, Father Angelo Casanova, although the steep shingle roof that he had installed was both ugly and inappropriate. It was finally replaced with proper tiling in the 1930's when the whole church was carefully and accurately restored.

SIMONEAU'S AT MONTEREY

A place does not clearly exist for the imagination, till we have moved elsewhere. The tenor of our experience, one day melting into another, unifies into a single picture; out of many sunsets, many dawns, and many starry rambles, we compound a *tertium quid*, a glorified quintessence; the honey of honey, the cream of cream; a classical landscape, artificially composed and far more lively, winning and veracious than the scene it represents. For single glances may, indeed, be memorable; they are the traits of which we afterwards compose our fancy likeness; but the eye cannot embrace a panorama; the eye, like the etcher's needle, cannot elaborate from nature; and literature, which is the language of our thoughts, must be gently elaborated in the course of time. Hence it is that a place grows upon our fancy after we have left it, taking more and more the colour of our predilections, growing, like our childhood, daily more beautiful through the cunning excisions of oblivion; until it means at last, for that inward eye of which the poet tells us, something at once familiar and express, like the remembered countenance of a friend. We know what the eyes are to the face; the inn where we dined is similarly all important in this memorial picture of a neighbourhood. It was the centre of our explorations, to which we still returned; it was the first high-light of an evening when we reentered, blinking, from a woodland ramble; it was there we went to eat when we were hungry, to be warmed when we were cold, to talk when our spirits mounted; and it was there, over the digestive coffee, that we reviewed at night the toils and pleasures of the day. A chronic wanderer, when he looks backward, counts his rosary of inns. On the chart of his terrigenous pilgrimage, he beholds his airy effigy arriving about sundown at one inn after another in every quarter of the world; there he unslings his knapsack, there he descends ungainly from his omnibus; there they dined [1] by the chimney where the snow-wind was hooting, there he breakfasted, with open shirt, in the green trellis at the garden end; but it was always from an inn that he departed, and towards an inn that he fared farther forth.

Out of all my private recollections of remembered inns and restaurants — and I believe it, other things equal, to be un-rivalled — one particular house of entertainment stands forth alone. I am grateful, indeed, to many a swinging signboard, to many a rusty wine-bush; but not with the same kind of gratitude. Some were beautifully situated, some had an ad-mirable table, some were the gathering-places of excellent companions; but take them for all in all, not one can be com-pared with Simoneau's at Monterey.

To the front, it was part barber's shop, part bar; to the back, there was a kitchen and a salle-a-manger. The intending diner found himself in a little, chilly, bare, adobé room, furnished with chairs and tables, and adorned with some oil sketches roughly brushed upon the wall in the manner of Barbizon and Cernay.[2] The table, at whatever hour you entered, was already laid with a not spotless napkin and, by way of épergne, with a dish of green peppers and tomatoes, pleasing alike to eye and palate. If you stayed there to meditate before a meal, you would hear Simoneau all about the kitchen, now rattling among the dishes, now clearing a semi-military chest with a "hroum-hroum," a drumming of his fists, and a snatch of music. Out of the single window, you beheld a court, with a well, and hens and chickens and stacks of empty bottles, and on the other side, a very massive and crumbling outhouse of

1. The change of person and tense is typical of a draft not finally prepared for the press.
2. Two of the artists' colonies that Stevenson frequented in the summer of 1875, when he met Fanny Osbourne at the nearby similar settlement of Grez.

adobé. It was a storied outhouse, one of the oldest buildings on the Pacific coast: the prison of Monterey, where many a poor soul has slept his last night, and Padres, long since dead themselves, have wrestled by the hour with those about to die. I have sat out there in the court, long times together, among the bottles or beside the well, for the sake of the warm sunshine; and, strange as it may seem, I never had the smallest visiting of inspirations from the neighbourhood of that grim relic. I forget to what trivial use it had then fallen; but it looked placid like a browsing cow.

There were two set meals a day; and there it was that our polyglot society assembled. There were rarely more than two of the same race together; though we were rich in pairs with two Frenchmen, two Portuguese and two Ligurians. Among Spanish, English and French, the sound of our talk was like a little Babel. But whatever tongue might be the speaker's fancy for the moment, the oaths that shone among his sentences were always English. By survival of the fittest, English oaths are destined to an immortality of service. Nothing in French, and only "carrajo" in Spanish, can struggle long for their existence in the company of our rugged, fierce and pithy execrations. And again, in whatever language the sentence might be couched, the western expletive "you bet" would be thrown out hoarsely in the midst. This friendly synthesis of tongues put everyone at home. We spoke neither English, Spanish nor French; we spoke Simoneaudean, the language of our common country.

François the baker filled the chair of presidence, his light eyes shining clearly under his rugged brows, his halting Provençal tongue sometimes wandering back upon old days in Chili or Brazil, sometimes uttering projects for the future of his joyous return to France and his family as that American Uncle, dear to playwrights. Our supper was François's breakfast, and our breakfast his supper; at which last, after his long, sweltering night's work and perhaps a glass of absinthe, I am bound to own he shone like the red sunrise among our starlight, morning faces.

Frank, the Italian Fisherman — though he usually took his meals among his fellow fishers, in a wooden house on stilts at the pier's end, redolent of nets and fish and apples and country wine on the tap — yet when things went well and the "take" was large, would join our company in the adobé parlour. He had served on the Lakes in Garibaldian days; and Garibaldi was always "my old man" with him, each of the three words rolled out with rough Italian gusto. He was the most politically minded man I ever knew. Unredeemed Italy was his pillow-thought, and he waded after his nets at sunrise with the concerns of an ambassador. Foreign politics, as the matter of a prolonged talk, ranks among the dullest; but Frank had a way of personifying European nations — Mr. Rooshia, Mr. Prooshia and Mr. Owstria[3] — which made the subject wonderfully lively. Finding that I could pronounce Italian, he would bring Italian journals up to papa Simoneau's, and set me reading aloud, while he, with a cigarette in his big fingers and a perfect fire of interest in his eye, sat drinking in the diplomatic items, scandalously mispronounced and delivered as a reader usually delivers things of which he understands about a third. It was only the other day that the reason of this mania flashed across my mind. Frank, the critic of Mr. Prooshia, had been denied the benefits of education.

Frank had a younger man who came with him, a Ligurian, Dutra, notable for little beyond pleasant looks. The elder Dutra was a regular boarder, principally distinguished for singing Mexican serenades and trying vainly to teach me Mexican courtesy; I could never so much as learn to lend my cigarette with the proper and, I must add, sensible and graceful manœuvre. Don A— I have forgot his name — a solemn gentleman, who had squandered a fortune, I was led to understand,

3. Frank's manner of speaking turns up as a generic characteristic of San Francisco's Italians in *The Wrecker,* Chap. 8.

in the pursuit of gallantry — was equally unsuccessful in his attempts to teach me Spanish; but he made a very grave figure at the board and gave our gatherings a flavour of respectability. The Captain of the Carmel whalers, a fierce, sensible Portuguese, joined us from time to time when he was in town on business. Once or twice, there came a melancholy example of a French savant, after beetles or plants, a man so filled with his own superiority that he could not address a fellow creature without offering or at least implying insult: a compound of the arrogance of science with the manners of the bagman, such as in fits of spleen, I suppose Haeckel to be like, poor man. And once only in my time — once was enough — there came down from his ranche upon the mountains, an incredible Swiss boy in the best spirits, I suppose, that ever were enjoyed by man. He broke dishes, he bawled, he told us stories of his wife (and he was newly married), he sang, he played on various instruments, most of which he broke; and in short, by the time I took my way homeward, the neighbourhood of Monterey prison house echoed like a Bedlam, and the next morning the whole company was pale and taciturn. As for the Swiss, if I am not misled, he took home with him to his mountain bride a notable headache and an empty purse. It is true he had been living for three months exclusively on tea and slapjacks.

The editor of the paper, Crevole Bronson, my patron as I shall proceed to show, was not frequently a diner, but he was a hanger on of our society, attracted by the character of our mirth which, for Monterey, was intellectual. Bronson, and his attendant youth, slept in the office of the journal in an atmosphere of printer's ink; the youth set up the exchanges, while Bronson, composing stick in hand, poured forth the leading articles. He had a disinterested love for polysyllables, and knew a great many. I can see him still, a very stout, large-faced, brown man with handsome eyes, leaning slightly forward against the case, the composing stick balanced in his hand, his spirit placidly pursuing longer words. His delight in the material of the art shows a rudimentary faculty; I cannot say that Bronson could write, but he wished to write, and he had an ideal of style. The Monterey paper was a losing business; its principal revenue was paid in kind by advertising shopkeepers; and one after another the editors wrestled for awhile, and then sold the paper, press and all, for something less than they had paid for it. Nor was it even amusing to conduct: the greater part of its columns were devoted to the exchanges and the advertisements by which it lived; and the only original matter which awoke much interest was in the form of personals. These take, in such a journal, one of two classical forms: As thus: "Jack Smith came over Tuesday, from Tres Pinos where he is doing a great hardware business. He was looking splendid, and left a bottle of whiskey at our office. Call again, Jack!" Or again as thus: "It is not true that Alexandro Gomez lost his way going home from the Fandango." The first ministers to the vanity of Jack; the second to the mirth of Alexandar's friends. But to a man of dumb literary aspirations, the field is somewhat narrow; and Bronson chafed against his boundaries, like Bonaparte in Elba. He never mentioned the word ambition; but he scarcely concealed his disappointment. He hurled polysyllables, somewhat vaguely, at the Monterey public . . .

All this time I have said nothing of papa Simoneau himself; always in his waistcoat and shirt sleeves, upright as a boy, with a rough, trooper-like smartness, vaunting his dishes if they were good, himself the first to condemn if they were unsuccessful; now red hot in a discussion, now playing his flute with antique graces, now shamelessly hurrying off the other boarders that he might sit down to chess with me: a man who had been most things from a man in business to a navvy, and kept his spirit and his kind heart through all.

I ask myself if I shall ever again sit down nightly with a pleasanter society; or if any human speech will ever sound more familiarly in my ears than the babel in that room beside the prison. And I am very sure, for one thing, I shall never find another landlord like my papa Simoneau. I was the spoiled child of the house; when my appetite failed, he broke his heart to find me dainties; if there was anything delicate in Monterey, papa Simoneau was sure to have some of it laid by for his favourite boarder. And then the talks that we had upon all subjects divine and human; the studies that we made in chess, Cunningham's gambit and what not; the long pleasant evenings in the corner by the stove! Once when I was three days confined to bed, I was wakened daily before sunrise by the cheery voice of Simoneau — I can hear it still — hailing me in the grey morning from the street, "*Stevenson — comment ça va?*" O mon bon Simoneau!, and the candles are blown out, and the shadows fall early round the prison, and we are all scattered to the four winds of heaven, and you yourself, as they write to me, are gone somewhere vaguely into the south, among the sand and the tarantulas, and I cannot even send you this word that your kindnesses are still remembered!

SAN FRANCISCO

The Pacific coast of the United States, as you may see by the map, and still better in that admirable book, *Two Years before the Mast*, by Dana, is one of the most exposed and shelterless on earth. The trade-wind blows fresh; the huge Pacific swell booms along degree after degree of an unbroken line of coast. South of the joint firth of the Columbia and Willamette, there flows in no considerable river; south of Puget Sound there is no protected inlet of the ocean. Along the whole sea-board of California there are but two unexceptionable anchorages, — the bight of the Bay of Monterey, and the inland sea that takes its name from San Francisco.

Whether or not it was here that Drake put in in 1597, we cannot tell. There is no other place so suitable; and yet the narrative of Francis Pretty[1] scarcely seems to suit the features of the scene. Viewed from seaward, the Golden Gates should give no very English impression to justify the name of a New Albion. On the west, the deep lies open; nothing near but the still vexed Farallones. The coast is rough and barren. Tamalpais, a mountain of a memorable figure, springing direct from the sea-level, over-plumbs the narrow entrance from the north. On the south, the loud music of the Pacific sounds along

1. Pretty is thought to have served as a gentleman-at-arms on Drake's *Golden Hinde*, and to him has been attributed "The Famous Voyage of Francis Drake into the South Sea and thence about the Whole Globe of the Earth," printed in Hakluyt's *Principal Navigations*. In it occurs the description Stevenson alludes to and a statement justifying Drake's coinage of the place name: "Our Generall called this Countrey, Nova Albion, and that for two causes: the one in respect of the white bankes and cliffes, which lie towards the sea: and the other, because it might have some affinitie with our Countrey in name which sometime was so called."

beaches and cliffs, and among broken reefs, the sporting-place
of the sea-lion. Dismal, shifting sandhills, wrinkled by the
wind, appear behind. Perhaps, too, in the days of Drake,
Tamalpais would be clothed to its peak with the majestic redwoods.

Within the memory of persons not yet old, a mariner might
have steered into these narrows — not yet the Golden Gates
— opened out the surface of the bay — here girt with hills,
there lying broad to the horizon — and beheld a scene as
empty of the presence, as pure from the handiwork, of man,
as in the days of our old sea-commander. A Spanish mission,
fort, and church took the place of those "houses of the people
of the country" which were seen by Pretty, "close to the
water-side." All else would be unchanged. Now, a generation
later, a great city covers the sandhills on the west, a growing
town lies along the muddy shallows of the east; steamboats
pant continually between them from before sunrise till the
small hours of the morning; lines of great sea-going ships lie
ranged at anchor; colours fly upon the islands; and from all
around the hum of corporate life, of beaten bells, and steam,
and running carriages, goes cheerily abroad in the sunshine.
Choose a place on one of the huge throbbing ferry-boats, and,
when you are midway between the city and the suburb; look
around. The air is fresh and salt as if you were at sea. On the
one hand is Oakland, gleaming white among its gardens. On
the other, to seaward, hill after hill is crowded and crowned
with the palaces of San Francisco; its long streets lie in regular
bars of darkness, east and west, across the sparkling picture; a
forest of masts bristles like bulrushes about its feet; nothing
remains of the days of Drake but the faithful trade-wind scattering the smoke, the fogs that will begin to muster about sundown, and the fine bulk of Tamalpais looking down on San
Francisco, like Arthur's Seat on Edinburgh.[2]

Thus, in the course of a generation only, this city and its
suburb have arisen. Men are alive by the score who have

2. Rocky eminence towering over Edinburgh.

hunted all over the foundations in a dreary waste. I have dined, near the "punctual centre" [3] of San Francisco, with a gentleman (then newly married), who told me of his former pleasures, wading with his fowling-piece in sand and scrub, on the site of the house where we were dining. In this busy, moving generation, we have all known cities to cover our boyish playgrounds, we have all started for a country walk and stumbled on a new suburb; but I wonder what enchantment of the Arabian Nights can have equalled this evocation of a roaring city, in a few years of a man's life, from the marshes and the blowing sand. Such swiftness of increase, as with an overgrown youth, suggests a corresponding swiftness of destruction. The sandy peninsula of San Francisco, mirroring itself on one side in the bay, beaten on the other by the surge of the Pacific, and shaken to the heart by frequent earthquakes, seems in itself no very durable foundation. According to Indian tales, perhaps older than the name of California, it once rose out of the sea in a moment, and sometime or other shall, in a moment, sink again.[4] No Indian, they say, cares to linger on that doubtful land. "The earth hath bubbles as the water has, and this is of them." [5] Here, indeed, all is new, nature as well as towns. The very hills of California have an unfinished look; the rains and the streams have not yet carved them to their perfect shape. The forests spring like mushrooms from the unexhausted soil; and they are mown down yearly by the forest fires. We are in early geological epochs, changeful and insecure; and we feel, as with a sculptor's model, that the author may yet grow weary of and shatter the rough sketch.

Fancy apart, San Francisco is a city beleaguered with alarms. The lower parts, along the bay side, sit on piles; old wrecks decaying, fish dwelling unsunned, beneath the populous houses;

3. Central point pricked by the stationary leg of a pair of compasses.
4. A legend of this general sort about the creation of the land may have been held by the Costanoans, who lived on the San Francisco peninsula, but there is no evidence that they avoided the region for this reason or that they expected it to sink suddenly.
5. *Macbeth*, I, iii, 78-79, slightly misquoted.

and a trifling subsidence might drown the business quarters in an hour. Earthquakes are not only common, they are sometimes threatening in their violence; the fear of them grows yearly on a resident; he begins with indifference, ends in sheer panic; and no one feels safe in any but a wooden house. Hence it comes that, in that rainless clime, the whole city is built of timber — a woodyard of unusual extent and complication; that fires spring up readily, and served by the unwearying trade-wind, swiftly spread; that all over the city there are fire-signal boxes; that the sound of the bell, telling the number of the threatened ward, is soon familiar to the ear; and that nowhere else in the world is the art of the fireman carried to so nice a point.

Next, perhaps, in order of strangeness to the rapidity of its appearance, is the mingling of the races that combine to people it. The town is essentially not Anglo-Saxon; still more essentially not American. The Yankee and the Englishman find themselves alike in a strange country. There are none of these touches — not of nature, and I dare scarcely say of art — by which the Anglo-Saxon feels himself at home in so great a diversity of lands. Here, on the contrary, are airs of Marseilles and of Pekin. The shops along the street are like the consulates of different nations. The passers-by vary in feature like the slides of a magic-lantern. For we are here in that city of gold to which adventurers congregated out of all the winds of heaven; we are in a land that till the other day was ruled and peopled by the countrymen of Cortes; and the sea that laves the piers of San Francisco is the ocean of the East and of the isles of summer. There goes the Mexican, unmistakable; there the blue-clad Chinaman with his white slippers; there the soft-spoken, brown Kanaka, or perhaps a waif from far-away Malaya. You hear French, German, Italian, Spanish, and English indifferently. You taste the food of all nations in the various restaurants; passing from a French *prix-fixe* where every one is French, to a roaring German ordinary where every one is German; ending, perhaps, in a cool and silent

Chinese tea-house. For every man, for every race and nation, that city is a foreign city; humming with foreign tongues and customs; and yet each and all have made themselves at home. The Germans have a German theatre and innumerable beer-gardens. The French Fall of the Bastille is celebrated with squibs and banners, and marching patriots, as noisily as the American Fourth of July. The Italians have their dear domestic quarter, with Italian caricatures in the windows, Chianti and polenta in the taverns. The Chinese are settled as in China. The goods they offer for sale are as foreign as the lettering on the signboard of the shop: dried fish from the China seas; pale cakes and sweetmeats — the like, perhaps, once eaten by Badroubadour;[6] nuts of unfriendly shape; ambiguous, outlandish vegetables, misshapen, lean, or bulbous — telling of a country where the trees are not as our trees, and the very back-garden is a cabinet of curiosities. The joss-house is hard by, heavy with incense, packed with quaint carvings and the paraphernalia of a foreign ceremonial. All these you behold, crowded together in the narrower arteries of the city, cool, sunless, a little mouldy, with the unfamiliar faces at your elbow, and the high, musical sing-song of that alien language in your ears. Yet the houses are of Occidental build; the lines of a hundred telegraphs pass, thick as a ship's rigging, overhead, a kite hanging among them, perhaps, or perhaps two, one European, one Chinese, in shape and colour; mercantile Jack, the Italian fisher, the Dutch merchant, the Mexican vaquero, go hustling by; at the sunny end of the street, a thoroughfare roars with European traffic; and meanwhile, high and clear, out breaks perhaps the San Francisco fire-alarm, and people pause to count the strokes, and in the stations of the double fire-service you know that the electric bells are ringing, the traps opening, and clapping to, and the engine, manned and harnessed, being whisked into the street, before the sound of

6. The Sultan's daughter who was wed to Aladdin after his lamp brought him great wealth. Stevenson's is an unusual variant of the name, more commonly spelled Badroulboudour or Beder-el-Budur.

the alarm has ceased to vibrate on your ear. Of all romantic places for a boy to loiter in, that Chinese quarter is the most romantic. There, on a half-holiday, three doors from home, he may visit an actual foreign land, foreign in people, language, things, and customs. The very barber of the Arabian Nights shall be at work before him, shaving heads;[7] he shall see Aladdin playing on the streets; who knows but among those nameless vegetables the fruit of the rose-tree itself may be exposed for sale? And the interest is heightened with a chill of horror. Below, you hear, the cellars are alive with mystery; opium dens, where the smokers lie one above another, shelf above shelf, close-packed and grovelling in deadly stupor; the seats of unknown vices and cruelties, the prisons of unacknowledged slaves and the secret lazarettos of disease.

With all this mass of nationalities, crime is common. There are rough quarters where it is dangerous o' nights; cellars of public entertainment which the wary pleasure-seeker chooses to avoid. Concealed weapons are unlawful, but the law is continually broken. One editor was shot dead while I was there;[8] another walked the streets accompanied by a bravo, his guardian angel. I have been quietly eating a dish of oysters in a restaurant, where, not more than ten minutes after I had left, shots were exchanged and took effect; and one night about ten o'clock, I saw a man standing watchfully at a street-corner with a long Smith-and-Wesson glittering in his hand behind his back. Somebody had done something he should not, and was being looked for with a vengeance. It is odd, too, that the seat of the last vigilance committee I know of — a mediæval

7. In *The Book of the Thousand and One Nights*, the character who figures in "The Tale of the Lame Man with the Barber of Baghdad" and "The Tale of the Barber of Baghdad and the Tales of his Six Brothers."

8. Charles De Young of the *Chronicle* was killed in his office on April 23, 1880, by Milton Kalloch, who was avenging his father, Rev. Isaac S. Kalloch, a former Baptist clergyman and currently mayor of San Francisco, who had been wounded previously by the editor as the result of a political feud.

Vehmgericht[9] — was none other than the Palace Hotel, the world's greatest caravanserai, served by lifts and lit with electricity; where, in the great glazed court, a band nightly discourses music from a grove of palms. So do extremes meet in this city of contrasts: extremes of wealth and poverty, apathy and excitement, the conveniences of civilisation and the red justice of Judge Lynch.

The streets lie straight up and down the hills, and straight across at right angles, these in sun, those in shadow, a trenchant pattern of gloom and glare; and what with the crisp illumination, the sea-air singing in your ears, the chill and glitter, the changing aspects both of things and people, the fresh sights at every corner of your walk — sights of the bay, of Tamalpais, of steep, descending streets, of the outspread city — whiffs of alien speech, sailors singing on shipboard, Chinese coolies toiling on the shore, crowds brawling all day in the street before the Stock Exchange — one brief impression follows and obliterates another, and the city leaves upon the mind no general and stable picture, but a profusion of airy and incongruous images, of the sea and shore, the east and west, the summer and the winter.

In the better parts of the most interesting city there is apt to be a touch of the commonplace. It is in the slums and suburbs that the city dilettante finds his game. And there is nothing more characteristic and original than the outlying quarters of San Francisco. The Chinese district is the most famous; but it is far from the only truffle in the pie. There is many another dingy corner, many a young antiquity, many a *terrain vague* with that stamp of quaintness that the city lover seeks and dwells on; and the indefinite prolongation of its streets, up hill and down dale, makes San Francisco a place apart. The same street in its career visits and unites so many different classes of society, here echoing with drays, there ly-

9. Secret tribunal of Westphalia, powerful from the end of the 12th to the middle of the 16th century.

ing decorously silent between the mansions of Bonanza millionaires, to founder at last among the drifting sands beside
Lone Mountain cemetery, or die out among the sheds and
lumber of the north. Thus you may be struck with a spot, set
it down for the most romantic of the city, and, glancing at
the name-plate, find it is in the same street that you yourself
inhabit in another quarter of the town.

The great net of straight thoroughfares lying at right angles,
east and west and north and south, over the shoulders of Nob
Hill, the hill of palaces, must certainly be counted the best part
of San Francisco. It is there that the millionaires are gathered
together vying with each other in display. From thence, looking down over the business wards of the city, we can descry a
building with a little belfry, and that is the Stock Exchange,
the heart of San Francisco: a great pump we might call it,
continually pumping up the savings of the lower quarters into
the pockets of the millionaires upon the hill. But these same
thoroughfares that enjoy for a while so elegant a destiny have
their lines prolonged into more unpleasant places. Some meet
their fate in the sands; some must take a cruise in the ill-famed
China quarters; some run into the sea; some perish unwept
among pig-sties and rubbish-heaps.

Nob Hill comes, of right, in the place of honour; but the
two other hills of San Francisco are more entertaining to ex-
plore. On both there are a world of old wooden houses snooz-
ing together all forgotten. Some are of the quaintest design,
others only romantic by neglect and age. Some have been almost undermined by new thoroughfares, and sit high up on
the margin of the sandy cutting, only to be reached by stairs.
Some are curiously painted, and I have seen one at least with
ancient carvings panelled in its wall. Surely they are not of
Californian building, but far voyagers from round the stormy
Horn, like those who sent for them and dwelt in them at first.
Brought to be the favourites of the wealthy, they have sunk
into these poor, forgotten districts, where, like old town toasts,
they keep each other silently in countenance. Telegraph Hill

and Rincon Hill, these are the two dozing quarters that I recommend to the city dilettante. There stand these forgotten houses, enjoying the unbroken sun and quiet. There, if there were such an author, would the San Francisco Fortuné de Boisgobey[10] pitch the first chapter of his mystery. But the first is the quainter of the two, and commands, moreover, a noble view. As it stands at the turn of the bay, its skirts are all waterside, and round from North Beach to the Bay Front you can follow doubtful paths from one quaint corner to another. Everywhere the same tumble-down decay and sloppy progress, new things yet unmade, old things tottering to their fall; everywhere the same out-at-elbows, many-nationed loungers at dim, irregular grog-shops; everywhere the same sea-air and isleted sea-prospect; and for a last and more romantic note, you have on the one hand Tamalpais standing high in the blue air, and on the other the tail of that long alignment of three-masted, full-rigged, deep-sea ships that make a forest of spars along the eastern front of San Francisco. In no other port is such a navy congregated. For the coast trade is so trifling, and the ocean trade from round the Horn so large, that the smaller ships are swallowed up, and can do nothing to confuse the majestic order of these merchant princes. In an age when the ship-of-the-line is already a thing of the past, and we can never again hope to go coasting in a cock-boat between the "wooden walls" of a squadron at anchor, there is perhaps no place on earth where the power and beauty of sea architecture can be so perfectly enjoyed as in this bay.

10. An indefatigable French romancer (1824–1891), whose eerie tales of intrigue were of the school of Ponson du Terrail, another writer enjoyed by Stevenson (see page 258).

THE SILVERADO SQUATTERS

The Silverado Squatters

Vixerunt nonnulli in agris, delectati re sua familiari.
His idem propositum fuit quod regibus, ut ne qua re
egerent, ne cui parerent, libertate uterentur: cujus pro-
prium est sic vivere ut velis.

CIC. DE OFF. I. XX.[1]

1. The Loeb Classical Library translation of this passage from Cicero's *De Officiis* that Stevenson selected for his title page reads: "Some of them, too, lived in the country and found their pleasure in the management of their private estates. Such men have had the same aims as kings — to suffer no want, to be subject to no authority, to enjoy their liberty, that is, in its essence, to live just as they please."

THE SILVERADO SQUATTERS

The scene of this little book is on a high mountain. There are, indeed, many higher; there are many of a nobler outline. It is no place of pilgrimage for the summary globe-trotter; but to one who lives upon its sides, Mount Saint Helena soon becomes a centre of interest. It is the Mont Blanc of one section of the Californian Coast Range, none of its near neighbours rising to one-half its altitude. It looks down on much green, intricate country. It feeds in the spring-time many splashing brooks. From its summit you must have an excellent lesson of geography: seeing, to the south, San Francisco Bay, with Tamalpais on the one hand and Monte Diablo on the other; to the west, and thirty miles away, the open ocean; eastward, across the corn-lands and thick tule swamps of Sacramento Valley, to where the Central Pacific railroad begins to climb the sides of the Sierras; and northward, for what I know, the white head of Shasta looking down on Oregon. Three counties, Napa County, Lake County, and Sonoma County, march across its cliffy shoulders. Its naked peak stands nearly four thousand five hundred feet above the sea; its sides are fringed with forest; and the soil, where it is bare, glows warm with cinnabar.

Life in its shadow goes rustically forward. Bucks, and bears, and rattlesnakes, and former mining operations, are the staple of men's talk. Agriculture has only begun to mount above the valley. And though in a few years from now the whole district may be smiling with farms, passing trains shaking the mountain to the heart, many-windowed hotels lighting up the night like factories, and a prosperous city occupying the site of sleepy Calistoga; yet in the meantime, around the foot of that mountain the silence of nature reigns in a great measure unbroken, and the people of hill and valley go sauntering about their business as in the days before the flood.

To reach Mount Saint Helena from San Francisco, the traveller has twice to cross the bay: once by the busy Oakland ferry, and again, after an hour or so of the railway, from Vallejo junction to Vallejo. Thence he takes rail once more to mount the long green strath of Napa Valley.

In all the contractions and expansions of that inland sea, the Bay of San Francisco, there can be few drearier scenes than the Vallejo Ferry. Bald shores and a low, bald islet enclose the sea; through the narrows the tide bubbles, muddy like a river. When we made the passage (bound, although yet we knew it not, for Silverado) the steamer jumped, and the black buoys were dancing in the jabble;[1] the ocean breeze blew killing chill; and, although the upper sky was still unflecked with vapour, the sea fogs were pouring in from seaward, over the hill-tops of Marin County, in one great, shapeless, silver cloud.

South Vallejo is typical of many Californian towns. It was a blunder; the site has proved untenable; and, although it is still such a young place by the scale of Europe, it has already begun to be deserted for its neighbour and namesake, North Vallejo. A long pier, a number of drinking-saloons, a hotel of a great size, marshy pools where the frogs keep up their croaking, and even at high noon the entire absence of any human face or voice — these are the marks of South Vallejo. Yet there was a tall building beside the pier, labelled the *Star Flour Mills*; and sea-going, full-rigged ships lay close alongshore, waiting for their cargo. Soon these would be plunging round the Horn, soon the flour from the Star Flour Mills would be landed on the wharves of Liverpool. For that, too, is one of England's outposts; thither, to this gaunt mill, across the At-

---

1. The word "jabble" provoked a question from Richard Watson Gilder, editor of the *Century Magazine* in which this text was first published but Stevenson assured him it was right — as indeed it is, meaning a splashing or dashing in small waves or ripples.

lantic and Pacific deeps and round about the icy Horn, this crowd of great, three-masted, deep-sea ships come, bringing nothing, and return with bread.

The Frisby House, for that was the name of the hotel, was a place of fallen fortunes, like the town. It was now given up to labourers, and partly ruinous. At dinner there was the ordinary display of what is called in the west a *two-bit house:* the tablecloth checked red and white, the plague of flies, the wire hencoops over the dishes, the great variety and invariable vileness of the food, and the rough, coatless men devouring it in silence. In our bedroom the stove would not burn, though it would smoke; and while one window would not open, the other would not shut. There was a view on a bit of empty road, a few dark houses, a donkey wandering with its shadow on a slope, and a blink of sea, with a tall ship lying anchored in the moonlight. All about that dreary inn frogs sang their ungainly chorus.

Early the next morning we mounted the hill along a wooden footway, bridging one marish spot after another. Here and there, as we ascended, we passed a house embowered in white roses. More of the bay became apparent, and soon the blue peak of Tamalpais rose above the green level of the island opposite. It told us we were still but a little way from the city of the Golden Gates, already, at that hour, beginning to awake among the sandhills. It called to us over the waters as with the voice of a bird. Its stately head, blue as a sapphire on the paler azure of the sky, spoke to us of wider outlooks and the bright Pacific. For Tamalpais stands sentry, like a lighthouse, over the Golden Gates, between the bay and the open ocean, and looks down indifferently on both. Even as we saw and hailed it from Vallejo, seamen, far out at sea, were scanning it with shaded eyes; and, as if to answer to the thought, one of the great ships below began silently to clothe herself with white sails, homeward bound for England.

For some way beyond Vallejo the railway led us through bald green pastures. On the west the rough highlands of Marin shut off the ocean; in the midst, in long, straggling, gleaming arms, the bay died out among the grass; there were few trees and few enclosures; the sun shone wide over open uplands, the displumed hills stood clear against the sky. But by and by these hills began to draw nearer on either hand, and first thicket and then wood began to clothe their sides; and soon we were away from all signs of the sea's neighbourhood, mounting an inland, irrigated valley. A great variety of oaks stood, now severally, now in a becoming grove, among the fields and vineyards. The towns were compact, in about equal proportions, of bright, new wooden houses and great and growing forest trees; and the chapel-bell on the engine sounded most festally that sunny Sunday, as we drew up at one green town after another, with the townsfolk trooping in their Sunday's best to see the strangers, with the sun sparkling on the clean houses, and great domes of foliage humming overhead in the breeze.

This pleasant Napa Valley is, at its north end, blockaded by our mountain. There, at Calistoga, the railroad ceases, and the traveller who intends faring farther, to the Geysers or to the springs in Lake County, must cross the spurs of the mountain by stage. Thus, Mount Saint Helena is not only a summit, but a frontier; and, up to the time of writing, it has stayed the progress of the iron horse.

In the Valley

CALISTOGA

It is difficult for a European to imagine Calistoga, the whole place is so new, and of such an Occidental pattern; the very name, I hear, was invented at a supper-party by the man who found the springs.[1]

The railroad and the highway come up the valley about parallel to one another. The street of Calistoga joins them, perpendicular to both — a wide street, with bright, clean, low houses, here and there a verandah over the sidewalk, here and there a horse-post, here and there lounging townsfolk. Other streets are marked out, and most likely named; for these towns in the New World begin with a firm resolve to grow larger, Washington and Broadway, and then First and Second, and so forth, being boldly plotted out as soon as the community indulges in a plan. But, in the meanwhile, all the life and most of the houses of Calistoga are concentrated upon that street between the railway station and the road. I never heard it called by any name, but I will hazard a guess that it is either Wash-

1. Long after the springs were discovered, the site was owned by Sam Brannan, a Mormon real estate promoter who planned to develop it as a resort. According to a popular story, he intended to declare that he would make the place California's equivalent of the New York spa Saratoga, but in a moment of enthusiasm, probably abetted by liquor, he instead stated, "I'll make this place the Calistoga of Sarifornia." The story may be apocryphal; perhaps Brannan simply called the place Calistoga in the typical American style of combining two well-known names to create a new but suggestively connotative one.

ington or Broadway. Here are the blacksmith's, the chemist's, the general merchant's, and Kong Sam Kee, the Chinese laundryman's; here, probably, is the office of the local paper (for the place has a paper — they all have papers); and here certainly is one of the hotels, Cheeseborough's, whence the daring Foss, a man dear to legend, starts his horses for the Geysers.[2]

It must be remembered that we are here in a land of stage-drivers and highwaymen: a land, in that sense, like England a hundred years ago. The highway robber — road-agent, he is quaintly called — is still busy in these parts. The fame of Vasquez is still young.[3] Only a few years go, the Lakeport stage was robbed a mile or two from Calistoga. In 1879, the dentist of Mendocino City, fifty miles away upon the coast, suddenly threw off the garments of his trade, like Grindoff, in *The Miller and His Men*, and flamed forth in his second dress as a captain of banditti.[4] A great robbery was followed by a long chase, a chase of days, if not of weeks, among the intricate hill-country; and the chase was followed by much desultory fighting, in which several — and the dentist, I believe, amongst the number — bit the dust. The grass was springing for the first time, nourished upon their blood, when I arrived in Calistoga. I am reminded of another highwayman of that same year. "He had been unwell," so ran his humorous defence, "and the doctor told him to take something, so he took the express-box."

The cultus of the stage-coachman always flourishes highest where there are thieves on the road, and where the guard travels armed, and the stage is not only a link between coun-

2. "Colonel" Clark Foss was locally famous for his swift, sure handling of his team and stagecoach over the mountainous toll road that he controlled.

3. See p. 162, n. 2.

4. Isaac Pocock's two-act melodrama *The Miller and His Men* (1813) deals with a villainous miller who is also the leader of a band of scoundrels. It is one of the dramas that Stevenson staged as a child in the toy theater he celebrates in "A Penny Plain and Twopence Coloured." The character of Grindoff would naturally have delighted the creator of Deacon Brodie and of Dr. Jekyll and Mr. Hyde.

try and city, and the vehicle of news, but has a faint warfaring aroma, like a man who should be brother to a soldier. California boasts her famous stage-drivers, and among the famous Foss is not forgotten. Along the unfenced, abominable mountain roads, he launches his team with small regard to human life or the doctrine of probabilities. Flinching travellers, who behold themselves coasting eternity at every corner, look with natural admiration at their driver's huge, impassive, fleshy countenance. He has the very face for the driver in Sam Weller's anecdote, who upset the election party at the required point.[5] Wonderful tales are current of his readiness and skill. One in particular, of how one of his horses fell at a ticklish passage of the road, and how Foss let slip the reins, and, driving over the fallen animal, arrived at the next stage with only three. This I relate as I heard it, without guarantee.

I only saw Foss once, though, strange as it may sound, I have twice talked with him. He lives out of Calistoga, at a ranche[6] called Fossville. One evening, after he was long gone home, I dropped into Cheeseborough's, and was asked if I should like to speak with Mr. Foss. Supposing that the interview was impossible, and that I was merely called upon to subscribe the general sentiment, I boldly answered "Yes." Next moment, I had one instrument at my ear, another at my mouth, and found myself, with nothing in the world to say, conversing with a man several miles off among desolate hills. Foss rapidly and somewhat plaintively brought the conversation to an end; and he returned to his night's grog at Fossville, while I strolled forth again on Calistoga high street. But it was an odd thing that here, on what we are accustomed to consider the very skirts of civilisation, I should have used the telephone for the

5. The adventure of Sam Weller's father is narrated by Dickens in *The Posthumous Papers of the Pickwick Club*, I, xiii; and the elder Weller is described (I, x) by his son: "My father, sir, wos a coachman. A widower he wos, and fat enough for anything — uncommon fat, to be sure . . . wery smart — top boots on — nosegay in his button-hole, broad-brimmed tile — green shawl — quite the gen'lm'n."

6. An anglicized form of "rancho" and an alternative of the more common "ranch."

first time in my civilised career. So it goes in these young countries; telephones, and telegraphs, and newspapers, and advertisements running far ahead among the Indians and the grizzly bears.

Alone, on the other side of the railway, stands the Springs Hotel, with its attendant cottages. The floor of the valley is extremely level to the very roots of the hills; only here and there a hillock, crowned with pines, rises like the barrow of some chieftain famed in war; and right against one of these hillocks is the Springs Hotel — is or was; for since I was there the place has been destroyed by fire, and has risen again from its ashes. A lawn runs about the house, and the lawn is in its turn surrounded by a system of little five-roomed cottages, each with a verandah and a weedy palm before the door. Some of the cottages are let to residents, and these are wreathed in flowers. The rest are occupied by ordinary visitors to the hotel; and a very pleasant way this is, by which you have a little country cottage of your own, without domestic burthens, and by the day or week.

The whole neighbourhood of Mount Saint Helena is full of sulphur and of boiling springs. The Geysers are famous; they were the great health resort of the Indians before the coming of the whites. Lake County is dotted with spas; Hot Springs and White Sulphur Springs are the names of two stations on the Napa Valley railroad; and Calistoga itself seems to repose on a mere film above a boiling, subterranean lake. At one end of the hotel enclosure are the springs from which it takes its name, hot enough to scald a child seriously while I was there. At the other end, the tenant of a cottage sank a well, and there also the water came up boiling. It keeps this end of the valley as warm as a toast. I have gone across to the hotel a little after five in the morning, when a sea-fog from the Pacific was hanging thick and grey, and dark and dirty overhead, and found the thermometer had been up before me, and had already climbed among the nineties; and in the stress of the day it was sometimes too hot to move about.

But in spite of this heat from above and below, doing one on both sides, Calistoga was a pleasant place to dwell in; beautifully green, for it was then that favoured moment in the Californian year, when the rains are over and the dusty summer has not yet set in; often visited by fresh airs, now from the mountain, now across Sonoma from the sea; very quiet, very idle, very silent but for the breezes and the cattle-bells afield. And there was something satisfactory in the sight of that great mountain that enclosed us to the north: whether it stood robed in sunshine, quaking to its topmost pinnacle with the heat and brightness of the day; or whether it set itself to weaving vapours, wisp after wisp growing, trembling, fleeting, and fading in the blue.

The tangled, woody, and almost trackless foothills that enclose the valley, shutting it off from Sonoma on the west, and from Yolo on the east[7] —rough as they were in outline, dug out by winter streams, crowned by cliffy bluffs and nodding pine-trees — were dwarfed into satellites by the bulk and bearing of Mount Saint Helena. She over-towered them by two-thirds of her own stature. She excelled them by the boldness of her profile. Her great bald summit, clear of trees and pasture, a cairn of quartz and cinnabar, rejected kinship with the dark and shaggy wilderness of lesser hill-tops.

7. The counties that flank Napa County, in which Calistoga is situated.

THE PETRIFIED FOREST

We drove off from the Springs Hotel about three in the afternoon. The sun warmed me to the heart. A broad, cool wind streamed pauselessly down the valley, laden with perfume. Up at the top stood Mount Saint Helena, a bulk of mountain, bare atop, with tree-fringed spurs, and radiating warmth. Once we saw it framed in a grove of tall and exquisitely graceful white oaks, in line and colour a finished composition. We passed a cow stretched by the roadside, her bell slowly beating time to the movement of her ruminating jaws, her big red face crawled over by half a dozen flies, a monument of content.

A little farther, and we struck to the left up a mountain road, and for two hours threaded one valley after another, green, tangled, full of noble timber, giving us every now and again a sight of Mount Saint Helena and the blue hilly distance, and crossed by many streams, through which we splashed to the carriage-step. To the right or the left, there was scarce any trace of man but the road we followed; I think we passed but one ranchero's house in the whole distance, and that was closed and smokeless. But we had the society of these bright streams — dazzlingly clear as is their wont, splashing from the wheels in diamonds, and striking a lively coolness through the sunshine. And what with the innumerable variety of greens, the masses of foliage tossing in the breeze, the glimpses of distance, the descents into seemingly impenetrable thickets, the continual dodging of the road which made haste to plunge again into the covert, we had a fine sense of woods, and spring-time, and the open air.

Our driver gave me a lecture by the way on Californian trees — a thing I was much in need of, having fallen among painters who know the name of nothing, and Mexicans who know the name of nothing in English. He taught me the madrona, the manzanita, the buck-eye, the maple; he showed me the crested mountain quail; he showed me where some young redwoods were already spiring heavenwards from the ruins of the old; for in this district all had already perished: redwoods and redskins, the two noblest indigenous living things, alike condemned.

At length, in a lonely dell, we came on a huge wooden gate with a sign upon it like an inn. "The Petrified Forest. Proprietor: C. Evans," ran the legend. Within, on a knoll of sward, was the house of the proprietor, and another smaller house hard by to serve as a museum, where photographs and petrifactions were retailed. It was a pure little isle of touristry among these solitary hills.

The proprietor was a brave old white-faced Swede. He had wandered this way, Heaven knows how, and taken up his acres — I forget how many years ago — all alone, bent double with sciatica, and with six bits in his pocket and an axe upon his shoulder. Long, useless years of seafaring had thus discharged him at the end, penniless and sick. Without doubt he had tried his luck at the diggings, and got no good from that; without doubt he had loved the bottle, and lived the life of Jack ashore. But at the end of these adventures, here he came; and, the place hitting his fancy, down he sat to make a new life of it, far from crimps and the salt sea. And the very sight of his ranche had done him good. It was "the handsomest spot in the Californy mountains." "Isn't it handsome, now?" he said. Every penny he makes goes into that ranche to make it handsomer. Then the climate, with the sea-breeze every afternoon in the hottest summer weather, had gradually cured the sciatica; and his sister and niece were now domesticated with him for company — or, rather, the niece came only once in the two days, teaching music the meanwhile in the valley. And then for a last piece of luck, "the handsomest spot in the Californy mountains" had produced a petrified forest, which Mr. Evans now shows at the modest figure of half a dollar a head, or two-thirds of his capital when he first came there with an axe and a sciatica.

This tardy favourite of fortune — hobbling a little, I think, as if in memory of the sciatica, but with not a trace that I can remember of the sea — thoroughly ruralised from head to foot, proceeded to escort us up the hill behind his house.

"Who first found the forest?" asked my wife.

"The first? I was that man," said he. "I was cleaning up the pasture for my beasts, when I found *this*" — kicking a great redwood, seven feet in diameter, that lay there on its side, hollow heart, clinging lumps of bark, all changed into grey stone, with veins of quartz between what had been the layers of the wood.

"Were you surprised?"

"Surprised? No! What would I be surprised about? What did I know about petrifactions — following the sea? Petrifaction! There was no such word in my language! I knew about putrefaction, though! I thought it was a stone; so would you if you was cleaning up pasture."

And now he had a theory of his own, which I did not quite grasp, except that the trees had not "grewed" there. But he mentioned, with evident pride, that he differed from all the scientific people who had visited the spot; and he flung about such words as "tufa" and "silica" with careless freedom.

When I mentioned I was from Scotland, "My old country," he said; "my old country" — with a smiling look and a tone of real affection in his voice. I was mightily surprised, for he was obviously Scandinavian, and begged him to explain. It seemed he had learned his English and done nearly all his sailing in Scottish ships. "Out of Glasgow," said he, "or Greenock; but that's all the same — they all hail from Glasgow." And he was so pleased with me for being a Scotsman, and his adopted compatriot, that he made me a present of a very beautiful piece of petrifaction — I believe the most beautiful and portable he had.

Here was a man, at least, who was a Swede, a Scot, and an American, acknowledging some kind allegiance to three lands. Mr. Wallace's Scoto-Circassian will not fail to come before the reader.[1] I have myself met and spoken with a Fifeshire German, whose combination of abominable accents struck me dumb. But, indeed, I think we all belong to many countries. And perhaps this habit of much travel, and the engendering of scattered friendships, may prepare the euthanasia of ancient nations.

And the forest itself? Well, on a tangled, briary hillside — for the pasture would bear a little further cleaning up, to my eyes — there lie scattered thickly various lengths of petrified trunk, such as the one already mentioned. It is very curious, of course, and ancient enough, if that were all. Doubtless the heart of the geologist beats quicker at the sight; but, for my part, I was mightily unmoved. Sight-seeing is the art of disappointment.

> 'There's nothing under heaven so blue,
> That's fairly worth the travelling to.'[2]

But, fortunately, Heaven rewards us with many agreeable prospects and adventures by the way; and sometimes, when we go out to see a petrified forest, prepares a far more delightful curiosity in the form of Mr. Evans, whom may all prosperity attend throughout a long and green old age.

1. Sir Donald Mackenzie Wallace, a foreign correspondent for the London *Times*, told in his book *Russia* (1877) of encountering near the Black Sea a descendant of the Moslems of Circassia who as a child had been converted by a Scottish missionary and given the name John Abercrombie. Despite his Circassian features, the old man told Wallace, "I'm a Scotchman tae!"

2. From "A Song of the Open Road," which Stevenson wrote in 1878 and published entire in *Underwoods* in 1887.

NAPA WINE

I was interested in Californian wine. Indeed, I am interested in all wines, and have been all my life, from the raisin-wine that a school-fellow kept secreted in his play-box up to my last discovery, those notable Valtellines,[1] that once shone upon the board of Cæsar.

Some of us, kind old Pagans, watch with dread the shadows falling on the age: how the unconquerable worm[2] invades the sunny terraces of France, and Bordeaux is no more, and the Rhone a mere Arabia Petræa. Château Neuf is dead, and I have never tasted it; Hermitage — a hermitage indeed from all life's sorrows — lies expiring by the river. And in the place of these imperial elixirs, beautiful to every sense, gem-hued, flower-scented, dream-compellers: — behold upon the quays at Cette[3] the chemicals arrayed; behold the analyst at Marseilles, raising

1. Solid-bodied red wines from Lombardy, near the Swiss border. Stevenson presumably came to know them in Davos while writing *The Silverado Squatters*. In classic times the comparable Rhaetic wine came from this region, and Suetonius calls it Augustus' favorite.

2. This term, playfully inverting Poe's "The Conqueror Worm" that overwhelms man, is particularly suitable to phylloxera, the root-burrowing louse that during the 1860's and 1870's ravaged French vineyards. Although the effects were devastating, Stevenson exaggerated about Bordeaux and the Rhone Valley, and even Château Neuf (in its post-phylloxera vintages more commonly called Châteauneuf-du-Pape) and Hermitage did not die out.

3. This seaport, about 100 miles west of Marseilles, was known not only for bulk handling of wine shipments and for the manufacture and export of chemicals but, worse yet, for unscrupulous mixture of these activities. Stendhal said that "with wine, sugar, iron filings, and certain floral essences they make here the wines of all countries," and a respectable wine-merchant of the 1870's declared that the great magician Houdin "would not be equal to such transformations" as went on in the city. Later the city's ethics changed, as did its name, to Sète.

hands in obsecration, attesting god Lyæus,[4] and the vats staved in, and the dishonest wines poured forth among the sea. It is not Pan only; Bacchus, too, is dead.

If wine is to withdraw its most poetic countenance, the sun of the white dinner-cloth, a deity to be invoked by two or three, all fervent, hushing their talk, degusting tenderly, and storing reminiscences — for a bottle of good wine, like a good act, shines ever in the retrospect — if wine is to desert us, go thy ways, old Jack! [5] Now we begin to have compunctions, and look back at the brave bottles squandered upon dinner-parties, where the guests drank grossly, discussing politics the while, and even the schoolboy "took his whack," like liquorice-water. And at the same time we look timidly forward, with a spark of hope, to where the new lands, already weary of producing gold, begin to green with vineyards. A nice point in human history falls to be decided by Californian and Australian wines.

Wine in California is still in the experimental stage; and when you taste a vintage, grave economical questions are involved. The beginning of vine-planting is like the beginning of mining for the precious metals: the wine-grower also "prospects." One corner of land after another is tried with one kind of grape after another. This is a failure; that is better; a third best. So, bit by bit, they grope about for their Clos Vougeot and Lafitte. Those lodes and pockets of earth, more precious than the precious ores, that yield inimitable fragrance and soft fire; those virtuous Bonanzas, where the soil has sublimated under sun and stars to something finer, and the wine is bottled poetry: these still lie undiscovered; chaparral conceals, thicket embowers them; the miner chips the rock and wanders farther, and the grizzly muses undisturbed. But there they bide

4. An alternate name for Dionysus, whom the honest analyst of Marseilles supplicates and by whom he also swears to the genuineness of a vintage or to the false contents of certain vats that should be staved and destroyed in the sea.

5. An allusion to Falstaff's playful, self-pitying tribute to his own good manhood (*Henry IV, Part I,* II, iv, 128).

their hour, awaiting their Columbus; and nature nurses and prepares them. The smack of Californian earth shall linger on the palate of your grandson.

Meanwhile the wine is merely a good wine; the best that I have tasted — better than a Beaujolais, and not unlike. But the trade is poor; it lives from hand to mouth, putting its all into experiments, and forced to sell its vintages. To find one properly matured, and bearing its own name, is to be fortune's favourite.

Bearing its own name, I say, and dwell upon the innuendo.

"You want to know why California wine is not drunk in the States?" a San Francisco wine-merchant said to me, after he had shown me through his premises. "Well, here's the reason."

And opening a large cupboard, fitted with many little drawers, he proceeded to shower me all over with a great variety of gorgeously tinted labels, blue, red, or yellow, stamped with crown or coronet, and hailing from such a profusion of *clos* and *châteaux*, that a single department could scarce have furnished forth the names. But it was strange that all looked unfamiliar.

"Châteaux X——?" said I. "I never heard of that."

"I daresay not," said he. "I had been reading one of X——'s novels."

They were all castles in Spain! But that sure enough is the reason why California wine is not drunk in the States.

Napa Valley has been long a seat of the wine-growing industry. It did not here begin, as it does too often, in the low valley lands along the river, but took at once to the rough foothills, where alone it can expect to prosper. A basking inclination, and stones, to be a reservoir of the day's heat, seem necessary to the soil for wine; the grossness of the earth must be evaporated, its marrow daily melted and refined for ages; until at length these clods that break below our footing, and to the eye appear but common earth, are truly and to the perceiving mind a masterpiece of nature. The dust of

Richebourg, [6] which the wind carries away, what an apotheosis of the dust! Not man himself can seem a stranger child of that brown, friable powder, than the blood and sun in that old flask behind the fagots.

A Californian vineyard, one of man's outposts in the wilderness, has features of its own. There is nothing here to remind you of the Rhine or Rhone, of the low Côte d'Or, or the infamous and scabby deserts of Champagne; but all is green, solitary, covert. We visited two of them, Mr. Schram's and Mr. M'Eckron's, sharing the same glen.

Some way down the valley below Calistoga we turned sharply to the south and plunged into the thick of the wood. A rude trail rapidly mounting; a little stream tinkling by on the one hand, big enough perhaps after the rains, but already yielding up its life; overhead and on all sides a bower of green and tangled thicket, still fragrant and still flower-bespangled by the early season, where thimble-berry played the part of our English hawthorn, and the buck-eyes were putting forth their twisted horns of blossom: through all this we struggled toughly upwards, canted to and fro by the roughness of the trail, and continually switched across the face by sprays of leaf or blossom. The last is no great inconvenience at home; but here in California it is a matter of some moment. For in all woods and by every wayside there prospers an abominable shrub or weed, called poison-oak, whose very neighbourhood is venomous to some, and whose actual touch is avoided by the most impervious.

The two houses, with their vineyards, stood each in a green niche of its own in this steep and narrow forest dell. Though they were so near, there was already a good difference in level; and Mr. M'Eckron's head must be a long way under the feet of Mr. Schram. No more had been cleared than was necessary for cultivation; close around each oasis ran the tangled wood;

6. A major vineyard of Vosne-Romanee, just south of Dijon, from whose soil comes one of the world's most famous and expensive wines.

the glen enfolds them; there they lie basking in sun and silence, concealed from all but the clouds and the mountain birds.

Mr. M'Eckron's is a bachelor establishment; a little bit of a wooden house, a small cellar hard by in the hillside, and a patch of vines planted and tended single-handed by himself. He had but recently begun; his vines were young, his business young also; but I thought he had the look of a man who succeeds. He hailed from Greenock: he remembered his father putting him inside Mons Meg, [7] and that touched me home; and we exchanged a word or two of Scots, which pleased me more than you would fancy.

Mr. Schram's, on the other hand, is the oldest vineyard in the valley, eighteen years old, I think; yet he began a penniless barber, and even after he had broken ground up here with his black malvoisies, continued for long to tramp the valley with his razor. Now, his place is the picture of prosperity; stuffed birds in the verandah, cellars far dug into the hillside, and resting on pillars like a bandit's cave: — all trimness, varnish, flowers, and sunshine, among the tangled wildwood. Stout, smiling Mrs. Schram, who has been to Europe and apparently all about the States for pleasure, entertained Fanny in the verandah while I was tasting wines in the cellar. To Mr. Schram this was a solemn office; his serious gusto warmed my heart; prosperity had not yet wholly banished a certain neophyte and girlish trepidation, and he followed every sip and read my face with proud anxiety. I tasted all. I tasted every variety and shade of Schramberger, red and white Schramberger, Burgundy Schramberger, Schramberger Hock, Schramberger Golden Chasselas, the latter with a notable bouquet, and I fear to think how many more. Much of it goes to London — most, I think; and Mr. Schram has a great notion of the English taste.

In this wild spot I did not feel the sacredness of ancient cultivation. It was still raw; it was no Marathon, and no

7. The great 15th-century Scottish cannon, now located at Edinburgh Castle, treated by the Scottish people as a symbol of that on which their safety has depended.

Johannisberg; yet the stirring sunlight, and the growing vines, and the vats and bottles in the cavern, made a pleasant music for the mind. Here, also, earth's cream was being skimmed and garnered; and the London customers can taste, such as it is, the tang of the earth in this green valley. So local, so quintessential is a wine, that it seems the very birds in the verandah might communicate a flavour, and that romantic cellar influence the bottle next to be uncorked in Pimlico, and the smile of jolly Mr. Schram might mantle in the glass.

But these are but experiments. All things in this new land are moving farther on: the wine-vats and the miner's blasting tools but picket for a night, like Bedouin pavilions; and to-morrow, to fresh woods! This stir of change and these perpetual echoes of the moving footfall haunt the land. Men move eternally, still chasing Fortune; and, Fortune found, still wander. As we drove back to Calistoga the road lay empty of mere passengers, but its green side was dotted with the camps of travelling families: one cumbered with a great waggonful of household stuff, settlers going to occupy a ranche they had taken up in Mendocino, or perhaps Tehama County; another, a party in dust coats, men and women, whom we found camped in a grove on the roadside, all on pleasure bent, with a Chinaman to cook for them, and who waved their hands to us as we drove by.

THE SCOT ABROAD

A few pages back I wrote that a man belonged, in these days, to a variety of countries; but the old land is still the true love, the others are but pleasant infidelities. Scotland is indefinable; it has no unity except upon the map. Two languages, many dialects, innumerable forms of piety, and countless local patriotisms and prejudices, part us among ourselves more widely than the extreme east and west of that great continent of America. When I am at home, I feel a man from Glasgow to be something like a rival, a man from Barra to be more than half a foreigner. Yet let us meet in some far country, and, whether we hail from the braes of Manor or the braes of Mar, some ready-made affection joins us on the instant. It is not race. Look at us. One is Norse, one Celtic, and another Saxon. It is not community of tongue. We have it not among ourselves; and we have it, almost to perfection, with English, or Irish, or American. It is no tie of faith, for we detest each other's errors. And yet somewhere, deep down in the heart of each one of us, something yearns for the old land and the old kindly people.

Of all mysteries of the human heart this is perhaps the most inscrutable. There is no special loveliness in that grey country, with its rainy, sea-beat archipelago; its fields of dark mountains; its unsightly places, black with coal; its treeless, sour, unfriendly-looking corn-lands; its quaint, grey, castled city, where the bells clash of a Sunday, and the wind squalls, and the salt showers fly and beat. I do not even know if I desire to live there; but let me hear, in some far land, a kindred voice sing out, "O why left I my hame?" and it seems at once as if no beauty under the kind heavens, and no society of the wise and good, can repay me for my absence from my country. And though I think I would rather die elsewhere, yet in my heart of hearts I long to be buried among good Scots clods. I will say it fairly, it grows on me with every year: there are no stars so lovely as Edinburgh street-lamps. When I forget thee, Auld Reekie, may my right hand forget its cunning!

The happiest lot on earth is to be born a Scotsman. You must pay for it in many ways, as for all other advantages on earth. You have to learn the Paraphrases and the Shorter Catechism; you generally take to drink; your youth, as far as I can find out, is a time of louder war against society, of more outcry and tears and turmoil, than if you had been born, for instance, in England. But somehow life is warmer and closer; the hearth burns more redly; the lights of home shine softer on the rainy street; the very names, endeared in verse and music, cling nearer round our hearts. An Englishman may meet an Englishman to-morrow, upon Chimborazo, and neither of them cares; but when the Scots wine-grower told me of Mons Meg it was like magic.

"From the dim shieling on the misty island
  Mountains divide us, and a world of seas;
Yet still our hearts are true, our hearts are Highland,
  And we, in dreams, behold the Hebrides." [1]

And, Highland and Lowland, all our hearts are Scottish.

Only a few days after I had seen M'Eckron, a message reached me in my cottage. It was a Scotsman who had come down a long way from the hills to market. He had heard there

[1]. Stevenson's recollection of this anonymous poem, "Canadian Boat Song," is somewhat garbled. The third line, for instance, should read: "Yet still the blood is strong, the heart is Highland." The poem is ostensibly a translation from Gaelic of a work sung by St. Lawrence boat-rowers far from their native Scotland. Printed in *Blackwood's* (1829), it has been variously attributed to Professor John Wilson ("Christopher North"), John G. Lockhart, and John Galt.

was a countryman in Calistoga, and came round to the hotel to see him. We said a few words to each other; we had not much to say — should never have seen each other had we stayed at home, separated alike in space and in society; and then we shook hands, and he went his way again to his ranche among the hills, and that was all.

Another Scotsman there was, a resident, who for the mere love of the common country, douce, serious, religious man, drove me all about the valley, and took as much interest in me as if I had been his son: more, perhaps; for the son has faults too keenly felt, while the abstract countryman is perfect — like a whiff of peats.

And there was yet another. Upon him I came suddenly, as he was calmly entering my cottage, his mind quite evidently bent on plunder: a man of about fifty, filthy, ragged, roguish, with a chimney-pot hat and a tail-coat, and a pursing of his mouth that might have been envied by an elder of the kirk. He had just such a face as I have seen a dozen times behind the plate.

"Hullo, sir!" I cried. "Where are you going?"

He turned round without a quiver.

"You're a Scotsman, sir?" he said gravely. "So am I; I come from Aberdeen. This is my card," presenting me with a piece of pasteboard which he had raked out of some gutter in the period of the rains. "I was just examining this palm," he continued, indicating the misbegotten plant before our door, "which is the largest sp*a*cimen I have yet observed in Califoarnia."

There were four or five larger within sight. But where was the use of argument? He produced a tape-line, made me help him to measure the tree at the level of the ground, and entered the figures in a large and filthy pocket-book, all with the gravity of Solomon. He then thanked me profusely, remarking that such little services were due between countrymen; shook hands with me, "for auld lang syne," as he said; and took himself solemnly away, radiating dirt and humbug as he went.[2]

A month or two after this encounter of mine, there came a Scot to Sacramento — perhaps from Aberdeen. Anyway, there never was any one more Scottish in this wide world. He could sing and dance — and drink, I presume; and he played the pipes with vigour and success. All the Scots in Sacramento became infatuated with him, and spent their spare time and money driving him about in an open cab, between drinks, while he blew himself scarlet at the pipes. This is a very sad story. After he had borrowed money from every one, he and his pipes suddenly disappeared from Sacramento, and when I last heard, the police were looking for him.

I cannot say how this story amused me, when I felt myself so thoroughly ripe on both sides to be duped in the same way.

It is at least a curious thing, to conclude, that the races which wander widest, Jews and Scots, should be the most clannish in the world. But perhaps these two are cause and effect: "For ye were strangers in the land of Egypt."

2. In the first printing in *Century Magazine* (November 1883, p. 31). there followed here two sentences: "A more impudent rascal I have never seen; and had he been American, I should have raged. But then — he came from Aberdeen."

With the Children of Israel

TO INTRODUCE MR. KELMAR

One thing in this new country very particularly strikes a stranger, and that is the number of antiquities. Already there have been many cycles of population succeeding each other, and passing away and leaving behind them relics. These, standing on into changed times, strike the imagination as forcibly as any pyramid or feudal tower. The towns, like the vineyards, are experimentally founded: they grow great and prosper by passing occasions; and when the lode comes to an end, and the miners move elsewhere, the town remains behind them, like Palmyra in the desert. I suppose there are, in no country in the world, so many deserted towns as here in California.

The whole neighbourhood of Mount Saint Helena, now so quiet and sylvan, was once alive with mining camps and villages. Here there would be two thousands souls under canvas; there one thousand or fifteen hundred ensconced, as if for ever, in a town of comfortable houses. But the luck had failed, the mines petered out; and the army of miners had departed, and left this quarter of the world to the rattlesnakes and deer and grizzlies, and to the slower but steadier advance of husbandry.

It was with an eye on one of these deserted places, Pine Flat, on the Geysers road, that we had come first to Calistoga. There is something singularly enticing in the idea of going, rent-free, into a ready-made house. And to the British mer-

chant, sitting at home at ease, it may appear that, with such
a roof over your head and a spring of clear water hard by,
the whole problem of the squatter's existence would be solved.
Food, however, has yet to be considered. I will go as far as
most people on tinned meats; some of the brightest moments
of my life were passed over tinned mulligatawny in the
cabin of a sixteen-ton schooner, storm-stayed in Portree Bay;
but after suitable experiments, I pronounce authoritatively
that man cannot live by tins alone. Fresh meat must be had
on an occasion. It is true that the great Foss, driving by along
the Geysers road, wooden-faced, but glorified with legend,
might have been induced to bring us meat, but the great Foss
could hardly bring us milk. To take a cow would have involved taking a field of grass and a milkmaid; after which it
would have been hardly worth while to pause, and we might
have added to our colony a flock of sheep and an experienced
butcher.

It is really very disheartening how we depend on other
people in this life. "*Mihi est propositum,*" as you may see by
the motto, "*idem quod regibus;*" [1] and behold, it cannot be carried out, unless I find a neighbour rolling in cattle.

Now, my principal adviser in this matter was one whom I
will call Kelmar. That was not what he called himself, but as
soon as I had set eyes on him, I knew it was or ought to be
his name; I am sure it will be his name among the angels.
Kelmar was the storekeeper, a Russian Jew, good-natured, in
a very thriving way of business, and, on equal terms, one of
the most serviceable of men. He also had something of the
expression of a Scottish country elder, who, by some pecu-
liarity, should chance to be a Hebrew. He had a projecting
under-lip, with which he continually smiled, or rather smirked.
Mrs. Kelmar was a singularly kind woman; and the oldest son

1. The motto is the quotation from Cicero that Stevenson had placed
on his title-page, whose second sentence he here adapts to himself by
putting it in the first person, present tense, to suggest that "my aim is
the same as that of kings."

had quite a dark and romantic bearing, and might be heard on summer evenings playing sentimental airs on the violin.

I had no idea, at the time I made his acquaintance, what an important person Kelmar was. But the Jew storekeepers of California, profiting at once by the needs and habits of the people, have made themselves in too many cases the tyrants of the rural population. Credit is offered, is pressed on the new customer, and when once he is beyond his depth, the tune changes, and he is from thenceforth a white slave. I believe, even from the little I saw, that Kelmar, if he chose to put on the screw, could send half the settlers packing in a radius of seven or eight miles round Calistoga. These are continually paying him, but are never suffered to get out of debt. He palms dull goods upon them, for they dare not refuse to buy; he goes and dines with them when he is on an outing, and no man is loudlier welcomed; he is their family friend, the director of their business, and, to a degree elsewhere unknown in modern days, their king.

For some reason, Kelmar always shook his head at the mention of Pine Flat, and for some days I thought he disapproved of the whole scheme and was proportionately sad. One fine morning, however, he met me, wreathed in smiles. He had found the very place for me — Silverado, another old mining town, right up the mountain. Rufe Hanson, the hunter, could take care of us — fine people the Hansons; we should be close to the Toll House, where the Lakeport stage called daily; it was the best place for my health, besides. Rufe had been consumptive, and was now quite a strong man, ain't it? In short, the place and all its accompaniments seemed made for us on purpose.

He took me to his back-door, whence, as from every point of Calistoga, Mount Saint Helena could be seen towering in the air. There, in the nick, just where the eastern foothills joined the mountain, and she herself began to rise above the zone of forest — there was Silverado. The name had already pleased me; the high station pleased me still more. I began to inquire with some eagerness. It was but a little while ago that Silverado was a great place. The mine — a silver mine, of course — had promised great things. There was quite a lively population, with several hotels and boarding-houses; and Kelmar himself had opened a branch store, and done extremely well — "Ain't it?" he said, appealing to his wife. And she said, "Yes; extremely well." Now there was no one living in the town but Rufe the hunter; and once more I heard Rufe's praises by the yard, and this time sung in chorus.

I could not help perceiving at the time that there was something underneath; that no unmixed desire to have us comfortably settled had inspired the Kelmars with this flow of words. But I was impatient to be gone, to be about my kingly projects; and when we were offered seats in Kelmar's waggon, I accepted on the spot. The plan of their next Sunday's outing took them, by good fortune, over the border into Lake County. They would carry us so far, drop us at the Toll House, present us to the Hansons, and call for us again on Monday morning early.

FIRST IMPRESSIONS OF SILVERADO

We were to leave by six precisely; that was solemnly pledged on both sides; and a messenger came to us the last thing at night, to remind us of the hour. But it was eight before we got clear of Calistoga: Kelmar, Mrs. Kelmar, a friend of theirs whom we named Abramina, her little daughter, my wife, myself, and, stowed away behind us, a cluster of ship's coffee-kettles. These last were highly ornamental in the sheen of their bright tin, but I could invent no reason for their presence. Our carriageful reckoned up, as near as we could get at it, some three hundred years to the six of us. Four of the six, besides, were Hebrews. But I never. in all my life, was conscious of so strong an atmosphere of holiday. No word was spoken but of pleasure; and even when we drove in silence, nods and smiles went round the party like refreshments.

The sun shone out of a cloudless sky. Close at the zenith rode the belated moon, still clearly visible, and, along one margin, even bright. The wind blew a gale from the north; the trees roared; the corn and the deep grass in the valley fled in whitening surges; the dust towered into the air along the road and dispersed like the smoke of battle. It was clear in our teeth from the first, and for all the windings of the road it managed to keep clear in our teeth until the end.

For some two miles we rattled through the valley, skirting the eastern foothills; then we struck off to the right, through haugh-land, and presently, crossing a dry water-course, entered the Toll Road, or, to be more local, entered on "the grade." The road mounts the near shoulder of Mount Saint Helena, bound northward into Lake County. In one place it skirts along the edge of a narrow and deep cañon, filled with trees, and I was glad, indeed, not to be driven at this point by the dashing Foss. Kelmar, with his unvarying smile, jogging to the motion of the trap, drove for all the world like a good, plain country clergyman at home; and I profess I blessed him unawares for his timidity.

Vineyards and deep meadows, islanded and framed with thicket, gave place more and more as we ascended to woods of oak and madrona, dotted with enormous pines. It was these pines, as they shot above the lower wood, that produced that pencilling of single trees I had so often remarked from the valley. Thence, looking up and from however far, each fir stands separate against the sky no bigger than an eyelash; and all together lend a quaint, fringed aspect to the hills. The oak is no baby; even the madrona, upon these spurs of Mount Saint Helena, comes to a fine bulk and ranks with forest trees; but the pines look down upon the rest for underwood. As Mount Saint Helena among her foothills, so these dark giants out-top their fellow-vegetables. Alas! if they had left the redwoods, the pines, in turn, would have been dwarfed. But the redwoods, fallen from their high estate, are serving as family bedsteads, or yet more humbly as field fences, along all Napa Valley.

A rough smack of resin was in the air, and a crystal mountain purity. It came pouring over these green slopes by the oceanful. The woods sang aloud, and gave largely of their healthful breath. Gladness seemed to inhabit these upper zones, and we had left indifference behind us in the valley. "I to the hills will lift mine eyes!" There are days in a life when thus to climb out of the lowlands seems like scaling heaven.[1]

1. In the first printing in *Century Magazine* (November 1883, p. 33) a new paragraph follows here: "Some way beyond the cañon, there stands a white house with *Saloon* painted on it, and a horse-trough with a spray of diamond water. On the other side of the road, we could see a few brown houses dotted in the bottom of the dell, and a great brown mill big as a factory, two stories high, and with tanks and ladders along the roof. This was Silverado mill and mill town; Lower Silverado, if you like; now long deserted and yielded up to squatters. Even the saloon was a saloon no longer; only its tenant, Old Wash, kept up the character of the place by the amount and strength of his potations."

As we continued to ascend, the wind fell upon us with increasing strength. It was a wonder how the two stout horses managed to pull us up that steep incline and still face the athletic opposition of the wind, or how their great eyes were able to endure the dust. Ten minutes after we went by, a tree fell, blocking the road; and even before us leaves were thickly strewn, and boughs had fallen, large enough to make the passage difficult. But now we were hard by the summit. The road crosses the ridge, just in the nick that Kelmar showed me from below, and then, without pause, plunges down a deep, thickly-wooded glen on the farther side. At the highest point a trail strikes up the main hill to the leftward; and that leads to Silverado. A hundred yards beyond, and in a kind of elbow of the glen, stands the Toll House Hotel. We came up the one side, were caught upon the summit by the whole weight of the wind as it poured over into Napa Valley, and a minute after had drawn up in shelter, but all buffeted and breathless, at the Toll House door.

A water-tank, and stables, and a grey house of two stories, with gable-ends and a verandah, are jammed hard against the hillside, just where a stream has cut for itself a narrow cañon, filled with pines. The pines go right up overhead; a little more and the stream might have played, like a fire-hose, on the Toll House roof. In front the ground drops as sharply as it rises behind. There is just room for the road and a sort of promontory of croquet ground, and then you can lean over the edge and look deep below you through the wood. I said croquet *ground*, not *green;* for the surface was of brown, beaten earth. The toll-bar itself was the only other note of originality: a long beam, turning on a post, and kept slightly horizontal by a counterweight of stones. Regularly about sundown this rude barrier was swung, like a derrick, across the road and made fast, I think, to a tree upon the farther side.

On our arrival there followed a gay scene in the bar. I was presented to Mr. Corwin, the landlord; to Mr. Jennings, the engineer, who lives there for his health; to Mr. Hoddy, a most pleasant little gentleman, once a member of the Ohio legislature, again the editor of a local paper, and now, with undiminished dignity, keeping the Toll House bar. I had a number of drinks and cigars bestowed on me, and enjoyed a famous opportunity of seeing Kelmar in his glory, friendly, radiant, smiling, steadily edging one of the ship's kettles on the reluctant Corwin. Corwin, plainly aghast, resisted gallantly, and for that bout victory crowned his arms.

At last we set forth for Silverado on foot. Kelmar and his jolly Jew girls were full of the sentiment of Sunday outings, breathed geniality and vagueness, and suffered a little vile boy from the hotel to lead them here and there about the woods.[2] For three people all so old, so bulky in body, and belonging to a race so venerable, they could not but surprise us by their extreme and almost imbecile youthfulness of spirit. They were only going to stay ten minutes at the Toll House; had they not twenty long miles of road before them on the other side? Stay to dinner? Not they! Put up the horses? Never. Let us attach them to the verandah by a wisp of straw-rope, such as would not have held a person's hat on that blustering day. And with all these protestations of hurry, they proved irresponsible like children. Kelmar himself, shrewd old Russian Jew, with a smirk that seemed just to have concluded a bargain to its satisfaction, intrusted himself and us devoutly to that boy. Yet the boy was patently fallacious; and for that matter a most unsympathetic urchin, raised apparently on gingerbread. He was bent on his own pleasure, nothing else; and Kelmar followed him to his ruin, with the same shrewd smirk. If the boy said there was "a hole there in the hill" — a hole, pure and simple, neither more nor less — Kelmar and his Jew girls would follow him a hundred yards to look com-

2. In the first printing in *Century Magazine* (November 1883, p. 34) this sentence is continued and another follows: ". . . without even explaining where he wished to go. So long as he might now and then draw up and descant upon the scenery to get his wind again, it was identically the same to that Ebrew Jew whether we ever arrived anywhere or not."

placently down that hole. For two hours we looked for houses; and for two hours they followed us, smelling trees, picking flowers, foisting false botany on the unwary. Had we taken five, with that vile lad to head them off on idle divagations, for five they would have smiled and stumbled through the woods.

However, we came forth at length, and as by accident, upon a lawn, sparse planted like an orchard, but with forest instead of fruit trees. That was the site of Silverado mining town. A piece of ground was levelled up, where Kelmar's store had been; and facing that we saw Rufe Hanson's house, still bearing on its front the legend *Silverado Hotel*. Not another sign of habitation. Silverado town had all been carted from the scene; one of the houses was now the school-house far down the road; one was gone here, one there, but all were gone away. It was now a sylvan solitude, and the silence was unbroken but by the great, vague voice of the wind. Some days before our visit, a grizzly bear had been sporting round the Hansons' chicken-house.

Mrs. Hanson was at home alone, we found. Rufe had been out after a "bar," had risen late, and was now gone, it did not clearly appear whither. Perhaps he had had wind of Kelmar's coming, and was now ensconced among the underwood, or watching us from the shoulder of the mountain. We, hearing there were no houses to be had, were for immediately giving up all hopes of Silverado. But this, somehow, was not to Kelmar's fancy. He first proposed that we should "camp someveres around, ain't it?" waving his hand cheerily as though to weave a spell; and when that was firmly rejected, he decided that we must take up house with the Hansons. Mrs. Hanson had been, from the first, flustered, subdued, and a little pale; but from this proposition she recoiled with haggard indignation. So did we, who would have preferred, in a manner of speaking, death. But Kelmar was not to be put by. He edged Mrs. Hanson into a corner, where for a long time he threatened her with his forefinger, like a character in Dickens; and the poor woman, driven to her entrenchments, at last remembered with a shriek that there were still some houses at the tunnel.

Thither we went; the Jews, who should already have been miles into Lake County, still cheerily accompanying us. For about a furlong we followed a good road along the hillside through the forest, until suddenly that road widened out and came abruptly to an end. A cañon, woody below, red, rocky, and naked overhead, was here walled across by a dump of rolling stones, dangerously steep, and from twenty to thirty feet in height. A rusty iron chute on wooden legs came flying, like a monstrous gargoyle, across the parapet. It was down this that they poured the precious ore; and below here the carts stood to wait their lading, and carry it millward down the mountain.

The whole cañon was so entirely blocked, as if by some rude guerilla fortification, that we could only mount by lengths of wooden ladder, fixed in the hillside. These led us round the farther corner of the dump; and when they were at an end, we still persevered over loose rubble and wading deep in poison-oak, till we struck a triangular platform, filling up the whole glen, and shut in on either hand by bold projections of the mountain. Only in front the place was open like the proscenium of a theatre, and we looked forth into a great realm of air, and down upon tree-tops and hill-tops, and far and near on wild and varied country. The place still stood as on the day it was deserted: a line of iron rails with a bifurcation; a truck in working order; a world of lumber, old wood, old iron; a blacksmith's forge on one side, half-buried in the leaves of dwarf madronas; and on the other, an old brown wooden house.

Fanny and I dashed at the house. It consisted of three rooms, and was so plastered against the hill, that one room was right atop of another, that the upper floor was more than twice as large as the lower, and that all three apartments must be entered from a different side and level. Not a window-sash remained. The door of the lower room was smashed, and one panel hung in splinters. We entered that, and found a fair amount of rubbish: sand and gravel that had been sifted in there by the mountain winds; straw, sticks, and stones; a table, a barrel; a plate-rack on the wall; two home-made bootjacks, signs of miners and their boots; and a pair of papers pinned on the boarding, headed respectively "Funnel No. 1," and "Funnel No. 2," but with the tails torn away.[3] The window, sashless of course, was choked with the green and sweetly smelling foliage of a bay; and through a chink in the floor, a spray of poison-oak had shot up and was handsomely prospering in the interior. It was my first care to cut away that poison-oak, Fanny standing by at a respectful distance. That was our first improvement by which we took possession.

The room immediately above could only be entered by a plank propped against the threshold, along which the intruder must foot it gingerly, clutching for support to sprays of poison-oak, the proper product of the country. Herein was, on either hand, a triple tier of beds, where miners had once lain; and the other gable was pierced by a sashless window and a doorless doorway opening on the air of heaven, five feet above the ground. As for the third room, which entered squarely from the ground level, but higher up the hill and farther up the cañon, it contained only rubbish and the uprights for another triple tier of beds.

The whole building was overhung by a bold, lionlike, red rock. Poison-oak, sweet bay trees, calcanthus, brush and chaparral, grew freely but sparsely all about it. In front, in the strong sunshine, the platform lay overstrewn with busy litter, as though the labours of the mine might begin again to-morrow in the morning.

Following back into the cañon, among the mass of rotting plant and through the flowering bushes, we came to a great crazy staging, with a wry windlass on the top; and clambering up, we could look into an open shaft, leading edgeways down

3. Since "Tunnel" is obviously intended, the word "Funnel" may be a printer's misreading of Stevenson's manuscript, unless Stevenson himself misread the papers in the cabin.

into the bowels of the mountain, trickling with water, and lit
by some stray sun-gleams, whence I know not. In that quiet
place the still far-away tinkle of the water-drops was loudly
audible. Close by, another shaft led edgeways up into the
superincumbent shoulder of the hill. It lay partly open; and
sixty or a hundred feet above our head we could see the strata
propped apart by solid wooden wedges, and a pine, half undermined, precariously nodding on the verge. Here also a
rugged, horizontal tunnel ran straight into the unsunned
bowels of the rock. This secure angle in the mountain's flank
was, even on this wild day, as still as my lady's chamber. But
in the tunnel a cold, wet draught tempestuously blew. Nor
have I ever known that place otherwise than cold and windy.[4]

Such was our first prospect of Juan Silverado. I own I had
looked for something different: a clique of neighbourly houses
on a village green, we shall say, all empty to be sure, but
swept and varnished; a trout stream brawling by; great elms or
chestnuts, humming with bees and nested in by song-birds;
and the mountains standing round about as at Jerusalem. Here,
mountain and house and the old tools of industry were all
alike rusty and down-falling. The hill was here wedged up,
and there poured forth its bowels in a spout of broken mineral;
man with his picks and powder, and nature with her own great
blasting tools of sun and rain, labouring together at the ruin
of that proud mountain. The view up the cañon was a glimpse
of devastation; dry red minerals sliding together, here and
there a crag, here and there dwarf thicket clinging in the general *glissade*, and over all a broken outline trenching on the
blue of heaven. Downwards indeed, from our rock eyrie, we
beheld the greener side of nature; and the bearing of the pines

4. In the first printing in *Century Magazine* (November 1883, p. 35)
a new paragraph follows here: "A little way back from there, some
clear cold water lay in a pool at the foot of a choked trough; and
forty or fifty feet higher up, through a thick jungle and hard by
another house where Chinamen had slept in the days of the prosperity
of Silverado, we were shown the intake of the pipe and the same bright
water welling from its spring."

and the sweet smell of bays and nutmegs commended themselves gratefully to our senses. One way and another, now the
die was cast. Silverado be it!

After we had got back to the Toll House, the Jews were
not long of striking forward. But I observed that one of the
Hanson lads came down, before their departure, and returned
with a ship's kettle. Happy Hansons! Nor was it until after
Kelmar was gone, if I remember rightly, that Rufe put in an
appearance to arrange the details of our installation.

The latter part of the day, Fanny and I sat in the verandah
of the Toll House, utterly stunned by the uproar of the wind
among the trees on the other side of the valley. Sometimes,
we would have it it was like a sea, but it was not various
enough for that; and again, we thought it like the roar of a
cataract, but it was too changeful for the cataract; and then
we would decide, speaking in sleepy voices, that it could be
compared with nothing but itself. My mind was entirely pre-
occupied by the noise. I hearkened to it by the hour, gapingly
hearkened, and let my cigarette go out. Sometimes the wind
would make a sally nearer hand, and send a shrill, whistling
crash among the foliage on our side of the glen; and sometimes
a back-draught would strike into the elbow where we sat, and
cast the gravel and torn leaves into our faces. But for the most
part, this great, streaming gale passed unweariedly by us into
Napa Valley, not two hundred yards away, visible by the tossing boughs, stunningly audible, and yet not moving a hair
upon our heads. So it blew all night long while I was writing
up my journal, and after we were in bed, under a cloudless,
star-set heaven; and so it was blowing still next morning
when we rose.

It was a laughable thought to us, what had become of our
cheerful, wandering Hebrews. We could not suppose they
had reached a destination. The meanest boy could lead them
miles out of their way to see a gopher-hole. Boys we felt to
be their special danger; none others were of that exact pitch
of cheerful irrelevancy to exercise a kindred sway upon their

minds: but before the attractions of a boy their most settled resolutions would be wax. We thought we could follow in fancy these three aged Hebrew truants wandering in and out on hill-top and in thicket, a demon boy trotting far ahead, their will-o'-the-wisp conductor; and at last, about midnight, the wind still roaring in the darkness, we had a vision of all three on their knees upon a mountaintop around a glow-worm.

THE RETURN

Next morning we were up by half-past five, according to agreement, and it was ten by the clock before our Jew boys returned to pick us up: Kelmar, Mrs. Kelmar, and Abramina, all smiling from ear to ear, and full of tales of the hospitality they had found on the other side. It had not gone unrewarded; for I observed with interest that the ship's kettles, all but one, had been "placed." Three Lake County families, at least, endowed for life with a ship's kettle. Come, this was no misspent Sunday. The absence of the kettles told its own story: our Jews said nothing about them; but, on the other hand, they said many kind and comely things about the people they had met. The two women, in particular, had been charmed out of themselves by the sight of a young girl surrounded by her admirers; all evening, it appeared, they had been triumphing together in the girl's innocent successes, and to this natural and unselfish joy they gave expression in language that was beautiful by its simplicity and truth.

Take them for all in all, few people have done my heart more good; they seemed so thoroughly entitled to happiness, and to enjoy it in so large a measure and so free from afterthought; almost they persuaded me to be a Jew. There was, indeed, a chink of money in their talk. They particularly commended people who were well-to-do. "*He* don't care — ain't it?" was their highest word of commendation to an individual fate; and here I seem to grasp the root of their philosophy — it was to be free from care, to be free to make these Sunday wanderings, that they so eagerly pursued after wealth; and all this carefulness was to be careless. The fine good-humour of all three seemed to declare they had attained their end. Yet there was the other side to it; and the recipients of kettles perhaps cared greatly.

No sooner had they returned than the scene of yesterday began again. The horses were not even tied with a straw rope this time — it was not worth while; and Kelmar disappeared into the bar, leaving them under a tree on the other side of the road. I had to devote myself. I stood under the shadow of that tree for, I suppose, hard upon an hour, and had not the heart to be angry. Once some one remembered me, and brought me out half a tumblerful of the playful, innocuous American cocktail. I drank it, and lo! veins of living fire ran down my leg; and then a focus of conflagration remained seated in my stomach, not unpleasantly, for a quarter of an hour. I love these sweet, fiery pangs, but I will not court them. The bulk of the time I spent in repeating as much French poetry as I could remember to the horses, who seemed to enjoy it hugely. And now it went —

> "O ma vieille Font-georges
> Où volent les rouges-gorges:"[1]

and again, to a more trampling measure —

> "Et tout tremble, Irun, Coïmbre,
> Santander, Almodovar,
> Sitôt qu'on entend le timbre
> Des cymbales de Bivar."[2]

The redbreasts and the brooks of Europe, in that dry and songless land; brave old names and wars, strong cities, cymbals, and bright armour, in that nook of the mountain, sacred only to the Indian and the bear! This is still the strangest thing in all man's travelling, that he should carry about with him in-

1. "Oh my old Font-Georges/Where the robins fly." Incorrectly quoted from Théodore de Banville, "A la Font-Georges" in *Les Stalactites*.

2. From Victor Hugo, "Le Romancero du Cid," Part VI, in *La Légende des siècles*, describing how the Spanish and Portuguese towns trembled at the advent of El Cid — Ruy Diaz de Bivar.

congruous memories. There is no foreign land; it is the traveller only that is foreign, and now and again, by a flash of recollection, lights up the contrasts of the earth.

But while I was thus wandering in my fancy, great feats had been transacted in the bar. Corwin the bold had fallen, Kelmar was again crowned with laurels, and the last of the ship's kettles had changed hands. If I had ever doubted the purity of Kelmar's motives, if I had ever suspected him of a single eye to business in his eternal dallyings, now at least, when the last kettle was disposed of, my suspicions must have been allayed. I dare not guess how much more time was wasted; nor how often we drove off, merely to drive back again and renew interrupted conversations about nothing, before the Toll House was fairly left behind. Alas! and not a mile down the grade there stands a ranche in a sunny vineyard, and here we must all dismount again and enter.

Only the old lady was at home, Mrs. Guele, a brown old Swiss dame, the picture of honesty; and with her we drank a bottle of wine and had an age-long conversation, which would have been highly delightful if Fanny and I had not been faint with hunger. The ladies each narrated the story of her marriage, our two Hebrews with the prettiest combination of sentiment and financial bathos. Abramina, specially, endeared herself with every word. She was as simple, natural, and engaging as a kid that should have been brought up to the business of a money-changer. One touch was so resplendently Hebraic that I cannot pass it over. When her "old man" wrote home for her from America, her old man's family would not intrust her with the money for the passage, till she had bound herself by an oath — on her knees, I think she said — not to employ it otherwise. This had tickled Abramina hugely, but I think it tickled me fully more.

Mrs. Guele told of her home-sickness up here in the long winters; of her honest, country-woman troubles and alarms upon the journey; how in the bank at Frankfort she had feared lest the banker, after having taken her cheque, should deny all knowledge of it — a fear I have myself every time I go to a bank; and how crossing the Lüneburger Heath, an old lady, witnessing her trouble and finding whither she was bound, had given her "the blessing of a person eighty years old," which would be sure to bring her safely to the States. "And the first thing I did," added Mrs. Guele, "was to fall down-stairs."

At length we got out of the house, and some of us into the trap, when — judgment of Heaven! — here came Mr. Guele from his vineyard. So another quarter of an hour went by; till at length, at our earnest pleading, we set forth again in earnest, Fanny and I white-faced and silent, but the Jews still smiling. The heart fails me. There was yet another stoppage! And we drove at last into Calistoga past two in the afternoon, Fanny and I having breakfasted at six in the morning, eight mortal hours before. We were a pallid couple; but still the Jews were smiling.

So ended our excursion with the village usurers; and, now that it was done, we had no more idea of the nature of the business, nor of the part we had been playing in it, than the child unborn. That all the people we had met were the slaves of Kelmar, though in various degrees of servitude; that we ourselves had been sent up the mountain in the interests of none but Kelmar; that the money we laid out, dollar by dollar, cent by cent, and through the hands of various intermediaries, should all hop ultimately into Kelmar's till; — these were facts that we only grew to recognise in the course of time and by the accumulation of evidence. At length all doubt was quieted, when one of the kettle-holders confessed. Stopping his trap in the moonlight, a little way out of Calistoga, he told me, in so many words, that he dare not show face there with an empty pocket. "You see, I don't mind if it was only five dollars, Mr. Stevens," he said, "but I must give Mr. Kelmar *something*."

Even now, when the whole tyranny is plain to me, I cannot find it in my heart to be as angry as perhaps I should be with the Hebrew tyrant. The whole game of business is beg-

gar my neighbour; and though perhaps that game looks uglier
when played at such close quarters and on so small a scale,
it is none the more intrinsically inhumane for that. The village
usurer is not so sad a feature of humanity and human progress
as the millionaire manufacturer, fattening on the toil and loss
of thousands, and yet declaiming from the platform against
the greed and dishonesty of landlords. If it were fair for
Cobden[3] to buy up land from owners whom he thought unconscious of its proper value, it was fair enough for my Russian Jew to give credit to his farmers. Kelmar, if he was unconscious of the beam in his own eye, was at least silent in the
matter of his brother's mote.

3. Richard Cobden, the 19th-century English statesman whose reforms
included the improved use of land, also speculated for himself by buying
property in Manchester.

THE ACT OF SQUATTING

There were four of us squatters — myself and my wife, the King and Queen of Silverado; Lloyd,[1] the Crown Prince; and Chuchu, the Grand Duke. Chuchu, a setter crossed with spaniel, was the most unsuited for a rough life. He had been nurtured tenderly in the society of ladies; his heart was large and soft; he regarded the sofa-cushion as a bed-rock necessary of existence. Though about the size of a sheep, he loved to sit in ladies' laps; he never said a bad word in all his blameless days; and if he had seen a flute, I am sure he could have played upon it by nature. It may seem hard to say it of a dog, but Chuchu was a tame cat.

The king and queen, the grand duke, and a basket of cold provender for immediate use, set forth from Calistoga in a double buggy; the crown prince, on horseback, led the way like an outrider. Bags and boxes and a second-hand stove were to follow close upon our heels by Hanson's team.

It was a beautiful still day; the sky was one field of azure. Not a leaf moved, not a speck appeared in heaven. Only from the summit of the mountain one little snowy wisp of cloud after another kept detaching itself, like smoke from a volcano, and blowing southward in some high stream of air: Mount Saint Helena still at her interminable task, making the weather, like a Lapland witch.

By noon we had come in sight of the mill: a great brown

1. Young Osbourne's middle name appears here (and on pp. 237, 265, and 278), rather than the usual Sam, the form used in this passage in the *Silverado Journal,* the first printing in *Century Magazine,* and the first book edition, published in 1883. Sidney Colvin presumably made the change because Osbourne dropped his first name in the mid or late 1880's.

building, half-way up the hill, big as a factory, two stories high, and with tanks and ladders along the roof; which, as a pendicle of Silverado mine, we held to be an outlying province of our own. Thither, then, we went, crossing the valley by a grassy trail; and there lunched out of the basket, sitting in a kind of portico, and wondering, while we ate, at this great bulk of useless building. Through a chink we could look far down into the interior, and see sunbeams floating in the dust and striking on tier after tier of silent, rusty machinery. It cost six thousand dollars, twelve hundred English sovereigns; and now, here it stands deserted, like the temple of a forgotten religion, the busy millers toiling somewhere else. All the time we were there, mill and mill-town showed no sign of life; that part of the mountain-side, which is very open and green, was tenanted by no living creature but ourselves and the insects; and nothing stirred but the cloud manufactory upon the mountain summit. It was odd to compare this with the former days, when the engine was in full blast, the mill palpitating to its strokes, and the carts came rattling down from Silverado, charged with ore.

By two we had been landed at the mine, the buggy was gone again, and we were left to our own reflections and the basket of cold provender, until Hanson should arrive. Hot as it was by the sun, there was something chill in such a homecoming, in that world of wreck and rust, splinter and rolling gravel, where for so many years no fire had smoked.

Silverado platform filled the whole width of the cañon. Above, as I have said, this was a wild, red, stony gully in the mountains; but below, it was a wooded dingle. And through this, I was told, there had gone a path between the mine and the Toll House — our natural north-west passage to civilisation. I found and followed it, clearing my way as I went through fallen branches and dead trees. It went straight down that steep cañon, till it brought you out abruptly over the roofs of the hotel. There was nowhere any break in the descent. It almost seemed as if, were you to drop a stone down the old iron chute at our platform, it would never rest until it hopped upon the Toll House shingles. Signs were not wanting of the ancient greatness of Silverado. The footpath was well marked, and had been well trodden in the old days by thirsty miners. And far down, buried in foliage, deep out of sight of Silverado, I came on a last outpost of the mine — a mound of gravel, some wreck of wooden aqueduct, and the mouth of a tunnel, like a treasure grotto in a fairy story. A stream of water, fed by the invisible leakage from our shaft, and dyed red with cinnabar or iron, ran trippingly forth out of the bowels of the cave; and, looking far under the arch, I could see something like an iron lantern fastened on the rocky wall. It was a promising spot for the imagination. No boy could have left it unexplored.

The stream thenceforward stole along the bottom of the dingle, and made, for that dry land, a pleasant warbling in the leaves. Once, I suppose, it ran splashing down the whole length of the cañon, but now its head-waters had been tapped by the shaft at Silverado, and for a great part of its course it wandered sunless among the joints of the mountain. No wonder that it should better its pace when it sees, far before it, daylight whitening in the arch, or that it should come trotting forth into the sunlight with a song.

The two stages had gone by when I got down, and the Toll House stood, dozing in sun and dust and silence, like a place enchanted. My mission was after hay for bedding, and that I was readily promised. But when I mentioned that we were waiting for Rufe, the people shook their heads. Rufe was not a regular man any way, it seemed; and if he got playing poker —— Well, poker was too many for Rufe. I had not yet heard them bracketed together; but it seemed a natural conjunction, and commended itself swiftly to my fears; and as soon as I returned to Silverado and had told my story, we practically gave Hanson up, and set ourselves to do what we could find do-able in our desert-island state.

The lower room had been the assayer's office. The floor was

thick with débris — part human, from the former occupants; part natural, sifted in by mountain winds. In a sea of red dust there swam or floated sticks, boards, hay, straw, stones, and paper; ancient newspapers, above all — for the newspaper, especially when torn, soon becomes an antiquity — and bills of the Silverado boarding-house, some dated Silverado, some Calistoga Mine. Here is one, verbatim; and if any one can calculate the scale of charges, he has my envious admiration.

Calistoga Mine, May 3rd, 1875.

John Stanley
   To S. Chapman, Cr.

To board from April 1st, to April 30	$25	75
" " " May 1st, to 3rd	2	00
	$27	75

Where is John Stanley mining now? Where is S. Chapman, within whose hospitable walls we were to lodge? The date was but five years old, but in that time the world had changed for Silverado; like Palmyra in the desert, it had outlived its people and its purpose; we camped, like Layard,[2] amid ruins, and these names spoke to us of prehistoric time. A bootjack, a pair of boots, a dog-hutch, and these bills of Mr. Chapman's, were the only speaking relics that we disinterred from all that vast Silverado rubbish-heap; but what would I not have given to unearth a letter, a pocket-book, a diary, only a ledger, or a roll of names, to take me back, in a more personal manner, to the past? It pleases me, besides, to fancy that Stanley or Chapman, or one of their companions, may light upon this chronicle, and be struck by the name, and read some news of their anterior home, coming, as it were, out of a subsequent epoch of history in that quarter of the world.

As we were tumbling the mingled rubbish on the floor,

2. Sir Austen Henry Layard, a famous English archaeologist who excavated the site of Nineveh, did not occur to Stevenson while he was at Silverado, for the allusion in his *Journal* is simply to Etruscan tombs.

kicking it with our feet, and groping for these written evidences of the past, Lloyd, with a somewhat whitened face, produced a paper bag. "What's this?" said he. It contained a granulated powder, something the colour of Gregory's Mixture,[3] but rosier; and as there were several of the bags, and each more or less broken, the powder was spread widely on the floor. Had any of us ever seen giant powder?[4] No, nobody had; and instantly there grew up in my mind a shadowy belief, verging with every moment nearer to certitude, that I had somewhere heard somebody describe it as just such a powder as the one around us. I have learnt since that it is a substance not unlike tallow, and is made up in rolls for all the world like tallow candles.

Fanny, to add to our happiness, told us a story of a gentleman who had camped one night, like ourselves, by a deserted mine. He was a handy, thrifty fellow, and looked right and left for plunder, but all he could lay his hands on was a can of oil. After dark he had to see to the horses with a lantern; and not to miss an opportunity, filled up his lamp from the oil-can. Thus equipped, he set forth into the forest. A little while after, his friends heard a loud explosion; the mountain echoes bellowed, and then all was still. On examination, the can proved to contain oil, with the trifling addition of nitroglycerine; but no research disclosed a trace of either man or lantern.

It was a pretty sight, after this anecdote, to see us sweeping out the giant powder. It seemed never to be far enough away. And, after all, it was only some rock pounded for assay.

So much for the lower room. We scraped some of the rougher dirt off the floor, and left it. That was our sitting-room and kitchen, though there was nothing to sit upon but the table, and no provision for a fire except a hole in the roof of the room above, which had once contained the chimney of a stove.

3. A popular Scottish medicine, also mentioned by Stevenson in "The Manse" in *Memories and Portraits*.
4. A form of dynamite.

To that upper room we now proceeded. There were the eighteen bunks in a double tier, nine on either hand, where from eighteen to thirty-six miners had once snored together all night long, John Stanley, perhaps, snoring loudest. There was the roof, with a hole in it through which the sun now shot an arrow. There was the floor, in much the same state as the one below, though, perhaps, there was more hay, and certainly there was the added ingredient of broken glass, the man who stole the window-frames having apparently made a miscarriage with this one. Without a broom, without hay or bedding, we could but look about us with a beginning of despair. The one bright arrow of day, in that gaunt and shattered barrack, made the rest look dirtier and darker, and the sight drove us at last into the open.

Here, also, the handiwork of man lay ruined: but the plants were all alive and thriving; the view below was fresh with the colours of nature; and we had exchanged a dim, human garret for a corner, even although it were untidy, of the blue hall of heaven. Not a bird, not a beast, not a reptile. There was no noise in that part of the world, save when we passed beside the staging, and heard the water musically falling in the shaft.

We wandered to and fro. We searched among that drift of lumber — wood and iron, nails and rails, and sleepers and the wheels of trucks. We gazed up the cleft into the bosom of the mountain. We sat by the margin of the dump, and saw, far below us, the green tree-tops standing still in the clear air. Beautiful perfumes, breaths of bay, resin, and nutmeg, came to us more often, and grew sweeter and sharper as the afternoon declined. But still there was no word of Hanson.

I set-to with pick and shovel, and deepened the pool behind the shaft, till we were sure of sufficient water for the morning; and by the time I had finished, the sun had begun to go down behind the mountain shoulder, the platform was plunged in quiet shadow, and a chill descended from the sky. Night began early in our cleft. Before us, over the margin of the dump, we could see the sun still striking aslant into the wooded nick below, and on the battlemented, pine-bescattered ridges on the farther side.

There was no stove, of course, and no hearth in our lodging, so we betook ourselves to the blacksmith's forge across the platform. If the platform be taken as a stage, and the out-curving margin of the dump to represent the line of the foot-lights, then our house would be the first wing on the actor's left, and this blacksmith's forge, although no match for it in size, the foremost on the right. It was a low, brown cottage, planted close against the hill, and overhung by the foliage and peeling boughs of a madrona thicket. Within, it was full of dead leaves and mountain dust and rubbish from the mine. But we soon had a good fire brightly blazing, and sat close about it on impromptu seats. Chuchu, the slave of sofa-cushions, whimpered for a softer bed; but the rest of us were greatly re-vived and comforted by that good creature — fire, which gives us warmth and light and companionable sounds, and colours up the emptiest building with better than frescoes. For a while it was even pleasant in the forge, with the blaze in the midst, and a look over our shoulders on the woods and mountains where the day was dying like a dolphin.

It was between seven and eight before Hanson arrived, with a waggonful of our effects and two of his wife's relatives to lend him a hand. The elder showed surprising strength. He would pick up a huge packing-case full of books, of all things, swing it on his shoulder, and away up the two crazy ladders and the break-neck spout of rolling mineral, familiarly termed a path, that led from the cart-track to our house. Even for a man unburthened, the ascent was toilsome and precarious; but Irvine scaled it with a light foot, carrying box after box, as the hero whisks the stage child up the practicable footway be-side the waterfall of the fifth act. With so strong a helper, the business was speedily transacted. Soon the assayer's office was thronged with our belongings, piled higgledy-piggledy, and upside down, about the floor. There were our boxes, indeed, but my wife had left her keys in Calistoga. There was the stove, but, alas! our carriers had forgot the chimney, and lost one of the plates along the road. The Silverado problem was scarce solved.

Rufe himself was grave and good-natured over his share of blame; he even, if I remember right, expressed regret. But his crew, to my astonishment and anger, grinned from ear to ear, and laughed aloud at our distress. They thought it "real funny" about the stove-pipe they had forgotten; "real funny" that they should have lost a plate. As for hay, the whole party refused to bring us any till they should have supped. See how late they were! Never had there been such a job as coming up that grade! Nor often, I suspect, such a game of poker as that before they started. But about nine, as a particular favour, we should have some hay.

So they took their departure, leaving me still staring, and we resigned ourselves to wait for their return. The fire in the forge had been suffered to go out, and we were one and all too weary to kindle another. We dined, or, not to take that word in vain, we ate after a fashion, in the nightmare disorder of the assayer's office, perched among boxes. A single candle lighted us. It could scarce be called a house-warming; for there was, of course, no fire, and with the two open doors and the open window gaping on the night, like breaches in a fortress, it began to grow rapidly chill. Talk ceased; nobody moved but the unhappy Chuchu, still in quest of sofa-cushions, who tumbled complainingly among the trunks. It required a certain happiness of disposition to look forward hopefully, from so dismal a beginning, across the brief hours of night, to the warm shining of to-morrow's sun.

But the hay arrived at last, and we turned, with our last spark of courage, to the bedroom. We had improved the entrance, but it was still a kind of rope-walking; and it would have been droll to see us mounting, one after another, by candle-light, under the open stars.

The western door — that which looked up the cañon, and through which we entered by our bridge of flying plank —

was still entire, a handsome, panelled door, the most finished piece of carpentry in Silverado. And the two lowest bunks next to this we roughly filled with hay for that night's use. Through the opposite, or eastern-looking gable, with its open door and window, a faint, diffused starshine came into the room like mist; and when we were once in bed, we lay, awaiting sleep, in a haunted, incomplete obscurity. At first the silence of the night was utter. Then a high wind began in the distance among the tree-tops, and for hours continued to grow higher. It seemed to me much such a wind as we had found on our visit; yet here in our open chamber we were fanned only by gentle and refreshing draughts, so deep was the cañon, so close our house was planted under the overhanging rock.

THE HUNTER'S FAMILY

There is quite a large race or class of people in America for whom we scarcely seem to have a parallel in England. Of pure white blood, they are unknown or unrecognisable in towns; inhabit the fringe of settlements and the deep, quiet places of the country; rebellious to all labour, and pettily thievish, like the English gipsies; rustically ignorant, but with a touch of wood-lore and the dexterity of the savage. Whence they came is a moot point. At the time of the war they poured north in thousands to escape the conscription; lived during summer on fruits, wild animals, and petty theft; and at the approach of winter, when these supplies failed, built great fires in the forest, and there died stoically by starvation. They are widely scattered, however, and easily recognised. Loutish, but not ill-looking, they will sit all day, swinging their legs on a field-fence, the mind seemingly as devoid of all reflection as a Suffolk peasant's, careless of politics, for the most part incapable of reading, but with a rebellious vanity and a strong sense of independence. Hunting is their most congenial business, or, if the occasion offers, a little amateur detection. In tracking a criminal, following a particular horse along a beaten highway, and drawing inductions from a hair or a footprint, one of these somnolent, grinning Hodges[1] will suddenly display activity of body and finesse of mind. By their names ye may know them, the women figuring as Loveina, Larsenia, Serena, Leanna, Orreana; the men answering to Alvin, Alva, or Orion, pronounced Orrion, with the accent on the first. Whether

1. Hodge is a common name for country bumpkins, including the loutish servant in *Gammer Gurton's Needle* and an insolent journeyman in Dekker's *The Shoemaker's Holiday*.

they are indeed a race, or whether this is the form of de-
generacy common to all backwoodsmen, they are at least
known by a generic byword, as Poor Whites or Low-downers.
I will not say that the Hanson family was Poor White, because the name savours of offence; but I may go as far as this
— they were, in many points, not unsimilar to the people
usually so called. Rufe himself combined two of the qualifica-
tions, for he was both a hunter and an amateur detective. It
was he who pursued Russel and Dollar, the robbers of the
Lake Port stage, and captured them the very morning after
the exploit, while they were still sleeping in a hay-field. Russel,
a drunken Scots carpenter, was even an acquaintance of his
own, and he expressed much grave commiseration for his
fate. In all that he said and did Rufe was grave. I never saw
him hurried. When he spoke, he took out his pipe with ceremonial deliberation, looked east and west, and then, in quiet
tones and few words, stated his business or told his story. His
gait was to match; it would never have surprised you if, at any
step, he had turned round and walked away again, so warily
and slowly, and with so much seeming hesitation did he go
about. He lay long in bed in the morning — rarely, indeed,
rose before noon; he loved all games, from poker to clerical
croquet; and in the Toll House croquet-ground I have seen
him toiling at the latter with the devotion of a curate. He took
an interest in education, was an active member of the local
school board, and when I was there he had recently lost the
school-house key. His waggon was broken, but it never
seemed to occur to him to mend it. Like all truly idle people,
he had an artistic eye. He chose the print stuff for his wife's
dresses, and counselled her in the making of a patchwork quilt,
always, as she thought, wrongly, but to the more educated
eye, always with bizarre and admirable taste — the taste of an
Indian. With all this, he was a perfect, unoffending gentleman
in word and act. Take his clay pipe from him, and he was
fit for any society but that of fools. Quiet as he was, there
burned a deep, permanent excitement in his dark-blue eyes;

and when this grave man smiled, it was like sunshine in a shady place.

Mrs. Hanson (*née*, if you please, Lovelands) was more commonplace than her lord. She was a comely woman, too, plump, fair-coloured, with wonderful white teeth; and in her print dresses (chosen by Rufe) and with a large sun-bonnet shading her valued complexion, made, I assure you, a very agreeable figure. But she was on the surface, what there was of her, outspoken and loud-spoken. Her noisy laughter had none of the charm of one of Hanson's rare, slow-spreading smiles; there was no reticence, no mystery, no manner about the woman: she was a first-class dairy-maid, but her husband was an unknown quantity between the savage and the nobleman. She was often in and out with us, merry, and healthy, and fair; he came far seldomer — only, indeed, when there was business, or, now and again, to pay a visit of ceremony, brushed up for the occasion, with his wife on his arm, and a clean clay pipe in his teeth. These visits, in our forest state, had quite the air of an event, and turned our red cañon into a salon.

Such was the pair who ruled in the old Silverado Hotel, among the windy trees, on the mountain shoulder overlooking the whole length of Napa Valley, as the man aloft looks down on the ship's deck. There they kept house, with sundry horses and fowls, and a family of sons, Daniel Webster, and I think George Washington, among the number. Nor did they want visitors. An old gentleman, of singular stolidity, and called Breedlove — I think he had crossed the plains in the same caravan with Rufe — housed with them for a while during our stay; and they had besides a permanent lodger, in the form of Mrs. Hanson's brother, Irvine Lovelands. I spell Irvine by guess, for I could get no information on the subject, just as I could never find out, in spite of many inquiries, whether or not Rufe was a contraction for Rufus. They were all cheerfully at sea about their names in that generation. And this is surely the more notable where the names are all so strange, and even the family names appear to have been coined. At one time, at least, the ancestors of all these Alvins and Alvas, Loveinas, Lovelands, and Breedloves, must have taken serious counsel and found a certain poetry in these denominations; that must have been, then, their form of literature. But still times change; and their next descendants, the George Washingtons and Daniel Websters, will at least be clear upon the point. And anyway, and however his name should be spelt, this Irvine Lovelands was the most unmitigated Caliban I ever knew.

Our very first morning at Silverado, when we were full of business, patching up doors and windows, making beds and seats, and getting our rough lodging into shape, Irvine and his sister made their appearance together, she for neighbour-liness and general curiosity; he, because he was working for me, to my sorrow, cutting firewood at I forget how much a day. The way that he set about cutting wood was characteristic. We were at that moment patching up and unpacking in the kitchen. Down he sat on one side, and down sat his sister on the other. Both were chewing pine-tree gum, and he, to my annoyance, accompanied that simple pleasure with profuse expectoration. She rattled away, talking up hill and down dale, laughing, tossing her head, showing her brilliant teeth. He looked on in silence, now spitting heavily on the floor, now putting his head back and uttering a loud, discordant, joyless laugh. He had a tangle of shock hair, the colour of wool; his mouth was a grin; although as strong as a horse, he looked neither heavy nor yet adroit, only leggy, coltish, and in the road. But it was plain he was in high spirits, thoroughly enjoying his visit; and he laughed frankly whenever we failed to accomplish what we were about. This was scarcely helpful: it was even, to amateur carpenters, embarrassing; but it lasted until we knocked off work and began to get dinner. Then Mrs. Hanson remembered she should have been gone an hour ago;

and the pair retired, and the lady's laughter died away among the nutmegs down the path. That was Irvine's first day's work in my employment — the devil take him!

The next morning he returned, and as he was this time alone, he bestowed his conversation upon us with great liberality. He prided himself on his intelligence; asked us if we knew the school ma'am. *He* didn't think much of her, anyway. He had tried her, he had. He had put a question to her. If a tree a hundred feet high were to fall a foot a day, how long would it take to fall right down? She had not been able to solve the problem. "She don't know nothing," he opined. He told us how a friend of his kept a school with a revolver, and chuckled mightily over that; his friend could teach school, he could. All the time he kept chewing gum and spitting. He would stand a while looking down; and then he would toss back his shock of hair, and laugh hoarsely, and spit, and bring forward a new subject. A man, he told us, who bore a grudge against him, had poisoned his dog. "That was a low thing for a man to do now, wasn't it? It wasn't like a man, that, nohow. But I got even with him: I pisoned *his* dog." His clumsy utterance, his rude embarrassed manner, set a fresh value on the stupidity of his remarks. I do not think I ever appreciated the meaning of two words until I knew Irvine — the verb *loaf*, and the noun *oaf*; between them, they complete his portrait. He could lounge, and wriggle, and rub himself against the wall, and grin, and be more in everybody's way than any other two people that I ever set my eyes on. Nothing that he did became him; and yet you were conscious that he was one of your own race, that his mind was cumbrously at work, revolving the problem of existence like a quid of gum, and in his own cloudy manner enjoying life, and passing judgment on his fellows. Above all things, he was delighted with himself. You would not have thought it, from his uneasy manners and troubled, struggling utterance; but he loved himself to the marrow, and was happy and proud like a peacock on a rail.

His self-esteem was, indeed, the one joint in his harness. He could be got to work, and even kept at work, by flattery. As long as my wife stood over him, crying out how strong he was, so long exactly he would stick to the matter in hand; and the moment she turned her back, or ceased to praise him, he would stop. His physical strength was wonderful; and to have a woman stand by and admire his achievements warmed his heart like sunshine. Yet he was as cowardly as he was powerful, and felt no shame in owning to the weakness. Something was once wanted from the crazy platform over the shaft, and he at once refused to venture there — did not like, as he said, "foolen' round them kind o' places," and let my wife go instead of him, looking on with a grin. Vanity, where it rules, is usually more heroic: but Irvine steadily approved himself, and expected others to approve him; rather looked down upon my wife, and decidedly expected her to look up to him, on the strength of his superior prudence.

Yet the strangest part of the whole matter was perhaps this, that Irvine was as beautiful as a statue. His features were, in themselves, perfect; it was only his cloudy, uncouth, and coarse expression that disfigured them. So much strength residing in so spare a frame was proof sufficient of the accuracy of his shape. He must have been built somewhat after the pattern of Jack Sheppard; but the famous housebreaker, we may be certain, was no lout.[2] It was by the extraordinary powers of his mind no less than by the vigour of his body that he broke his strong prison with such imperfect implements, turning the very obstacles to service. Irvine, in the same case, would have sat down and spat, and grumbled curses. He had the soul of a fat sheep, but, regarded as an artist's model, the exterior of a Greek god. It was a cruel thought to persons less favoured in their birth, that this creature, endowed — to use the language of theatres — with extraordinary "means," should so manage to misemploy them that he looked ugly and almost deformed. It was only by an effort of abstrac-

2. This notorious highwayman and thief, hanged in 1724, was the subject of a tract by Defoe and a romance by Harrison Ainsworth.

tion, and after many days, that you discovered what he was.

By playing on the oaf's conceit, and standing closely over him, we got a path made round the corner of the dump to our door, so that we could come and go with decent ease; and he even enjoyed the work, for in that there were boulders to be plucked up bodily, bushes to be uprooted, and other occasions for athletic display; but cutting wood was a different matter. Anybody could cut wood; and, besides, my wife was tired of supervising him, and had other things to attend to. And, in short, days went by, and Irvine came daily, and talked and lounged and spat; but the firewood remained intact as sleepers on the platform or growing trees upon the mountain side. Irvine, as a woodcutter, we could tolerate; but Irvine as a friend to the family, at so much a day, was too bald an imposition, and at length, on the afternoon of the fourth or fifth day of our connection, I explained to him, as clearly as I could, the light in which I had grown to regard his presence. I pointed out to him that I could not continue to give him a salary for spitting on the floor; and this expression, which came after a good many others, at last penetrated his obdurate wits. He rose at once, and said if that was the way he was going to be spoke to, he reckoned he would quit. And, no one interposing, he departed.

So far, so good. But we had no firewood. The next afternoon I strolled down to Rufe's and consulted him on the subject. It was a very droll interview, in the large, bare north room of the Silverado Hotel, Mrs. Hanson's patchwork on a frame, and Rufe, and his wife, and I, and the oaf himself, all more or less embarrassed. Rufe announced there was nobody in the neighbourhood but Irvine who could do a day's work for anybody. Irvine, thereupon, refused to have any more to do with my service; he "wouldn't work no more for a man as had spoke to him's I had done." I found myself on the point of the last humiliation — driven to beseech the creature whom I had just dismissed with insult: but I took the high hand in despair, said there must be no talk of Irvine coming back unless matters were to be differently managed; that I would rather chop firewood for myself than be fooled; and, in short, the Hansons being eager for the lad's hire, I so imposed upon them with merely affected resolution that they ended by begging me to re-employ him again, on a solemn promise that he should be more industrious. The promise, I am bound to say, was kept. We soon had a fine pile of firewood at our door; and if Caliban gave me the cold shoulder and spared me his conversation, I thought none the worse of him for that, nor did I find my days much longer for the deprivation.

The leading spirit of the family was, I am inclined to fancy, Mrs. Hanson. Her social brilliancy somewhat dazzled the others, and she had more of the small change of sense. It was she who faced Kelmar, for instance; and perhaps, if she had been alone, Kelmar would have had no rule within her doors. Rufe, to be sure, had a fine, sober, open-air attitude of mind, seeing the world without exaggeration — perhaps, we may even say, without enough; for he lacked, along with the others, that commercial idealism which puts so high a value on time and money. Sanity itself is a kind of convention. Perhaps Rufe was wrong; but, looking on life plainly, he was unable to perceive that croquet or poker were in any way less important than, for instance, mending his waggon. Even his own profession, hunting, was dear to him mainly as a sort of play; even that he would have neglected, had it not appealed to his imagination. His hunting-suit, for instance, had cost I should be afraid to say how many bucks — the currency in which he paid his way; it was all befringed, after the Indian fashion, and it was dear to his heart. The pictorial side of his daily business was never forgotten. He was even anxious to stand for his picture in those buckskin hunting clothes; and I remember how he once warmed almost into enthusiasm, his dark-blue eyes growing perceptibly larger, as he planned the composition in which he should appear, "with the horns of some real big bucks, and dogs, and a camp on a crick" (creek, stream).

There was no trace in Irvine of this woodland poetry. He

did not care for hunting, nor yet for buckskin suits. He had never observed scenery. The world, as it appeared to him, was almost obliterated by his own great grinning figure in the foreground: Caliban-Malvolio. And it seems to me as if, in the persons of these brothers-in-law, we had the two sides of rusticity fairly well represented: the hunter living really in nature; the clodhopper living merely out of society: the one bent up in every corporal agent to capacity in one pursuit, doing at least one thing keenly and thoughtfully, and thoroughly alive to all that touches it; the other in the inert and bestial state, walking in a faint dream, and taking so dim an impression of the myriad sides of life that he is truly conscious of nothing but himself. It is only in the fastnesses of nature, forests, mountains, and the back of man's beyond, that a creature endowed with five senses can grow up into the perfection of this crass and earthy vanity. In towns or the busier country-sides he is roughly reminded of other men's existence; and if he learns no more, he learns at least to fear contempt. But Irvine had come scatheless through life, conscious only of himself, of his great strength and intelligence; and in the silence of the universe to which he did not listen, dwelling with delight on the sound of his own thoughts.

THE SEA FOGS

A change in the colour of the light usually called me in the morning. By a certain hour, the long vertical chinks in our western gable, where the boards had shrunk and separated, flashed suddenly into my eyes as stripes of dazzling blue, at once so dark and splendid that I used to marvel how the qualities could be combined. At an earlier hour the heavens in that quarter were still quietly coloured, but the shoulder of the mountain which shuts in the cañon already glowed with sunlight in a wonderful compound of gold and rose and green; and this too would kindle, although more mildly and with rainbow tints, the fissures of our crazy gable. If I were sleeping heavily, it was the bold blue that struck me awake; if more lightly, then I would come to myself in that earlier and fairer light.

One Sunday morning, about five, the first brightness called me. I rose and turned to the east, not for my devotions, but for air. The night had been very still. The little private gale that blew every evening in our cañon, for ten minutes or perhaps a quarter of an hour, had swiftly blown itself out; in the hours that followed not a sigh of wind had shaken the tree-tops; and our barrack, for all its breaches, was less fresh that morning than of wont. But I had no sooner reached the window than I forgot all else in the sight that met my eyes, and I made but two bounds into my clothes, and down the crazy plank to the platform.

The sun was still concealed below the opposite hill-tops, though it was shining already, not twenty feet above my head, on our own mountain slope. But the scene, beyond a few near features, was entirely changed. Napa Valley was gone;

gone were all the lower slopes and woody foothills of the range; and in their place, not a thousand feet below me, rolled a great level ocean. It was as though I had gone to bed the night before, safe in a nook of inland mountains, and had awakened in a bay upon the coast. I had seen these inundations from below; at Calistoga I had risen and gone abroad in the early morning, coughing and sneezing, under fathoms on fathoms of grey sea-vapour, like a cloudy sky — a dull sight for the artist, and a painful experience for the invalid. But to sit aloft one's self in the pure air and under the unclouded dome of heaven, and thus look down on the submergence of the valley, was strangely different, and even delightful to the eyes. Far away were hill-tops like little islands. Nearer, a smoky surf beat about the foot of precipices and poured into all the coves of these rough mountains. The colour of that fog-ocean was a thing never to be forgotten. For an instant, among the Hebrides and just about sundown, I have seen something like it on the sea itself. But the white was not so opaline; nor was there, what surprisingly increased the effect, that breathless, crystal stillness over all. Even in its gentlest moods the salt sea travails, moaning among the weeds or lisping on the sand; but that vast fog-ocean lay in a trance of silence, nor did the sweet air of the morning tremble with a sound.

As I continued to sit upon the dump, I began to observe that this sea was not so level as at first sight it appeared to be. Away in the extreme south, a little hill of fog arose against the sky above the general surface, and as it had already caught the sun, it shone on the horizon like the topsails of some giant ship. There were huge waves, stationary, as it seemed, like waves in a frozen sea; and yet, as I looked again, I was not sure but they were moving after all, with a slow and august advance. And while I was yet doubting, a promontory of the hills some four or five miles away, conspicuous by a bouquet of tall pines, was in a single instant overtaken and swallowed up. It appeared in a little, with its pines, but this time as an islet, and

only to be swallowed up once more, and then for good. This
set me looking nearer, and I saw that in every cove along the
line of mountains the fog was being piled in higher and higher,
as though by some wind that was inaudible to me. I could trace
its progress, one pine-tree first growing hazy and then disappearing after another; although sometimes there was none of
this forerunning haze, but the whole opaque white ocean gave
a start and swallowed a piece of mountain at a gulp. It was to
flee these poisonous fogs that I had left the seaboard, and
climbed so high among the mountains. And now, behold, here
came the fog to besiege me in my chosen altitudes, and yet
came so beautifully that my first thought was of welcome.

The sun had now gotten much higher, and through all the
gaps of the hills it cast long bars of gold across that white
ocean. An eagle, or some other very great bird of the mountain,
came wheeling over the nearer pine-tops, and hung, poised and
something sideways, as if to look abroad on that unwonted
desolation, spying, perhaps with terror, for the eyries of her
comrades. Then, with a long cry, she disappeared again towards Lake County and the clearer air. At length it seemed
to me as if the flood were beginning to subside. The old
landmarks, by whose disappearance I had measured its advance,
here a crag, there a brave pine-tree, now began, in the inverse
order, to make their reappearance into daylight. I judged all
danger of the fog was over. This was not Noah's flood; it was
but a morning spring, and would now drift out seaward
whence it came. So, mightily relieved, and a good deal ex-
hilarated by the sight, I went into the house to light the fire.

I suppose it was nearly seven when I once more mounted the
platform to look abroad. The fog-ocean had swelled up
enormously since last I saw it; and a few hundred feet below
me, in the deep gap where the Toll House stands and the road
runs through into Lake County, it had already topped the
slope, and was pouring over and down the other side like
driving smoke. The wind had climbed along with it; and

though I was still in calm air, I could see the trees tossing below me, and their long, strident sighing mounted to me where I stood.

Half an hour later, the fog had surmounted all the ridge on the opposite side of the gap, though a shoulder of the mountain still warded it out of our cañon. Napa Valley and its bounding hills were now utterly blotted out. The fog, sunny white in the sunshine, was pouring over into Lake County in a huge ragged cataract, tossing tree-tops appearing and disappearing in the spray. The air struck with a little chill, and set me coughing. It smelt strong of the fog, like the smell of a washing-house, but with a shrewd tang of the sea-salt.

Had it not been for two things — the sheltering spur which answered as a dyke, and the great valley on the other side which rapidly engulfed whatever mounted — our own little platform in the cañon must have been already buried a hundred feet in salt and poisonous air. As it was, the interest of the scene entirely occupied our minds. We were set just out of the wind, and but just above the fog; we could listen to the voice of the one as to music on the stage; we could plunge our eyes down into the other as into some flowing stream from over the parapet of a bridge; thus we looked on upon a strange, impetuous, silent, shifting exhibition of the powers of nature, and saw the familiar landscape changing from moment to moment like figures in a dream.

The imagination loves to trifle with what is not. Had this been indeed the deluge, I should have felt more strongly, but the emotion would have been similar in kind. I played with the idea, as the child flees in delighted terror from the creations of his fancy. The look of the thing helped me. And when at last I began to flee up the mountain, it was indeed partly to escape from the raw air that kept me coughing, but it was also part in play.

As I ascended the mountain side I came once more to overlook the upper surface of the fog; but it wore a different appearance from what I had beheld at daybreak. For, first, the sun now fell on it from high overhead, and its surface shone and undulated like a great nor'land moor country, sheeted with untrodden morning snow. And next, the new level must have been a thousand or fifteen hundred feet higher than the old, so that only five or six points of all the broken country below me still stood out. Napa Valley was now one with Sonoma on the west. On the hither side, only a thin, scattered fringe of bluffs was unsubmerged; and through all the gaps the fog was pouring over, like an ocean, into the blue, clear, sunny country on the east. There it was soon lost; for it fell instantly into the bottom of the valleys, following the watershed; and the hill-tops in that quarter were still clear cut upon the eastern sky.

Through the Toll House gap and over the near ridges on the other side the deluge was immense. A spray of thin vapour was thrown high above it, rising and falling, and blown into fantastic shapes. The speed of its course was like a mountain torrent. Here and there a few tree-tops were discovered and then whelmed again; and for one second the bough of a dead pine beckoned out of the spray like the arm of a drowning man. But still the imagination was dissatisfied, still the ear waited for something more. Had this indeed been water (as it seemed so to the eye) with what a plunge of reverberating thunder would it have rolled upon its course, disembowelling mountains and deracinating pines! And yet water it was, and sea-water at that—true Pacific billows, only somewhat rarefied, rolling in mid-air among the hill-tops.

I climbed still higher, among the red rattling gravel and dwarf underwood of Mount Saint Helena, until I could look right down upon Silverado, and admire the favoured nook in which it lay. The sunny plain of fog was several hundred feet higher; behind the protecting spur a gigantic accumulation of cottony vapour threatened, with every second, to blow over and submerge our homestead; but the vortex setting past the Toll House was too strong; and there lay our little platform, in the arms of the deluge, but still enjoying its unbroken sunshine. About eleven, however, thin spray came flying over the friendly buttress, and I began to think the fog had hunted out its Jonah after all. But it was the last effort. The wind veered while we were at dinner, and began to blow squally from the mountain summit; and by half-past one all that world of sea-fogs was utterly routed and flying here and there into the south in little rags of cloud. And instead of a lone sea-beach, we found ourselves once more inhabiting a high mountain-side, with the clear green country far below us, and the light smoke of Calistoga blowing in the air.

This was the great Russian campaign for that season. Now and then, in the early morning, a little white lakelet of fog would be seen far down in Napa Valley; but the heights were not again assailed, nor was the surrounding world again shut off from Silverado.

THE TOLL HOUSE

The Toll House, standing alone by the wayside under nodding pines, with its streamlet and water-tank; its backwoods, toll-bar, and well-trodden croquet-ground; the ostler standing by the stable door chewing a straw; a glimpse of the Chinese cook in the back parts; and Mr. Hoddy in the bar, gravely alert and serviceable, and equally anxious to lend or borrow books; — dozed all day in the dusty sunshine, more than half asleep. There were no neighbours, except the Hansons up the hill. The traffic on the road was infinitesimal; only, at rare intervals, a couple in a waggon, or a dusty farmer on a spring-board, toiling over "the grade" to that metropolitan hamlet, Calistoga; and, at the fixed hours, the passage of the stages.

The nearest building was the school-house, down the road; and the school-ma'am boarded at the Toll House, walking thence in the morning to the little brown shanty where she taught the young ones of the district, and returning thither pretty weary in the afternoon. She had chosen this outlying situation, I understood, for her health. Mr. Corwin was consumptive; so was Rufe; so was Mr. Jennings, the engineer. In short, the place was a kind of small Davos: consumptive folk consorting on a hill-top in the most unbroken idleness. Jennings never did anything that I could see, except now and then to fish, and generally to sit about in the bar and the verandah, waiting for something to happen. Corwin and Rufe did as little as possible; and if the school-ma'am, poor lady, had to work pretty hard all morning, she subsided when it was over into much the same dazed beatitude as all the rest.

Her special corner was the parlour — a very genteel room, with Bible prints, a crayon portrait of Mrs. Corwin in the height of fashion, a few years ago, another of her son (Mr. Corwin was not represented), a mirror, and a selection of dried grasses. A large book was laid religiously on the table — *From Palace to Hovel*,[1] I believe, its name — full of the raciest experiences in England. The author had mingled freely with all classes, the nobility particularly meeting him with open arms; and I must say that traveller had ill requited his reception. His book, in short, was a capital instance of the Penny Messalina school of literature; and there arose from it, in that cool parlour, in that silent wayside mountain inn, a rank atmosphere of gold and blood and "Jenkins," and the "Mysteries of London,"[2] and sickening, inverted snobbery, fit to knock you down. The mention of this book reminds me of another and far racier picture of our island life. The latter parts of *Rocambole*[3] are surely too sparingly consulted in the country which they celebrate. No man's education can be said to be complete, nor can he pronounce the world yet emptied of enjoyment, till he has made the acquaintance of "the Reverend Patterson, director of the Evangelical Society." To follow the evolutions of that reverend gentleman, who goes through scenes in which even Mr. Duffield[4] would hesitate to place

1. *Palace and Hovel; Or, Phases of London Life* (1870), by the New York *World* correspondent Daniel Joseph Kirwan, according to its subtitle told of the author's observations of the "social customs and modes of living of the rich and the reckless, the destitute and the depraved in the metropolis of Great Britain."

2. The work that Stevenson simply calls "Jenkins" seems to belong to the popular shockers of the latter-day Gothic school, which appeared in penny weekly form, as did its counterpart W. M. Reynolds' *The Mysteries of London* (1845), which in 624 issues told of adventures and intrigues among the upper class.

3. *Rocambole*, which Stevenson read in San Francisco, is a romance somewhat similar to Reynolds' work. It was written by Vicomte Ponson du Terrail and was originally published in cheap serial form. Mostly set in France, part of it deals with the hero's experiences in England, where Rev. Patterson, who "exercised a power perhaps greater than the Archbishop of Canterbury," becomes involved in many sordid situations.

4. Mr. Duffield is probably Alexander James Duffield (1821–1890), author of *Peru in the Guano Age*, which opens with a contrast between

a bishop, is to rise to new ideas. But, alas! there was no Patterson about the Toll House. Only, alongside of *From Palace to Hovel*, a sixpenny "Ouida" figured. So literature, you see, was not unrepresented.

The school-ma'am had friends to stay with her, other schoolma'ams enjoying their holidays, quite a bevy of damsels. They seemed never to go out, or not beyond the verandah, but sat close in the little parlour, quietly talking or listening to the wind among the trees. Sleep dwelt in the Toll House, like a fixture: summer sleep, shallow, soft, and dreamless. A cuckoo-clock, a great rarity in such a place, hooted at intervals about the echoing house; and Mr. Jennings would open his eyes for a moment in the bar, and turn the leaf of a newspaper, and the resting school-ma'ams in the parlour would be recalled to the consciousness of their inaction. Busy Mrs. Corwin and her busy Chinaman might be heard indeed, in the penetralia, pounding dough or rattling dishes; or perhaps Rufe had called up some of the sleepers for a game of croquet, and the hollow strokes of the mallet sounded far away among the woods; but with these exceptions, it was sleep and sunshine and dust, and the wind in the pine-trees, all day long.

A little before stage-time that castle of indolence awoke. The ostler threw his straw away and set to his preparations. Mr. Jennings rubbed his eyes; happy Mr. Jennings, the something he had been waiting for all day about to happen at last! The boarders gathered in the verandah, silently giving ear, and gazing down the road with shaded eyes. And as yet there was no sign for the senses, not a sound, not a tremor of the mountain road. The birds, to whom the secret of the hooting cuckoo is unknown, must have set down to instinct this premonitory bustle.

And then the first of the two stages swooped upon the Toll

---

the modern era of clerical and lay corruption — the Guano Age — and the morality of a past Golden Age, and coauthor of the novel *Masston: A Story of These Modern Days*, also touching upon contemporary corruption.

House with a roar and in a cloud of dust; and the shock had not yet time to subside, before the second was abreast of it. Huge concerns they were, well-horsed and loaded, the men in their shirt-sleeves, the women swathed in veils, the long whip cracking like a pistol; and as they charged upon that slumbering hostelry, each shepherding a dust-storm, the dead place blossomed into life and talk and clatter. This the Toll House? — with its city throng, its jostling shoulders, its infinity of instant business in the bar? The mind would not receive it! The heartfelt bustle of that hour is hardly credible; the thrill of the great shower of letters from the post-bag, the childish hope and interest with which one gazed in all these strangers' eyes. They paused there but to pass: the blue-clad China boy, the San Francisco magnate, the mystery in the dust-coat, the secret memoirs in tweed, the ogling, well-shod lady with her troop of girls; they did but flash and go; they were hull-down for us behind life's ocean, and we but hailed their topsails on the line. Yet, out of our great solitude of four-and-twenty mountain hours, we thrilled to their momentary presence; gauged and divined them, loved and hated; and stood light-headed in that storm of human electricity. Yes, like Piccadilly Circus, this is also one of life's crossing-places. Here I beheld one man, already famous, or infamous, a centre of pistol-shots: and another who, if not yet known to rumour, will fill a column of the Sunday paper when he comes to hang — a burly, thickset, powerful Chinese desperado, six long bristles upon either lip; redolent of whisky, playing cards, and pistols; swaggering in the bar with the lowest assumption of the lowest European manners; rapping out blackguard English oaths in his canorous Oriental voice; and combining in one person the depravities of two races and two civilisations. For all his lust and vigour he seemed to look cold upon me from the valley of the shadow of the gallows. He imagined a vain thing; and while he drained his cocktail, Holbein's Death was at his elbow. Once, too, I fell in talk with another of these flitting strangers — like the rest, in his shirt-sleeves and all begrimed with dust — and the next minute we were discussing Paris and London, theatres and wines. To him, journeying from one human place to another, this was a trifle; but to me! No, Mr. Lillie, I have not forgotten it.

And presently the city tide was at its flood and began to ebb. Life runs in Piccadilly Circus, say, from nine to one, and then, there also, ebbs into the small hours of the echoing policeman and the lamps and stars. But the Toll House is far up stream, and near its rural springs; the bubble of the tide but touches it. Before you had yet grasped your pleasure, the horses were put to, the loud whips volleyed, and the tide was gone. North and south had the two stages vanished, the towering dust subsided in the woods; but there was still an interval before the flush had fallen on your cheeks, before the ear became once more contented with the silence, or the seven sleepers of the Toll House dozed back to their accustomed corners. Yet a little, and the ostler would swing round the great barrier across the road; and in the golden evening that dreamy inn begin to trim its lamps and spread the board for supper.

As I recall the place — the green dell below; the spires of pine; the sun-warm, scented air; that grey, gabled inn, with its faint stirrings of life amid the slumber of the mountains — I slowly awake to a sense of admiration, gratitude, and almost love. A fine place, after all, for a wasted life to doze away in — the cuckoo-clock hooting of its far home country; the croquet mallets, eloquent of English lawns; the stages daily bringing news of the turbulent world away below there; and perhaps once in the summer, a salt fog pouring overhead with its tale of the Pacific.

A STARRY DRIVE

In our rule at Silverado there was a melancholy interregnum. The queen and the crown prince with one accord fell sick; and, as I was sick to begin with, our lone position on Mount Saint Helena was no longer tenable, and we had to hurry back to Calistoga and a cottage on the green. By the time we had begun to realise the difficulties of our position. We had found what an amount of labour it cost to support life in our red cañon; and it was the dearest desire of our hearts to get a China boy to go along with us when we returned. We could have given him a whole house to himself — self-contained, as they say in the advertisements; and on the money question we were prepared to go far. Kong Sam Kee, the Calistoga washerman, was intrusted with the affair; and from day to day it languished on, with protestations on our part and mellifluous excuses on the part of Kong Sam Kee.

At length, about half-past eight of our last evening, with the waggon ready harnessed to convey us up the grade, the washerman, with a somewhat sneering air, produced the boy. He was a handsome, gentlemanly lad, attired in rich dark blue, and shod with snowy white; but, alas! he had heard rumours of Silverado. He knew it for a lone place on the mountainside, with no friendly wash-house near by, where he might smoke a pipe of opium o' nights with other China boys, and lose his little earnings at the game of tan; and he first backed out for more money; and then, when that demand was satisfied, refused to come point-blank. He was wedded to his wash-houses; he had no taste for the rural life; and we must go to our mountain servantless. It must have been near half an hour before we reached that conclusion, standing in the midst of

Calistoga high street under the stars, and the China boy and Kong Sam Kee singing their pigeon English in the sweetest voices and with the most musical inflections.

We were not, however, to return alone; we brought with us a painter guest,[1] who proved to be a most good-natured comrade and a capital hand at an omelette. I do not know in which capacity he was most valued — as a cook or a companion; and he did excellently well in both.

The Kong Sam Kee negotiation had delayed us unduly; it must have been half-past nine before we left Calistoga, and night came fully ere we struck the bottom of the grade. I have never seen such a night. It seemed to throw calumny in the teeth of all the painters that ever dabbled in starlight. The sky itself was of a ruddy, powerful, nameless, changing colour, dark and glossy like a serpent's back. The stars, by innumerable millions, stuck boldly forth like lamps. The milky way was bright, like a moonlit cloud; half heaven seemed milky way. The greater luminaries shone each more clearly than a winter's moon. Their light was dyed in every sort of colour — red, like fire; blue, like steel; green, like the tracks of sunset; and so sharply did each stand forth in its own lustre that there was no appearance of that flat, star-spangled arch we know so well in pictures, but all the hollow of heaven was one chaos of contesting luminaries — a hurly-burly of stars. Against this the hills and rugged tree-tops stood out redly dark.

As we continued to advance, the lesser lights and milky ways first grew pale, and then vanished; the countless hosts of heaven dwindled in number by successive millions; those that still shone had tempered their exceeding brightness and fallen back into their customary wistful distance; and the sky declined from its first bewildering splendour into the appearance of a common night. Slowly this change proceeded, and still there was no sign of any cause. Then a whiteness like mist was thrown over the spurs of the mountain. Yet a while, and, as

1. Joseph Strong, who was Fanny Stevenson's son-in-law and the artist who drew the frontispiece for *The Silverado Squatters.*

we turned a corner, a great leap of silver light and net of forest shadows fell across the road and upon our wondering waggonful; and, swimming low among the trees, we beheld a strange, misshapen, waning moon, half-tilted on her back.

"Where are ye when the moon appears?" [2] so the old poet sang, half-taunting, to the stars, bent upon a courtly purpose.

> "As the sunlight round the dim earth's midnight tower of
>   shadow pours,
>   Streaming past the dim, wide portals,
>   Viewless to the eyes of mortals,
> Till it floods the moon's pale islet or the morning's golden
>   shores."

So sings Mr. Trowbridge, [3] with a noble inspiration. And so had the sunlight flooded that pale islet of the moon, and her lit face put out, one after another, that galaxy of stars. The wonder of the drive was over; but, by some nice conjunction of clearness in the air and fit shadow in the valley where we travelled, we had seen for a little while that brave display of the midnight heavens. It was gone, but it had been; nor shall I ever again behold the stars with the same mind. He who has seen the sea commoved with a great hurricane thinks of it very differently from him who has seen it only in a calm. And the difference between a calm and a hurricane is not greatly more striking than that between the ordinary face of night and the splendour that shone upon us in that drive. Two in our waggon knew night as she shines upon the tropics, but even that bore no comparison. The nameless colour of the sky, the hues of the star-fire, and the incredible projection of the stars themselves, starting from their orbits, so that the eye seemed to

2. Surely Stevenson is recalling, "What are you, when the Moon shall rise?" from Sir Henry Wotton's lyric "On His Mistress, the Queen of Bohemia," for in its first stanza the poet taunts the "meaner beauties of the night" as a way of praising his beloved.

3. John Townsend Trowbridge, a contemporary American poet. His "Under Moon and Stars" is accurately quoted, except that in his collected *Poetical Works* (1903) no comma appears at the end of the third line and the original has "flood" for "floods."

distinguish their positions in the hollow of space — these were things that we had never seen before and shall never see again.

Meanwhile, in this altered night, we proceeded on our way among the scents and silence of the forest, reached the top of the grade, wound up by Hanson's, and came at last to a stand under the flying gargoyle of the chute. Lloyd, who had been lying back, fast asleep, with the moon on his face, got down, with the remark that it was pleasant "to be home." The waggon turned and drove away, the noise gently dying in the woods, and we clambered up the rough path, Caliban's great feat of engineering, and came home to Silverado.

The moon shone in at the eastern doors and windows, and over the lumber on the platform. The one tall pine beside the ledge was steeped in silver. Away up the cañon, a wild cat welcomed us with three discordant squalls. But once we had lit a candle, and began to review our improvements, homely in either sense, and count our stores, it was wonderful what a feeling of possession and permanence grew up in the hearts of the lords of Silverado. A bed had still to be made up for our guest, and the morning's water to be fetched, with clinking pail; and as we set about these household duties, and showed off our weath and conveniences before the stranger, and had a glass of wine, I think, in honour of our return, and trooped at length one after another up the flying bridge of plank, and lay down to sleep in our shattered, moon-pierced barrack, we were among the happiest sovereigns in the world, and certainly ruled over the most contented people. Yet, in our absence, the palace had been sacked. Wild cats, so the Hansons said, had broken in and carried off a side of bacon, a hatchet, and two knives.

EPISODES IN THE STORY
OF A MINE

No one could live at Silverado and not be curious about the
story of the mine. We were surrounded by so many evidences
of expense and toil, we lived so entirely in the wreck of that
great enterprise, like mites in the ruins of a cheese, that the
idea of the old din and bustle haunted our repose. Our own
house, the forge, the dump, the chutes, the rails, the windlass,
the mass of broken plant; the two tunnels, one far below in
the green dell, the other on the platform where we kept our
wine; the deep shaft, with the sun-glints and the water-drops;
above all, the ledge, that great gaping slice out of the mountain
shoulder, propped apart by wooden wedges, on whose immediate margin, high above our heads, the one tall pine precariously nodded — these stood for its greatness; while the
dog-hutch, bootjacks, old boots, old tavern bills, and the very
beds that we inherited from bygone miners, put in human
touches and realised for us the story of the past.

I have sat on an old sleeper, under the thick madronas near
the forge, with just a look over the dump on the green world
below, and seen the sun lying broad among the wreck, and
heard the silence broken only by the tinkling water in the shaft,
or a stir of the royal family about the battered palace, and my
mind has gone back to the epoch of the Stanleys and the
Chapmans, with a grand *tutti* of pick and drill, hammer and
anvil, echoing about the cañon; the assayer hard at it in our
dining-room; the carts below on the road, and their cargo of
red mineral bounding and thundering down the iron chute.
And now all gone — all fallen away into this sunny silence
and desertion: a family of squatters dining in the assayer's

office, making their beds in the big sleeping-room erstwhile so crowded, keeping their wine in the tunnel that once rang with picks.

But Silverado itself, although now fallen in its turn into decay, was once but a mushroom, and had succeeded to other mines and other flitting cities. Twenty years ago, away down the glen on the Lake County side, there was a place, Jonestown by name, with two thousand inhabitants dwelling under canvas, and one roofed house for the sale of whiskey. Round on the western side of Mount Saint Helena there was at the same date a second large encampment, its name, if it ever had one, lost for me. Both of these have perished, leaving not a stick and scarce a memory behind them. Tide after tide of hopeful miners have thus flowed and ebbed about the mountain, coming and going, now by lone prospectors, now with a rush. Last in order of time came Silverado, reared the big mill in the valley, founded the town which is now represented, monumentally, by Hanson's, pierced all these slaps and shafts and tunnels, and in turn declined and died away.

> "Our noisy years seem moments in the being
> Of the eternal silence." [1]

As to the success of Silverado in its time of being, two reports were current. According to the first, six hundred thousand dollars were taken out of that great upright seam, that still hung open above us on crazy wedges. Then the ledge pinched out, and there followed, in quest of the remainder, a great drifting and tunnelling in all directions, and a great consequent effusion of dollars, until, all parties being sick of the expense, the mine was deserted, and the town decamped. According to the second version, told me with much secrecy of manner, the whole affair, mine, mill, and town, were parts of one majestic swindle. There had never come any silver out of any portion of the mine; there was no silver to come. At midnight trains of pack-horses might have been observed winding by devious

1. Wordsworth, "Ode on the Intimations of Immortality," ll. 155–156.

tracks about the shoulder of the mountain. They came from far away, from Amador or Placer, laden with silver in "old cigar-boxes." They discharged their load at Silverado, in the hour of sleep; and before the morning they were gone again with their mysterious drivers to their unknown source. In this way, twenty thousand pounds' worth of silver was smuggled in under cover of night, in these old cigar-boxes; mixed with Silverado mineral; carted down to the mill; crushed, amalgamated, and refined, and despatched to the city as the proper product of the mine. Stockjobbing, if it can cover such expenses, must be a profitable business in San Francisco.

I give these two versions as I got them. But I place little reliance on either, my belief in history having been greatly shaken. For it chanced that I had come to dwell in Silverado at a critical hour; great events in its history were about to happen — did happen, as I am led to believe; nay, and it will be seen that I played a part in that revolution myself. And yet from first to last I never had a glimmer of an idea what was going on; and even now, after full reflection, profess myself at sea. That there was some obscure intrigue of the cigar-box order, and that I, in the character of a wooden puppet, set pen to paper in the interest of somebody, — so much, and no more, is certain.

Silverado, then under my immediate sway, belonged to one whom I will call a Mr. Ronalds. I only knew him through the extraordinarily distorting medium of local gossip, now as a momentous jobber; now as a dupe to point an adage; and again, and much more probably, as an ordinary Christian gentleman like you or me, who had opened a mine and worked it for a while with better and worse fortune. So, through a defective window-pane, you may see the passer-by shoot up into a hunchbacked giant or dwindle into a pot-bellied dwarf.

To Ronalds, at least, the mine belonged; but the notice by which he held it would run out upon the 30th of June — or rather, as I suppose, it had run out already, and the month of grace would expire upon that day, after which any American citizen might post a notice of his own, and make Silverado his. This, with a sort of quiet slyness, Rufe told me at an early period of our acquaintance. There was no silver, of course; the mine "wasn't worth nothing, Mr. Stevens," but there was a deal of old iron and wood around, and to gain possession of this old wood and iron, and get a right to the water, Rufe proposed, if I had no objections, to "jump the claim."

Of course I had no objection. But I was filled with wonder. If all he wanted was the wood and iron, what, in the name of fortune, was to prevent him taking them? "His right there was none to dispute." [2] He might lay hands on all to-morrow, as the wild cats had laid hands upon our knives and hatchet. Besides, was this mass of heavy mining plant worth transportation? If it was, why had not the rightful owners carted it away? If it was, would they not preserve their title to these moveables, even after they had lost their title to the mine? And if it were not, what the better was Rufe? Nothing would grow at Silverado; there was even no wood to cut; beyond a sense of property, there was nothing to be gained. Lastly, was it at all credible that Ronalds would forget what Rufe remembered? The days of grace were not yet over: any fine morning he might appear, paper in hand, and enter for another year on his inheritance. However, it was none of my business; all seemed legal; Rufe or Ronalds, all was one to me.

On the morning of the 27th, Mrs. Hanson appeared with the milk as usual, in her sun-bonnet. The time would be out on Tuesday,[3] she reminded us, and bade me be in readiness to play my part, though I had no idea what it was to be. And suppose Ronalds came? we asked. She received the idea with derision, laughing aloud with all her fine teeth. He could not find the mine to save his life, it appeared, without Rufe to guide him. Last year, when he came, they heard him "up and down the road a-hollerin' and a-raisin' Cain." And at last he

2. William Cowper, "Verses supposed to be written by Alexander Selkirk."
3. Actually, the 30th of June fell on a Wednesday in 1880.

had to come to the Hansons in despair, and bid Rufe, "Jump into your pants and shoes, and show me where this old mine is, anyway!" Seeing that Ronalds had laid out so much money in the spot, and that a beaten road led right up to the bottom of the dump, I thought this a remarkable example. The sense of locality must be singularly in abeyance in the case of Ronalds.

That same evening, supper comfortably over, our guest busy at work on a drawing of the dump and the opposite hills, we were all out on the platform together, sitting there, under the tented heavens, with the same sense of privacy as if we had been cabined in a parlour, when the sound of brisk foot-steps came mounting up the path. We pricked our ears at this, for the tread seemed lighter and firmer than was usual with our country neighbours. And presently, sure enough, two town gentlemen, with cigars and kid gloves, came debouching past the house. They looked in that place like a blasphemy.

"Good-evening," they said. For none of us had stirred; we all sat stiff with wonder.

"Good-evening," I returned; and then, to put them at their ease, "A stiff climb," I added.

"Yes," replied the leader; "but we have to thank you for this path."

I did not like the man's tone. None of us liked it. He did not seem embarrassed by the meeting, but threw us his remarks like favours, and strode magisterially by us towards the shaft and tunnel.

Presently we heard his voice raised to his companion. "We drifted every sort of way, but couldn't strike the ledge." Then again: "It pinched out here." And once more: "Every miner that ever worked upon it says there's bound to be a ledge somewhere."

These were the snatches of his talk that reached us, and they had a damning significance. We, the lords of Silverado, had come face to face with our superior. It is the worst of all quaint and of all cheap ways of life that they bring us at last to the pinch of some humiliation. I liked well enough to be a squatter when there was none but Hanson by; before Ronalds, I will own, I somewhat quailed. I hastened to do him fealty, said I gathered he was the Squattee, and apologised. He threatened me with ejection, in a manner grimly pleasant — more pleasant to him, I fancy, than to me; and then he passed off into praises of the former state of Silverado. "It was the busiest little mining town you ever saw:" a population of between a thousand and fifteen hundred souls, the engine in full blast, the mill newly erected; nothing going but champagne, and hope the order of the day. Ninety thousand dollars came out; a hundred and forty thousand were put in, making a net loss of fifty thousand. The last days, I gathered, the days of John Stanley, were not so bright; the champagne had ceased to flow, the population was already moving elsewhere, and Silverado had begun to wither in the branch before it was cut at the root. The last shot that was fired knocked over the stove chimney, and made that hole in the roof of our barrack, through which the sun was wont to visit slug-a-beds towards afternoon. A noisy last shot, to inaugurate the days of silence.

Throughout this interview my conscience was a good deal exercised; and I was moved to throw myself on my knees and own the intended treachery. But then I had Hanson to consider. I was in much the same position as Old Rowley, that royal humorist, whom "the rogue had taken into his confidence." [4] And again, here was Ronalds on the spot. He must know the day of the month as well as Hanson and I. If a broad hint were necessary, he had the broadest in the world. For a large board had been nailed by the crown prince on the very front of our house, between the door and window, painted in

4. Old Rowley was the favorite stallion of Charles II, and because of his powers and proclivities, the king himself was given the nickname with a bawdy connotation. The source of Stevenson's quotation and his reference have not been identified, although the allusion may be either to the confession of an officer, one Blood, who told the monarch that he had been involved in a plot to assassinate him, to the Titus Oates plot, or to some other of the many machinations that touched upon Charles.

cinnabar — the pigment of the country — with doggerel rhymes and contumelious pictures, and announcing, in terms unnecessarily figurative, that the trick was already played, the claim already jumped, and the author of the placard the legitimate successor of Mr. Ronalds. But no, nothing could save that man; *quem deus vult perdere, prius dementat.*[5] As he came so he went, and left his rights depending.

Late at night, by Silverado reckoning, and after we were all abed, Mrs. Hanson returned to give us the newest of her news. It was like a scene in a ship's steerage: all of us abed in our different tiers, the single candle struggling with the darkness, and this plump, handsome woman, seated on an upturned valise beside the bunks, talking and showing her fine teeth, and laughing till the rafters rang. Any ship, to be sure, with a hundredth part as many holes in it as our barrack, must long ago have gone to her last port. Up to that time I had always imagined Mrs. Hanson's loquacity to be mere incontinence, that she said what was uppermost for the pleasure of speaking, and laughed and laughed again as a kind of musical accompaniment. But I now found there was an art in it. I found it less communicative than silence itself. I wished to know why Ronalds had come; how he had found his way without Rufe; and why, being on the spot, he had not refreshed his title. She talked interminably on, but her replies were never answers. She fled under a cloud of words; and when I had made sure that she was purposely eluding me, I dropped the subject in my turn, and let her rattle where she would.

She had come to tell us that, instead of waiting for Tuesday, the claim was to be jumped on the morrow. How? If the time were not out, it was impossible. Why? If Ronalds had come and gone, and done nothing, there was the less cause for hurry. But again I could reach no satisfaction. The claim was to be jumped next morning, that was all that she would condescend upon.

And yet it was not jumped the next morning, nor yet the

5. "Whom a god wishes to destroy, he first makes mad."

next, and a whole week had come and gone before we heard more of this exploit. That day week, however, a day of great heat, Hanson, with a little roll of paper in his hand, and the eternal pipe alight; Breedlove, his large, dull friend, to act, I suppose, as witness; Mrs. Hanson, in her Sunday best; and all the children, from the oldest to the youngest; — arrived in a procession, tailing one behind another up the path. Caliban was absent, but he had been chary of his friendly visits since the row; and with that exception, the whole family was gathered together as for a marriage or a christening. Strong was sitting at work, in the shade of the dwarf madronas near the forge; and they planted themselves about him in a circle, one on a stone, another on the waggon rails, a third on a piece of plank. Gradually the children stole away up the cañon to where there was another chute, somewhat smaller than the one across the dump; and down this chute, for the rest of the afternoon, they poured one avalanche of stones after another, waking the echoes of the glen. Meantime, we elders sat together on the platform, Hanson and his friend smoking in silence like Indian sachems, Mrs. Hanson rattling on as usual with an adroit volubility, saying nothing, but keeping the party at their ease like a courtly hostess.

Not a word occurred about the business of the day. Once, twice, and thrice I tried to slide the subject in, but was discouraged by the stoic apathy of Rufe, and beaten down before the pouring verbiage of his wife. There is nothing of the Indian brave about me, and I began to grill with impatience. At last, like a highway robber, I cornered Hanson, and bade him stand and deliver his business. Thereupon he gravely rose, as though to hint that this was not a proper place, nor the subject one suitable for squaws, and I, following his example, led him up the plank into our barrack. There he bestowed himself on a box, and unrolled his papers with fastidious deliberation. There were two sheets of note-paper, and an old mining notice, dated May 30th, 1879, part print, part manuscript, and the latter much obliterated by the rains. It was by this

identical piece of paper that the mine had been held last year.[6]
For thirteen months it had endured the weather and the change
of seasons on a cairn behind the shoulder of the cañon; and it was
now my business, spreading it before me on the table, and sitting
on a valise, to copy its terms, with some necessary changes,
twice over on the two sheets of note-paper. One was then to
be placed on the same cairn — "a mound of rocks" the notice
put it; and the other to be lodged for registration.

Rufe watched me, silently smoking, till I came to the place
for the locator's name at the end of the first copy; and when I
proposed that he should sign, I thought I saw a scare in his
eye. "I don't think that'll be necessary," he said slowly; "just
you write it down." Perhaps this mighty hunter, who was the
most active member of the local school-board, could not write.
There would be nothing strange in that. The constable of
Calistoga is, and has been for years, a bedridden man, and, if
I remember rightly, blind. He has more need of the emolu-
ments than another, it was explained; and it was easy for him
to "depytise," with a strong accent on the last. So friendly
and so free are popular institutions.

When I had done my scrivening, Hanson strolled out, and
addressed Breedlove, "Will you step up here a bit?" and after
they had disappeared a little while into the chaparral and
madrona thicket, they came back again, *minus* a notice, and the
deed was done. The claim was jumped; a track of mountain-
side, fifteen hundred feet long by six hundred wide, with all
the earth's precious bowels, had passed from Ronalds to
Hanson, and, in the passage, changed its name from the "Mam-
moth" to the "Calistoga." I had tried to get Rufe to call it

6. As Stevenson points out in his *Journal* (p. 79), the date to reclaim
the mine had somehow been overlooked so that "for a month back
it had been anyone's to jump who chose." Yet he also makes clear
that it was jumped the day after the visit from the former owner, rather
than on the later date indicated in the book. The little newspaper that
young Sam printed in the Chinaman's house declares: "The Silverado
mine was jumped on the 27th of June by Rufe Hanson for water
purposes, No bloodshed expected."

after his wife, after himself, and after Garfield, the Republican Presidential candidate of the hour — since then elected, and, alas! dead — but all was in vain. The claim had once been called the Calistoga before, and he seemed to feel safety in returning to that.

And so the history of that mine became once more plunged in darkness, lit only by some monster pyrotechnical displays of gossip. And perhaps the most curious feature of the whole matter is this: that we should have dwelt in this quiet corner of the mountains, with not a dozen neighbours, and yet struggled all the while, like desperate swimmers, in this sea of falsities and contradictions. Wherever a man is, there will be a lie.

TOILS AND PLEASURES

I must try to convey some notion of our life, of how the days passed and what pleasure we took in them, of what there was to do and how we set about doing it, in our mountain hermitage. The house, after we had repaired the worst of the damages, and filled in some of the doors and windows with white cotton cloth, became a healthy and a pleasant dwelling-place, always airy and dry, and haunted by the outdoor perfumes of the glen. Within, it had the look of habitation, the human look. You had only to go into the third room, which we did not use, and see its stones, its sifting earth, its tumbled litter; and then return to our lodging, with the beds made, the plates on the rack, the pail of bright water behind the door, the stove crackling in a corner, and perhaps the table roughly laid against a meal, — and man's order, the little clean spots that he creates to dwell in, were at once contrasted with the rich passivity of nature. And yet our house was everywhere so wrecked and shattered, the air came and went so freely, the sun found so many portholes, the golden outdoor glow shone in so many open chinks, that we enjoyed, at the same time, some of the comforts of a roof and much of the gaiety and brightness of *al fresco* life. A single shower of rain, to be sure, and we should have been drowned out like mice. But ours was a Californian summer, and an earthquake was a far likelier accident than a shower of rain.

Trustful in this fine weather, we kept the house for kitchen and bedroom, and used the platform as our summer parlour. The sense of privacy, as I have said already, was complete. We could look over the dump on miles of forest and rough hill-top; our eyes commanded some of Napa Valley, where

the train ran, and the little country townships sat so close together along the line of the rail. But here there was no man
to intrude. None but the Hansons were our visitors. Even they
came but at long intervals, or twice daily at a stated hour,
with milk. So our days, as they were never interrupted, drew
out to the greater length; hour melted insensibly into hour;
the household duties, though they were many, and some of
them laborious, dwindled into mere islets of business in a sea
of sunny day-time; and it appears to me, looking back, as
though the far greater part of our life at Silverado had been
passed, propped upon an elbow, or seated on a plank, listening
to the silence that there is among the hills.

My work, it is true, was over early in the morning. I rose
before any one else, lit the stove, put on the water to boil, and
strolled forth upon the platform to wait till it was ready.
Silverado would then be still in shadow, the sun shining on the
mountain higher up. A clean smell of trees, a smell of the
earth at morning, hung in the air. Regularly, every day, there
was a single bird, not singing, but awkwardly chirruping
among the green madronas, and the sound was cheerful, natural,
and stirring. It did not hold the attention, nor interrupt the
thread of meditation, like a blackbird or a nightingale; it was
mere woodland prattle, of which the mind was conscious like
a perfume. The freshness of these morning seasons remained
with me far on into the day.

As soon as the kettle boiled, I made porridge and coffee;
and that, beyond the literal drawing of water, and the preparation of kindling, which it would be hyperbolical to call the
hewing of wood, ended my domestic duties for the day.
Thenceforth my wife laboured single-handed in the palace, and
I lay or wandered on the platform at my own sweet will. The
little corner near the forge, where we found a refuge under the
madronas from the unsparing early sun, is indeed connected in
my mind with some nightmare encounters over Euclid and the
Latin Grammar. These were known as the Crown Prince's
lessons. He was supposed to be the victim and the sufferer;

but here there must have been some misconception, for whereas I generally retired to bed after one of these engagements, he was no sooner set free than he dashed up to the Chinaman's house, where he had installed a printing-press, that great element of civilisation, and the sound of his labours would be faintly audible about the cañon half the day.

To walk at all was a laborious business; the foot sank and slid, the boots were cut to pieces, among sharp, uneven, rolling stones. When we crossed the platform in any direction, it was usual to lay a course, following as much as possible the line of waggon rails. Thus, if water were to be drawn, the water-carrier left the house along some tilting planks that we had laid down, and not laid down very well. These carried him to that great highroad, the railway; and the railway served him as far as to the head of the shaft. But from thence to the spring and back again he made the best of his unaided way, staggering among the stones, and wading in low growth of the calcanthus, where the rattlesnakes lay hissing at his passage. Yet I liked to draw water. It was pleasant to dip the grey metal pail into the clean, colourless, cool water; pleasant to carry it back, with the water lipping at the edge, and a broken sunbeam quivering in the midst.

But the extreme roughness of the walking confined us in common practice to the platform, and, indeed, to those parts of it that were most easily accessible along the line of rails. The rails came straight forward from the shaft, here and there overgrown with little green bushes, but still entire, and still carrying a truck, which it was Lloyd's delight to trundle to and fro by the hour with various ladings. About midway down the platform the railroad trended to the right, leaving our house and coasting along the far side within a few yards of the madronas and the forge, and not far from the latter, ended in a sort of platform on the edge of the dump. There, in old days, the trucks were tipped, and their load sent thundering down the chute. There, besides, was the only spot where we could approach the margin of the dump. Anywhere else, you took your life in your right hand when you came within a yard and a half to peer over. For at any moment the dump might begin to slide and carry you down and bury you below its ruins. Indeed, the neighbourhood of an old mine is a place beset with dangers. For as still as Silverado was, at any moment the report of rotten wood might tell us that the platform had fallen into the shaft; the dump might begin to pour into the road below; or a wedge slip in the great upright seam, and hundreds of tons of mountain bury the scene of our encampment.

I have already compared the dump to a rampart, built certainly by some rude people, and for prehistoric wars. It was likewise a frontier. All below was green and woodland, the tall pines soaring one above another, each with a firm outline and full spread of bough. All above was arid, rocky, and bald. The great spout of broken mineral, that had dammed the cañon up, was a creature of man's handiwork, its material dug out with a pick and powder, and spread by the service of the trucks. But nature herself, in that upper district, seemed to have had an eye to nothing besides mining; and even the natural hillside was all sliding gravel and precarious boulder. Close at the margin of the well, leaves would decay to skeletons and mummies, which at length some stronger gust would carry clear of the cañon and scatter in the subjacent woods. Even moisture and decaying vegetable matter could not, with all nature's alchemy, concoct enough soil to nourish a few poor grasses. It is the same, they say, in the neighbourhood of all silver mines; the nature of that precious rock being stubborn with quartz and poisonous with cinnabar. Both were plenty in our Silverado. The stones sparkled white in the sunshine with quartz; they were all stained red with cinnabar. Here, doubtless, came the Indians of yore to paint their faces for the warpath; and cinnabar, if I remember rightly, was one of the few articles of Indian commerce.[1] Now, the Crown Prince had it in his undisturbed possession, to pound down and slake and

1. Stevenson was right in recalling that cinnabar was traded, to be used for vermilion paint by some California tribes.

paint his rude designs with. But to me it had always a fine flavour of poetry, compounded out of Indian story and Haw-thornden's allusion: —

> "Desire, alas! desire a Zeuxis new,
> From Indies borrowing gold, from Eastern skies
> Most bright cinoper . . ." [2]

Yet this is but half the picture; our Silverado platform has another side to it. Though there was no soil, and scarce a blade of grass, yet out of these tumbled gravel-heaps and broken boulders a flower-garden bloomed as at home in a conservatory. Calcanthus crept, like a hardy weed, all over our rough parlour, choking the railway, and pushing forth its rusty, aromatic cones from between two blocks of shattered mineral. Azaleas made a big snow-bed just above the well. The shoulder of the hill waved white with Mediterranean heath. In the crannies of the ledge and about the spurs of the tall pine, a red flowering stone-plant hung in clusters. Even the low, thorny chaparral was thick with pea-like blossom. Close at the foot of our path nutmegs prospered, delightful to the sight and smell. At sunrise, and again late at night, the scent of the sweet bay-trees filled the cañon, and the down-blowing night-wind must have borne it hundreds of feet into the outer air.

All this vegetation, to be sure, was stunted. The madrona was here no bigger than the manzanita; the bay was but a stripling shrub; the very pines, with four or five exceptions in all our upper cañon, were not so tall as myself, or but a little taller, and the most of them came lower than my waist. For a pros-perous forest tree we must look below, where the glen was crowded with green spires. But for flowers and ravishing per-fume we had none to envy: our heap of road-metal was thick with bloom, like a hawthorn in the front of June; our red, baking angle in the mountain, a laboratory of poignant scents.

2. From an untitled sonnet by William Drummond of Hawthornden, accurately quoted except that the original has "western" instead of "Eastern skies."

It was an endless wonder to my mind, as I dreamed about the platform, following the progress of the shadows, where the madrona with its leaves, the azalea and calcanthus with their blossoms, could find moisture to support such thick, wet, waxy growths, or the bay-tree collect the ingredients of its perfume. But there they all grew together, healthy, happy, and happy-making, as though rooted in a fathom of black soil.

Nor was it only vegetable life that prospered. We had, indeed, few birds, and none that had much of a voice or anything worthy to be called a song. My morning comrade had a thin chirp, unmusical and monotonous, but friendly and pleasant to hear. He had but one rival: a fellow with an ostentatious cry of near an octave descending, not one note of which properly followed another. This is the only bird I ever knew with a wrong ear; but there was something enthralling about his performance. You listened and listened, thinking each time he must surely get it right; but no, it was always wrong, and always wrong the same way. Yet he seemed proud of his song, delivered it with execution and a manner of his own, and was charming to his mate. A very incorrect, incessant human whistler had thus a chance of knowing how his own music pleased the world. Two great birds — eagles, we thought — dwelt at the top of the cañon, among the crags that were printed on the sky. Now and again, but very rarely, they wheeled high over our heads in silence, or with a distant, dying scream; and then, with a fresh impulse, winged fleetly forward, dipped over a hill-top, and were gone. They seemed solemn and ancient things, sailing the blue air; perhaps coeval with the mountain where they haunted, perhaps emigrants from Rome, where the glad legions may have shouted to behold them on the morn of battle.

But if birds were rare, the place abounded with rattlesnakes — the rattlesnake's nest, it might have been named. Wherever we brushed among the bushes, our passage woke their angry buzz. One dwelt habitually in the wood-pile, and sometimes, when we came for firewood, thrust up his small head between two logs, and hissed at the intrusion. The rattle has a legendary credit; it is said to be awe-inspiring, and, once heard, to stamp itself for ever in the memory. But the sound is not at all alarming; the hum of many insects and the buzz of the wasp convince the ear of danger quite as readily. As a matter of fact, we lived for weeks in Silverado, coming and going, with rattles sprung on every side, and it never occurred to us to be afraid. I used to take sun-baths and do calisthenics in a certain pleasant nook among azalea and calcanthus, the rattles whizzing on every side like spinning-wheels, and the combined hiss or buzz rising louder and angrier at any sudden movement; but I was never in the least impressed, nor ever attacked. It was only towards the end of our stay, that a man down at Calistoga, who was expatiating on the terrifying nature of the sound, gave me at last a very good imitation; and it burst on me at once that we dwelt in the very metropolis of deadly snakes, and that the rattle was simply the commonest noise in Silverado. Immediately on our return, we attacked the Hansons on the subject. They had formerly assured us that our cañon was favoured, like Ireland, with an entire immunity from poisonous reptiles; but, with the perfect inconsequence of the natural man, they were no sooner found out than they went off at score in the contrary direction, and we were told that in no part of the world did rattlesnakes attain to such a monstrous bigness as among the warm, flower-dotted rocks of Silverado. This is a contribution rather to the natural history of the Hansons than to that of snakes.

One person, however, better served by his instinct, had known the rattle from the first; and that was Chuchu, the dog. No rational creature has ever led an existence more poisoned by terror than that dog's at Silverado. Every whiz of the rattle made him bound. His eyes rolled; he trembled; he would be often wet with sweat.[3] One of our great mysteries was his

3. The contention that a dog's skin can become wet with perspiration was more than once questioned by readers. On Dec. 15, 1883, while at Hyères, Stevenson drafted a reply stating: "As for the animal in

terror of the mountain. A little way above our nook, the
azaleas and almost all the vegetation ceased. Dwarf pines not
big enough to be Christmas-trees grew thinly among loose
stones and gravel scaurs. Here and there a big boulder sat
quiescent on a knoll, having paused there till the next rain in
his long slide down the mountain. There was here no am-
buscade for the snakes, you could see clearly where you trod;
and yet the higher I went, the more abject and appealing became Chuchu's terror. He was an excellent master of that
composite language in which dogs communicate with men,
and he would assure me, on his honour, that there was some
peril on the mountain; appeal to me, by all that I held holy,
to turn back; and at length, finding all was in vain, and that
I still persisted, ignorantly foolhardy, he would suddenly whip
round and make a bee-line down the slope for Silverado, the
gravel showering after him. What was he afraid of? There
were admittedly brown bears and Californian lions on the
mountain; and a grizzly visited Rufe's poultry-yard not long
before, to the unspeakable alarm of Caliban, who dashed out to
chastise the intruder, and found himself, by moonlight, face
to face with such a Tartar. Something at least there must have
been; some hairy, dangerous brute lodged permanently among
the rocks a little to the north-west of Silverado, spending his
summer thereabout, with wife and family.

And there was, or there had been, another animal. Once,
under the broad daylight, on that open stony hillside, where
the baby pines were growing, scarcely tall enough to be a
badge for a MacGregor's bonnet, I came suddenly upon his

question, in my book, a spaniel crossed with a setter, was certainly an
exception, take this crucial instance! The first time he was ever
travelled by rail, sitting in a romantic flutter on a lady's lap, he
became gradually wet from head to foot. I should be glad to learn if
he was an exception, or if the common opinion is groundless." The
manuscript of this answer belonged to Herman LeRoy Edgar and was
sold on Feb. 1, 1924, at the American Art Association of New York
City, from whose catalogue description of it, numbered 449, the text is
here quoted. The present whereabouts of the manuscript have not
been discovered.

innocent body, lying mummified by the dry air and sun: a pigmy kangaroo. I am ingloriously ignorant of these subjects; had never heard of such a beast; thought myself face to face with some incomparable sport of nature; and began to cherish hopes of immortality in science. Rarely have I been conscious of a stranger thrill than when I raised that singular creature from the stones, dry as a board, his innocent heart long quiet, and all warm with sunshine. His long hind-legs were stiff, his tiny forepaws clutched upon his breast, as if to leap; his poor life cut short upon that mountain by some unknown accident. But the kangaroo rat, it proved, was no such unknown animal; and my discovery was nothing.[4]

Crickets were not wanting. I thought I could make out exactly four of them, each with a corner of his own, who used to make night musical at Silverado. In the matter of voice they far excelled the birds, and their ringing whistle sounded from rock to rock, calling and replying the same thing, as in a meaningless opera. Thus children in full health and spirits shout together, to the dismay of neighbours; and their idle, happy, deafening vociferations rise and fall, like the song of the crickets. I used to sit at night on the platform, and wonder why these creatures were so happy; and what was wrong with man that he also did not wind up his days with an hour or two of shouting; but I suspect that all long-lived animals are solemn. The dogs alone are hardly used by nature; and it seems a manifest injustice for poor Chuchu to die in his teens, after a life so shadowed and troubled, continually shaken with alarm, and the tear of elegant sentiment permanently in his eye.

There was another neighbour of ours at Silverado, small but very active, a destructive fellow. This was a black, ugly fly — a bore, the Hansons called him — who lived by hundreds in the boarding of our house. He entered by a round hole, more

4. Although more usually found in the southwest desert country of the United States than in northern California, the kangaroo rat (genus, *Dipodomys;* family, *Heteromyidae*) is not an uncommon rodent.

neatly pierced than a man could do it with a gimlet, and he seems to have spent his life in cutting out the interior of the plank, but whether as a dwelling or a store-house, I could never find. When I used to lie in bed in the morning for a rest — we had no easy-chairs in Silverado — I would hear, hour after hour, the sharp cutting sound of his labours, and from time to time a dainty shower of sawdust would fall upon the blankets. There lives no more industrious creature than a bore.

And now that I have named to the reader all our animals and insects without exception — only I find I have forgotten the flies — he will be able to appreciate the singular privacy and silence of our days. It was not only man who was excluded: animals, the song of birds, the lowing of cattle, the bleating of sheep, clouds even, and the variations of the weather, were here also wanting; and as, day after day, the sky was one dome of blue, and the pines below us stood motionless in the still air, so the hours themselves were marked out from each other only by the series of our own affairs, and the sun's great period as he ranged westward through the heavens. The two birds cackled a while in the early morning; all day the water tinkled in the shaft, the bores ground sawdust in the planking of our crazy palace — infinitesimal sounds; and it was only with the return of night that any change would fall on our surroundings, or the four crickets begin to flute together in the dark.

Indeed, it would be hard to exaggerate the pleasure that we took in the approach of evening. Our day was not very long, but it was very tiring. To trip along unsteady planks or wade among shifting stones, to go to and fro for water, to clamber down the glen to the Toll House after meat and letters, to cook, to make fires and beds, were all exhausting to the body. Life out of doors, besides, under the fierce eye of day, draws largely on the animal spirits. There are certain hours in the afternoon when a man, unless he is in strong health or enjoys a vacant mind, would rather creep into a cool corner of a house and sit upon the chairs of civilisation. About that time the sharp stones, the planks, the upturned boxes of Silverado, began to grow irksome to my body; I set out on that hopeless, never-ending quest for a more comfortable posture; I would be fevered and weary of the staring sun; and just then he would begin courteously to withdraw his countenance, the shadows lengthened, the aromatic airs awoke, and an indescribable but happy change announced the coming of the night.

The hours of evening, when we were once curtained in the friendly dark, sped lightly. Even as with the crickets, night brought to us a certain spirit of rejoicing. It was good to taste the air; good to mark the dawning of the stars, as they increased their glittering company; good, too, to gather stones, and send them crashing down the chute, a wave of light. It seemed, in some way, the reward and the fulfilment of the day. So it is when men dwell in the open air; it is one of the simple pleasures that we lose by living cribbed and covered in a house, that, though the coming of the day is still the most inspiriting, yet day's departure, also, and the return of night, refresh, renew, and quiet us; and in the pastures of the dusk we stand, like cattle, exulting in the absence of the load.

Our nights were never cold, and they were always still, but for one remarkable exception. Regularly, about nine o'clock, a warm wind sprang up, and blew for ten minutes, or maybe a quarter of an hour, right down the cañon, fanning it well out, airing it as a mother airs the night-nursery before the children sleep. As far as I could judge, in the clear darkness of the night, this wind was purely local: perhaps dependent on the configuration of the glen. At least, it was very welcome to the hot and weary squatters; and if we were not abed already, the springing up of this Lilliputian valley-wind would often be our signal to retire.

I was the last to go to bed, as I was still the first to rise. Many a night I have strolled about the platform, taking a bath of darkness before I slept. The rest would be in bed, and even from the forge I could hear them talking together from bunk to bunk. A single candle in the neck of a pint bottle was their only illumination; and yet the old cracked house seemed literally bursting with the light. It shone keen as a knife through all the vertical chinks; it struck upward through the broken shingles; and through the eastern door and window it fell in a great splash upon the thicket and the overhanging rock. You would have said a conflagration, or at the least a roaring forge; and behold it was but a candle. Or perhaps it was yet more strange to see the procession moving bedwards round the corner of the house, and up the plank that brought us to the bedroom door; under the immense spread of the starry heavens, down in a crevice of the giant mountain, these few human shapes, with their unshielded taper, made so disproportionate a figure in the eye and mind. But the more he is alone with nature, the greater man and his doings bulk in the consideration of his fellow-men. Miles and miles away upon the opposite hill-tops, if there were any hunter belated or any traveller who had lost his way, he must have stood, and watched and wondered, from the time the candle issued from the door of the assayer's office till it had mounted the plank and disappeared again into the miners' dormitory.

THE JOHN HARVARD LIBRARY

*The intent of
Waldron Phoenix Belknap, Jr.,
as expressed in an early will, was for
Harvard College to use the income from a
permanent trust fund he set up, for "editing and
publishing rare, inaccessible, or hitherto unpublished
source material of interest in connection with the
history, literature, art (including minor and useful
art), commerce, customs, and manners or way of
life of the Colonial and Federal Periods of the United
States . . . In all cases the emphasis shall be on the
presentation of the basic material." A later testament
broadened this statement, but Mr. Belknap's interests remained constant until his death.*

*In linking the name of the first benefactor of
Harvard College with the purpose of this later,
generous-minded believer in American culture the
John Harvard Library seeks to emphasize the importance of Mr. Belknap's purpose. The John Harvard
Library of the Belknap Press of Harvard University
Press exists to make books and documents
about the American past more readily
available to scholars and the
general reader.*